THE FLAMES OF CALAIS

A Soldier's Battle 1940

By the same author

THEY HAVE THEIR EXITS

LITTLE CYCLONE

SATURDAY AT M.I.9

THE FLAMES OF CALAIS

A Soldier's Battle 1940

by

AIREY NEAVE

LEO COOPER

First published in 1972 by Hodder and Stoughton Limited
Republished in 2003
and reprinted in this format in 2018 by
Pen & Sword MILITARY
An imprint of Pen & Sword Books Ltd
Yorkshire – Philadelphia

ISBN: 978 1 52674 851 5

A CIP catalogue record for this book is available from the British Library

Printed and bound in in England by CPI UK

Pen & Sword Books Limited incorporates the imprints of Atlas, Archaeology, Aviation, Discovery, Family History, Fiction, History, Maritime, Military, Military Classics, Politics, Select, Transport, True Crime, Air World, Frontline Publishing, Leo Cooper, Remember When, Seaforth Publishing, The Praetorian Press, Wharncliffe Local History, Wharncliffe Transport, Wharncliffe True Crime and White Owl.

For a complete list of Pen & Sword titles please contact
PEN & SWORD BOOKS LIMITED
47 Church Street, Barnsley, South Yorkshire, S70 2AS, England
E-mail: enquiries@pen-and-sword.co.uk • Website: www.pen-and-sword.co.uk
Or
PEN AND SWORD BOOKS
1950 Lawrence Rd, Havertown, PA 19083, USA
E-mail: Uspen-and-sword@casematepublishers.com
Website: www.penandswordbooks.com

ACKNOWLEDGMENTS

When Calais was captured on the afternoon of the 26th May 1940, nearly all of the garrison who were not killed or did not die of their wounds, were taken prisoner. There are therefore very few contemporary documents. Reports written in prisoner-of-war camps and official minutes and telegrams are preserved in the Public Record Office.

Brigadier Claude Nicholson died in captivity in 1943 before a report written under his direction was complete. I am grateful to his widow, the Hon. Mrs. MacDonald, and his brother, Sir Godfrey Nicholson, for personal information. Lieutenant-General Sir Euan Miller, Major A. W. Allan, Brigadier R. C. Keller, Lieutenant-Colonel R. M. Goldney and Lieutenant-Colonel John Ellison-Macartney, who held commands at Calais, read the manuscript for me and greatly added to my knowledge of the battle.

I received particular help from the Earl of Avon, Mrs. Chandos Hoskyns, Mrs. Joan St. George Saunders, Mrs. Venetia Pollock, Miss Joy Robilliard, Group Captain A. F. Anderson, Sir Everard Radcliffe, Major Quentin Carpendale, Mr. Duncan Nash and Lieutenant-Commander C. Brammall. I also wish to thank the Ministry of Defence, Lieutenant-Colonel Roger Nixon and Mr. J. M. Leslie (Regimental Headquarters Royal Green Jackets), Colonel R. H. Hordern (Royal Armoured Corps Tank Museum), The House of Commons Library and the Imperial War Museum.

The old part of Calais was totally destroyed in the war, which made research difficult. My wife did most of it, in all weathers, and my son William took the latest photographs. The Town of Calais gave every assistance through M. Saint of the Archives and M.

Rérolle of the Musée, as did Mr. John Selwyn (H.M. Vice-Consul), M. S. Maupin of the Hôtel Meurice, Mme. Veuve, André Gershell, M. Georges Wiart and M. André Berthe.

For the German side of the story I have to thank Dr. Stahl of the Militarchiv section of the Bundesarchiv for copies of the War Diaries and other papers. These and the German photographs were obtained with the help of Major A. T. R. Shelley and Captain von Merveldt, 2nd Royal Green Jackets. The documents were translated by Mrs. Annelise Springer who also did much of the typing; so did Mrs. Patricia Saunders and Mrs. Jenny Richardson.

Most of this account of the defence of Calais is based on unpublished official and private papers but the following books and articles were of great use to me:

Eric Linklater: *The Defence of Calais* (H.M.S.O.)
David Divine: *The Nine Days of Dunkirk* (Faber & Faber)
Lord Avon: *The Eden Memoirs—The Reckoning* (Cassell & Co.)
Decisive Battles of World War II: The German View (André Deutsch)
Goutard: *The Battle of France 1940* (Muller)
Maxime Weygand: *Recalled to Service* (Heinemann)
The Ironside Diaries (Constable)
Liddell Hart: *The Other Side of the Hill* (Cassell & Co.), *The Tanks*, Vol. II (Cassell & Co.)
Chalmers: *Full Cycle—The Biography of Admiral Sir Bertram Ramsay* (Hodder and Stoughton)
Guy Bataille: *Le Boulonnais dans la Tourmente* (Pierru)
Winston Churchill: *The Second World War*, Vol. II (Cassell & Co.)
The Rev. Clifford Lever: *On My Heart Too* (Epworth Press)
Heinz Guderian: *Panzer Leader* (Michael Joseph)
Gordon Instone: *Freedom the Spur* (Burke)
Alistair Horne: *To Lose a Battle* (Macmillan)
Major A. W. Allan: Articles on Calais in the *Rifle Brigade Chronicle 1945*
J. A. Evitts: *Calais 1940 Remembered* (Private)
Annals of the King's Royal Rifle Corps, Vol. VI (Brigadier G. H. Mills and Lieut.-Col. R. F. Nixon)

I am grateful to the many survivors of the battle who wrote to me. I only regret that the names of so many who deserve our gratitude are not included, but I hope that through this book their "memorable resistance" will no longer be forgotten.

Airey Neave

CONTENTS

ILLUSTRATIONS

MAPS

PART I
CONTRADICTORY ORDERS

Principal events covered by Part I

10th May 1940	Guderian's XIXth Army Corps crosses the Luxembourg frontier.
19th May	Guderian captures Amiens
20th May	Admiral Ramsay in charge of all cross-channel shipping
21st May	British counter-attack at Arras
22nd May	The Third Royal Tank Regiment and Queen Victoria's Rifles land at Calais
23rd May	Brigadier Nicholson with the 60th Rifles and the Rifle Brigade lands at Calais. The Third Royal Tank Regiment and the First Searchlight Regiment in action against the First Panzer Division

CHAPTER ONE

Was Churchill Right?

CALAIS burned. From the Citadel to the Courgain every street was on fire. A giant, choking, cloud of smoke drifted over the harbour, so that only the spire of Notre Dame and the clock tower of the Hôtel de Ville could be seen from the shore.

At 3 p.m. on the 26th May 1940, Very lights were fired from the Cellulose Factory and German infantry stormed over the quays and platforms of the Gare Maritime. These were men of the 69th German Rifle Regiment of the Tenth Panzer Division. Within half an hour, they captured the Bastion de l'Estran and forced the Rifle Brigade to surrender at Bastion 1. It was a savage fight with heavy loss on both sides.

At 4 p.m., the 86th Rifle Regiment had surrounded the old Citadel of Richelieu and Vauban. Led by a Feldwebel with a revolver, they crossed the courtyard and captured Brigadier Claude Nicholson, the garrison commander, who had twice refused to surrender. German tanks were in the streets of the old town or Calais-Nord firing at point-blank range. The hasty road-blocks could no longer be held. Heat, thirst and wounds ended all organised resistance. From post to post, went the last order to the 60th Rifles and those who fought with them.

"Every man for himself!"

It was a bitter ending for those who had fought for four days against hopeless odds. The British and French dead lay at the final barricades, on the quays and in the bastions. The wounded in the cellars cried out for water. In the tunnel under Bastion 1, a young soldier blew his brains out rather than surrender. From burning houses and trenches, came the survivors, dead-beat, but defiant. Many had bullet wounds hastily bandaged and their white unshaven faces showed the strain of the long bombardment. When it was nearly dark, a sad but dignified column of prisoners-of-war marched off to five years of imprisonment in Nazi Germany. These were the men who had held Calais to the last hour.

Lying half-conscious on my bloodstained stretcher in the tunnel, I saw the shadow of a large figure in German uniform leaning over me. I remember now most vividly the sense of peace after the shattering roar of the battle. Until this moment the fight had raged without respite in the blazing streets.

It had been a soldier's battle. A fight to the death. In places, entire sections lay still at their posts. Why had this happened? Why were 3,000 Englishmen and 800 Frenchmen sacrificed in full view of the Kent coast, while the British Expeditionary Force was within thirty miles of them and ships of the Royal Navy stood off Calais?

By the 26th May the British Expeditionary Force, or B.E.F., was in no position to help the defenders of Calais. They were withdrawing to Dunkirk. "Operation Dynamo" which led to the "miraculous" evacuation of 330,000 Allied soldiers began that evening, while the fires of Calais still burned. When the XIXth Army Corps of three Panzer divisions under General Heinz Guderian swept through the Ardennes on the 10th May, and in nine days reached the sea, the British were trapped. They could either stand and fight or retreat to the Channel ports. But so fast did Guderian move that he outstripped all intelligence.

In London, the War Office sent muddled and contradictory orders to France. The plan to evacuate the B.E.F. emerged day by day. At first only "useless mouths" and wounded were to be disembarked. The ports of Calais and Boulogne were got ready for their departure. Within a few hours, as Guderian turned north towards the Channel ports, the whole of the B.E.F., with the French Army of the North, were threatened with encirclement and capitulation. It was nearly the end of the war in Europe.

Hasty orders were given to defend Boulogne and Calais. Since the 19th May, the anti-aircraft forces of Calais had been strengthened. On the 22nd May, the Third Royal Tank Regiment and the Queen Victoria's Rifles were landed. They were followed on the 23rd, by two regular battalions, the Second Battalion, The King's Royal Rifle Corps (The 60th Rifles) and the First Battalion, The Rifle Brigade with an anti-tank battery. From the 23rd May, all these troops came under Brigadier Nicholson's command.

Nicholson faced an impossible task. By the 23rd May, two Panzer divisions were close to Calais and both missed the opportunity of taking it before he could improvise the defence. For the next four days, he held off the Tenth Panzer Division which was reinforced by masses of artillery and, at the last, by 100 dive-bombing Stukas. The garrison fought to the last. Many among the 3,000 British troops were untrained for battle. They had neither proper equipment, arms or ammunition. The two regular infantry battalions fought brilliantly, though one of them had only half its weapons and transport. The Tanks and the Territorials bravely supported them to the end. But Nicholson had no field artillery and very few tanks. His only additional support were 800 French soldiers and sailors and a handful of Dutch and Belgians. And yet his little force delayed Guderian for many critical hours.

The War Office knew the situation in Calais, for they were in touch with the defenders till the last moment. Nicholson had asked repeatedly for artillery, ammunition and food: he had explained his position and the enemy's; he had been visited by two generals, an admiral and a naval commodore. How was it that the War Office could be so ignorant of the size, strength and movement of the Germans that they could ask these few ill-equipped men to fight to the death? If they knew that they were so unfairly matched why did they not send the reinforcements for which Nicholson pleaded?

After Nicholson had landed, he received a stream of infuriating orders. He was first ordered to move west to Boulogne to help the 20th Guards Brigade. This was followed by a plan to escort 350,000 rations in lorries east to Dunkirk. The tanks were to go to Boulogne. At the same time, they were ordered to St. Omer in the opposite direction. Nicholson had only been in Calais for a few hours, when the War Office evacuated "non-fighting" soldiers. They also decided on the evacuation "in principle" of his brigade. Orders were written for its withdrawal to the Gare Maritime. Twelve hours later, Winston

Churchill, the Prime Minister, countermanded the evacuation and told Nicholson to fight on. Despite this order, destroyers of the Royal Navy stood off Calais until a few hours before its fall. Most of the defenders still expected to be taken off. Then, at 9 p.m. on the 25th May, Churchill, Anthony Eden, Secretary of State for War, and General Sir Edmund Ironside, Chief of the Imperial General Staff, sat down and drafted this message:

"Every hour you continue to exist is of greatest help to B.E.F. Government has therefore decided you must continue to fight. Have greatest admiration for your splendid stand."[1]

A minesweeper fought its way into Calais harbour at midnight on the 25th May to deliver it. When dawn came, the destroyers, which had been in sight of the garrison, had returned to Dover. Now there was no escape. During the next few hours, a furious battle raged in Calais-Nord and round the Gare Maritime.

How had Churchill, Eden and Ironside arrived at this terrible decision? They were certainly aware that it involved the sacrifice of many lives.

The British were not the only people to give curious and irrational orders. The German High Command, staggered by the speed of Guderian's initial advance, were out of touch with events and badly informed. Both sides made decisions about Calais which were to cost them dear.

The Germans were worried about their long, unwieldy, supply line. They could not believe that the war could be over so quickly, that the British and the French Armies in the north of France would depart without a fight. When the British counter-attacked at Arras on the 21st May, the Germans were temporarily unnerved. They believed that more such attacks would follow. Guderian had already been compelled to stop his advance for twenty-four hours. His plan to take Dunkirk by surprise on the 21st May had to be abandoned. But other opportunities existed to seize it, before Hitler personally halted the advance of all Panzer divisions at 11.30 a.m. on the 24th May.

[1] Churchill on p. 73 of *The Second World War*, Vol. II, says that the decision was taken on the 26th May. This must be an error. The signal was dispatched on the night of the 25th.

Guderian had hoped to ignore Calais and race for Dunkirk, but it finally had to be taken. The fierce resistance used up four essential days when one or more of his Panzer divisions might have been across the Aa Canal. Or would the prize have been snatched from him in any case? If Calais had not been held would Hitler have kept the Panzers back from Dunkirk and left it to the Luftwaffe? When Calais was finally taken, all three of Guderian's Panzer divisions rested and were ordered south, to fight elsewhere. They took no part in the final battle for Dunkirk. Was it the defence of Calais which saved the B.E.F. or were they saved by German error? Was it Hitler and Field-Marshal von Rundstedt who halted the Panzers on the line of the Aa Canal on the morning of the 24th May, who made possible the evacuation of the B.E.F.? Does this mean that the sacrifice of Calais was vain and useless?

The battle of Calais is clearly open to many interpretations. As the Narrator, I have made my own analysis. I believe the episode was the result of indecision and misinformation on both sides. Neither regarded it as a main objective. Neither expected it. It is this accidental aspect which I seek to examine in this book.

Should it have occurred at all? If it was no longer possible to use Calais—as it had been intended—to take off part of the B.E.F., should it not then have been evacuated in good time? Did leaving 3,000 Englishmen to die or be taken prisoner there really show "solidarity" with our French Allies? Why was it not realised, until long after the battle began, that every hour Nicholson held out would be crucial for the B.E.F.? Churchill was often wrong about Calais but when others faltered, he insisted that it should be fought to the death. It was his personal decision and he believed that it saved the B.E.F. Nine days after its fall, he made one of his finest speeches in the House of Commons.[2] His classic peroration: "We will fight on the beaches . . . We will never surrender," sustained the free world in the struggle to come.

Of Calais he said: "The British Brigadier was given an hour to surrender. He spurned the offer [cheers] and four days of intense street

[2] 5th June 1940.

fighting passed before a silence reigned over Calais which marked the end of a memorable resistance."

Churchill did not know the fate of the survivors but he said: "Their sacrifice was not in vain. At least two armoured divisions which otherwise would have been turned against the British Expeditionary Force had to be sent there to overcome them. They added another page to the glories of the Light Division and the time gained enabled the Gravelines Waterline to be flooded and held by French troops and thus it was that the port of Dunkirk was kept open."

After the war, Churchill wrote:

"Calais was the crux. Many other causes might have prevented the deliverance of Dunkirk, but it is certain the three days gained by the defence of Calais enabled the Gravelines Waterline to be held, and that without this, even in spite of Hitler's vacillations and Rundstedt's orders, all would have been cut off and lost."[3] Was he right?

Since nearly all the 3,000 defenders, who were not killed or died afterwards of wounds, were taken prisoner, it has been impossible to obtain exact figures of the casualties. About sixty men escaped, some in boats across the Channel. But official records of the regiments which took part are sketchy. The survivors were not liberated until 1945 and much happened in the interval. Many came back to find the "memorable resistance", so eloquently described by Churchill, had been forgotten.

It is believed that 204 men of the 60th Rifles, the Rifle Brigade and the Queen Victoria's Rifles were killed in action. The Third Royal Tank Regiment, with the Anti-tank, Anti-aircraft, Searchlight regiments and other units are believed to have had about a hundred dead. Many bodies were buried in the ruins and never traced. There are no casualty returns and no figure for the wounded has ever been confirmed. Two hundred wounded were evacuated by sea before the end and those left behind exceeded 500.[4] The regular infantry battalions, the 60th Rifles and the Rifle Brigade suffered the worst. Their casualties in killed and wounded were at least sixty per cent of their

[3] *The Second World War*, Vol. II, p. 73.

[4] A reason for the relatively low casualties for such a fierce battle was that many bombs and shells buried themselves in the sand dunes without causing injury.

strength. The German Military Archives have no separate figures for the casualties of the First and Tenth Panzer Division at Calais, nor has it been possible to ascertain the exact losses of the French Army and Navy.

At the age of twenty four, I was one of those wounded and taken prisoner. For the next six weeks I was in hospital in Calais-St. Pierre, then taken to Lille. By the middle of July, I had joined the hopeless march of prisoners to Germany. Driven by despair and boredom, and a natural impatience, I planned escapes. I got away from the fortress of Bydgoszcz near Thoru in Poland in April 1941. The attempt was a near disaster, for the Gestapo caught me with the sketch of a German military aerodrome. I was surprised when they accepted my flimsy explanation.

In January 1942, I escaped from Colditz Castle in Saxony and reached London four months later. For the next three years, I was one of the chief organisers of secret escape lines in occupied Europe.

In this book I have tried to give an impression of the battle, though in military terms my contribution was insignificant. It seems of more consequence to pose questions about the defence of Calais, which for more than thirty years have required an answer.

Sadly, Nicholson's own account of his brigade was unfinished when he died in Germany in 1943. We do not have his story of those four extraordinary days, but I have been able to talk and correspond with many still alive today who survived the flames.

The War Diaries of Guderian's Army Corps and of the First and Tenth Panzer Divisions show the German side of the battle. Yet there are many aspects of this fateful action which military historians have ignored. The reader may judge whether it was vain, but few, I think, will disagree with Guderian himself that it was heroic.

It has often been difficult to discover what happened in the fantastic fighting. I have set out the evidence and sought to answer my own questions. First, it is necessary to place Calais in the context of the campaign in France. I begin by following Guderian and his three Panzer divisions from their starting-point on the Luxembourg frontier at 5.30 a.m. on the 10th May 1940.

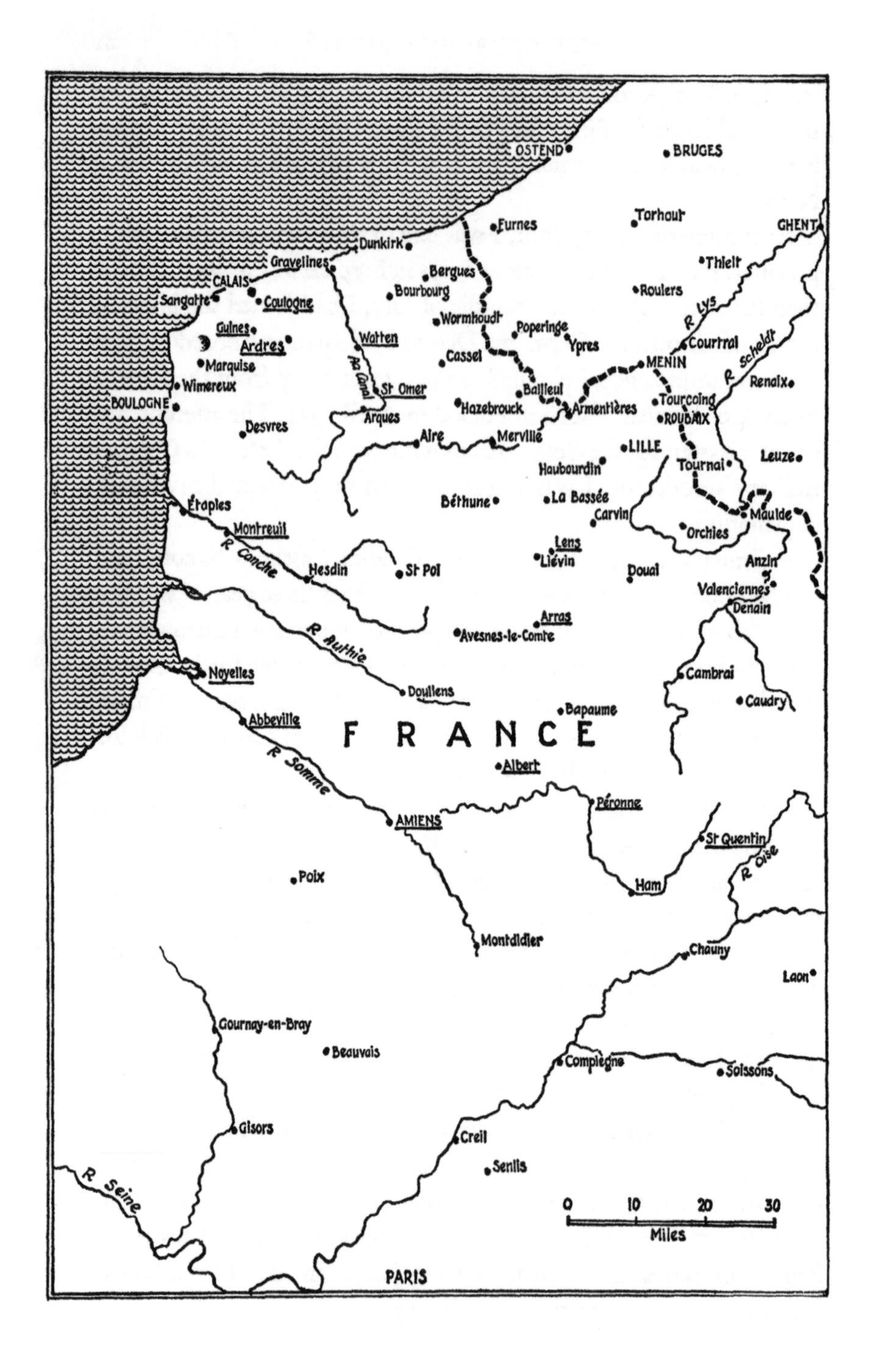

OSTEND
BRUGES
Torhout
GHENT
Furnes
Dunkirk
Thielt
Gravelines
Bergues
CALAIS
Bourbourg
Roulers
Sangatte
Coulogne
R Lys
Wormhoudt
Guines
Poperinge
Ardres
Watten
Courtrai
Ypres
Marquise
Cassel
MENIN
R Scheldt
Aa Canal
St Omer
Bailleul
Renaix
Wimereux
Tourcoing
BOULOGNE
Hazebrouck
Armentières
ROUBAIX
Arques
Desvres
Aire
Merville
LILLE
Haubourdin
Leuze
Tournai
Béthune
La Bassée
Etaples
Carvin
Maulde
Montreuil
Orchies
Lens
R Canche
Liévin
Anzin
Hesdin
St Pol
Douai
Valenciennes
Denain
Arras
R Authie
Avesnes-le-Comte
Noyelles
Cambrai
Doullens
Caudry
Bapaume
Abbeville
FRANCE
Albert
R Somme
Péronne
AMIENS
St Quentin
R Oise
Poix
Ham
Montdidier
Chauny
Laon
Gournay-en-Bray
Beauvais
Compiègne
Soissons
Gisors
Creil
Senlis
R Seine
0
10
20
30
Miles
PARIS

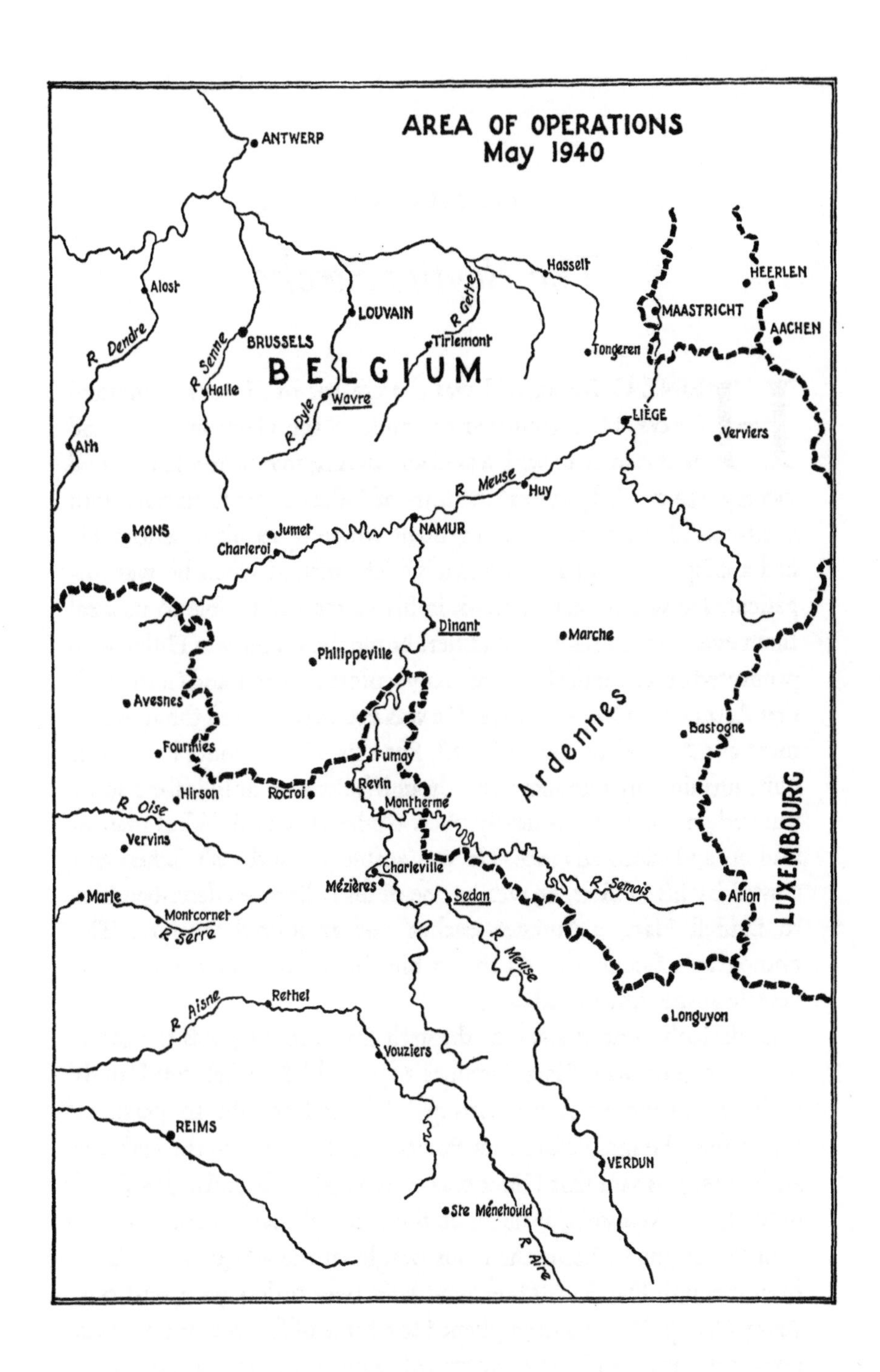
AREA OF OPERATIONS
May 1940
ANTWERP
Alost
R Dendre
R Senne
BRUSSELS
LOUVAIN
R Gette
Hasselt
HEERLEN
MAASTRICHT
AACHEN
Tirlemont
Tongeren
BELGIUM
Halle
R Dyle
Wavre
LIÈGE
Verviers
Ath
R Meuse
Huy
MONS
Jumet
Charleroi
NAMUR
Dinant
Marche
Philippeville
Avesnes
Ardennes
Bastogne
Fourmies
Fumay
Hirson
Rocroi
Revin
Monthermé
LUXEMBOURG
R Oise
Vervins
Charleville
R Semois
Mézières
Sedan
Arlon
Marle
Montcornet
R Serre
R Meuse
R Aisne
Rethel
Longuyon
Vouziers
REIMS
VERDUN
Ste Ménehould
R Aire

CHAPTER TWO

The Scythe Stroke

HEINZ GUDERIAN was the creator of Hitler's Armoured Forces. He introduced the tank to the German Army and used it in 1940 with a skill and daring that nearly led to total victory. He was fifty-two at the time of Calais, short in stature, with a self-confidence in his own judgment which upset his superiors. He had a crisp style and a moustache which bristled when he was impatient. He was by nature frank in his views and unable to conceal them even in the presence of Hitler. None the less, it was Hitler who promoted him over the heads of many seniors to command Germany's first Armoured Corps, in 1938. He was even considered for appointment as Chief of the General Staff. For this job he would have been quite unsuited by temperament, though he was to hold it for a short time when the war was nearly over. Guderian was the ideal man to lead an audacious advance. He was ambitious and rash. Liked and trusted by his soldiers, he was, as one of his colleagues described him to Liddell Hart, a "master-teacher" of armoured warfare. The photograph facing page 65 shows him in his armoured command vehicle at the time of Calais.

Guderian's famous advance through Luxembourg was the result of a change of plan. Since October 1939 Field-Marshal von Rundstedt, commanding Army Group "A", had sought to persuade Hitler that the main assault on France should be made through the Ardennes. It is said that Hitler was convinced by Rundstedt's Chief of Staff, von Manstein, at lunch on the 17th February 1940.

In the original scheme the main weight of the attack would have been through Flanders. Three days later new orders were sent out. Army Group "A" was strengthened to a force of forty-four divisions, seven armoured and three motorised. The attack was to be led by

Panzer Group von Kleist, consisting of two corps, one of three Panzer divisions under Guderian and one of two divisions under General Hoth. From their early morning start on the 10th May, the Germans brushed aside all resistance. They swept through the "impassable" Ardennes and raced to the River Meuse. In attacking on this narrow front with practically all their armour, they took remarkable risks but it was not long before they gained huge victories.

On the 14th May, the British War Cabinet received an agitated message from Paul Reynaud, the French Prime Minister. Five Panzer divisions of Army Group "A" had crossed the Meuse after a concentrated thrust through the Ardennes. Two of Guderian's divisions, the First and the Tenth, with the Second not far behind, had occupied the northern bank of the river on the evening of the 12th May and captured Sedan. Next day, two more Panzer divisions crossed the Meuse at Dinant. One was the Seventh Panzer Division under Rommel. Their orders were to win bridgeheads over the river for the following infantry.

At 7.30 a.m. on the 15th May, Churchill was woken by the telephone at his bedside. It was Paul Reynaud, speaking in English.

"We have been defeated."

As Churchill did not immediately respond he said again: "We are beaten: we have lost the battle."

"Surely," asked Churchill, "it can't have happened so soon?"

But Paul Reynaud replied: "The front is broken near Sedan: they are pouring through in great numbers with tanks and armoured cars."

It was the truth. But Churchill, remembering the German breakthrough of the 21st March 1918, believed that the offensive would have to halt for lack of supplies. He reckoned without the revolution, strongly influenced by Guderian himself, in the use of fast-moving heavy armour.

At 3 p.m. on the 16th May, Churchill flew to Paris to meet Paul Reynaud and General Georges Gamelin the French commander-in-chief. Gamelin explained that Guderian's three Panzer divisions were already advancing on Amiens, apparently making for Abbeville and the coast. There was nothing to stop them. "But where," asked Churchill, "are the strategic reserves of the French Army?"

"There are none left," replied Gamelin.[1]

Churchill was dumbfounded. "The absence of any reserve was one of the greatest surprises I have had in my life." At 9 p.m., he telegraphed the War Cabinet, emphasising "the mortal gravity of the hour".

Churchill saw two great dangers. First, that the B.E.F. would be largely left "in the air" since, having advanced to meet the Germans in Belgium, it would be difficult to withdraw to their old line on the frontier around Lille. Second, that the German thrust would soon destroy the French Army. He telegraphed the War Cabinet to agree to send ten fighter squadrons of the R.A.F. for which Gamelin had pleaded. Early next day, he sought to comfort Paul Reynaud in his Paris apartment, with the news of their agreement.

On his return to London, next morning, the 17th May, Churchill ordered the Chiefs of Staff to consider the possible withdrawal of the B.E.F. from France. On the same day, General Sir Edmund Ironside, Chief of the Imperial General Staff, proposed to the Admiralty that all small vessels should be collected to evacuate the men of the B.E.F. if the worst should happen. They would have to be taken off without their equipment unless they could reach Cherbourg and Brest, for the ports of Dunkirk, Calais and Boulogne could not handle heavy vehicles and stores.

Despite his spectacular success, Guderian was already in difficulties with his superior commanders. He had told Hitler in March 1940 that he would complete his armoured breakthrough and only stop when he reached the coast. Hitler seemed to agree and it never occurred to Guderian that he would order the advance to be halted.

On the 17th May, Guderian was planning to move forward from a position fifty-five miles from Sedan. Early that morning he received a shock. General von Kleist, the Panzer Group commander, arrived and furiously reprimanded him for disobedience. He was ordered to hand over his command. Matters were smoothed over that afternoon by General List, commander of the Twelfth German Army,

[1] Churchill: *The Second World War*, Vol. II, p. 42.

which was following behind. List explained that the order had come from Hitler himself. This was not the last time that Hitler and his staff became nervous at the unheard-of speed of Guderian's advance and interfered with his plans. But he was permitted "a reconnaissance in force" which carried him over the Oise, seventy miles from Sedan. On the 18th May, the Second Panzer Division was in St. Quentin and, the First, after capturing Péronne on the 19th May, moved up to take Amiens.

It was now clear that nothing would stop Guderian from reaching the sea. He was planning to capture the Channel ports and cut off the B.E.F. For this purpose, he intended to send the Tenth Panzer Division direct to Dunkirk, which, he believed, could be easily taken.

By the 19th May, General Lord Gort, the commander-in-chief of the B.E.F., realised that withdrawal to the Channel ports, including Calais, had become a "last alternative". Not everyone agreed. In London, the General Staff were slow to react to the German break-through, in retrospect, astonishingly slow. At a War Office meeting that morning, they were mainly concerned with alternative supply routes for the B.E.F. The "hazardous evacuation of very large forces" was considered "unlikely".

The use of Calais and Boulogne in preference to Dunkirk was debated and the possible evacuation of base units and hospital staffs *in three days' time*. Orders were sent to the Adjutant-General of the B.E.F., Lieut.-General Sir Douglas Brownrigg, to arrange for the return of all "useless mouths" to England. This uncomplimentary term covered the training and administrative units who formed part of the B.E.F. and whose existence would be a drain on its food supplies. Some were trapped and died bravely in defence of the Channel ports. Plans were made that evening at Brownrigg's headquarters at the Imperial Hotel, Boulogne. Finally, there were the wounded to be brought by hospital train and ambulance from the battle zone in Belgium and Northern France. Brownrigg appointed Colonel R. T. Holland, a General Staff officer, as Base Commandant of Calais, to organise the departure of the "useless mouths" and the wounded. Since the outbreak of war, the town had been a transit camp for men on compassionate leave.

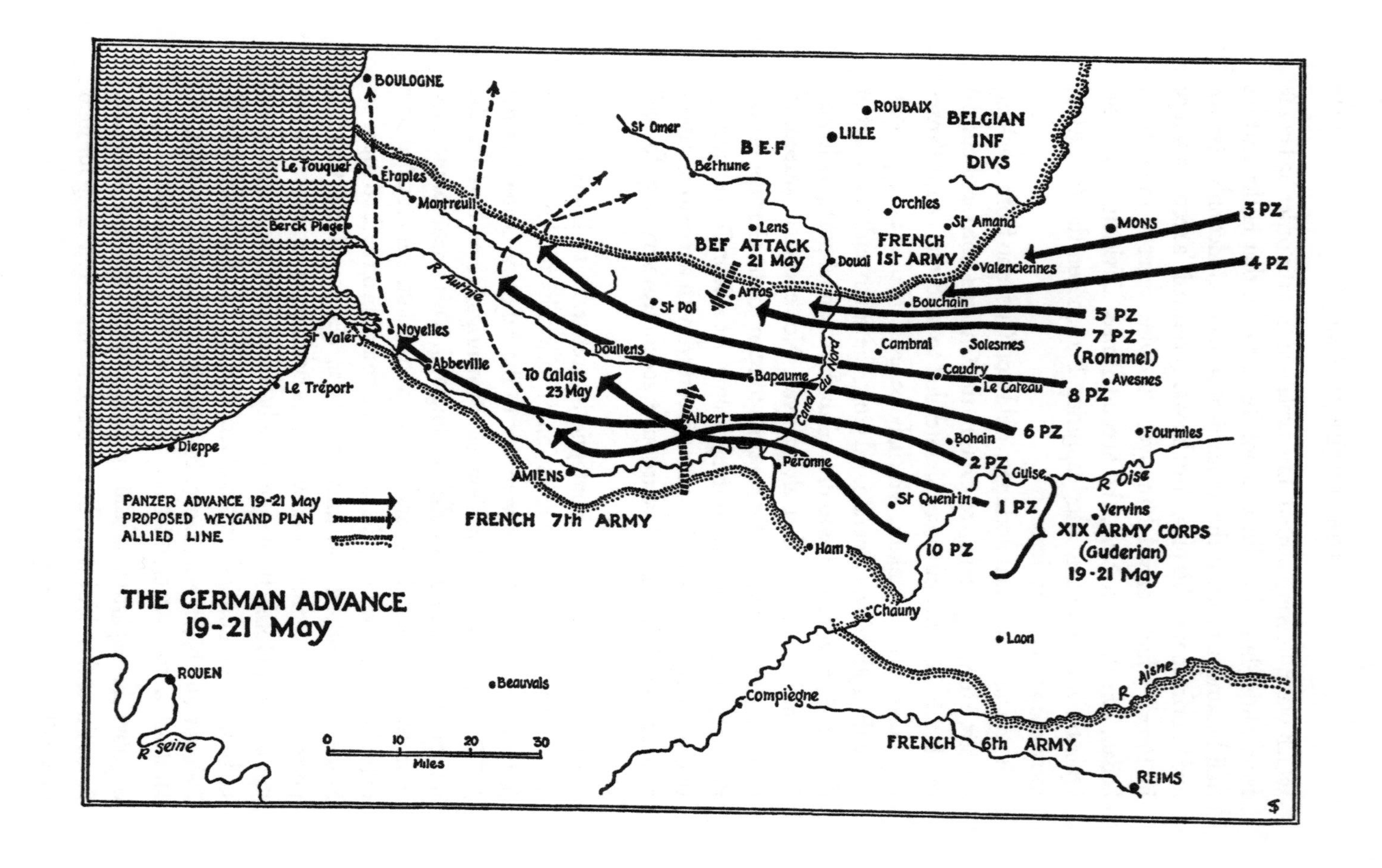
THE GERMAN ADVANCE
19-21 May
PANZER ADVANCE 19-21 May
PROPOSED WEYGAND PLAN
ALLIED LINE
BOULOGNE
Le Touquet
Étaples
Montreuil
Berck Plage
St Valéry
Noyelles
Abbeville
Le Tréport
Dieppe
AMIENS
R Authie
Doullens
To Calais
23 May
St Omer
Béthune
B E F
BEF ATTACK
21 May
Lens
Arras
St Pol
Bapaume
Albert
Péronne
Ham
Douai
Canal du Nord
ROUBAIX
LILLE
BELGIAN
INF
DIVS
Orchies
St Amand
FRENCH
1st ARMY
Valenciennes
Bouchain
MONS
3 PZ
4 PZ
5 PZ
7 PZ
(Rommel)
Cambrai
Solesmes
Caudry
Le Cateau
Avesnes
8 PZ
6 PZ
Bohain
Fourmies
2 PZ
Guise
R Oise
St Quentin
1 PZ
10 PZ
Vervins
XIX ARMY CORPS
(Guderian)
19-21 May
FRENCH 7th ARMY
Chauny
Laon
ROUEN
R Seine
Beauvais
0
10
20
30
Miles
Compiègne
R Aisne
FRENCH 6th ARMY
REIMS

Orders were now given for its anti-aircraft defences to be greatly strengthened. The 6th (Heavy) A.A. Battery R.A., the 172nd Light A.A. Battery R.A. and the First and Second Searchlight Batteries were therefore moved up from Arras and deployed in a semi-circle round the Outer Perimeter of Calais.

When Colonel Holland arrived in Calais at 10 a.m. on the morning of the 20th May, there were no firm plans to defend the Channel ports from German tanks, or to evacuate the B.E.F. He set up a transit camp and the flow of "useless mouths" began. In the next four days, there was a bizarre two-way traffic in the Channel. Soldiers and airmen were evacuated on Channel steamers from the Gare Maritime. On the same steamers came troops from Dover to fight the Germans. Holland found about 150 British non-combatants in the town and a platoon of the Argyll and Sutherland Highlanders who were guarding an R.A.F. radar station on the road to Dunkirk.

The French troops were commanded by Capitaine de Frégate Carlos de Lambertye, a naval reserve officer, with headquarters at Fort Risban on the west side of the Avant Port. He had one and a half infantry companies, all reservists, one machine-gun company and two "soixante quinze" (75 mm) field guns based on the Citadel. The coastal defence guns, in forts and bastions on the sea front, were manned by French sailors.

Until the 22nd May the War Office were unable to decide whether to defend the Channel ports, or use them to evacuate the "non-fighting" elements of the B.E.F. It was not until the last ship left Calais on the 24th May, that the port ceased to be used, except for the evacuation of wounded. It may be that the War Office expected the Panzer divisions to move on Paris where Churchill had seen the burning of official documents in the gardens of the Quai d'Orsay. He wrote that by the 20th May the direction of the German thrust had become "obvious".[2] Amiens and Abbeville had been captured and, during the night, one Panzer division had reached the sea at Noyelles. Guderian was now poised to capture the Channel ports and the B.E.F. was all but surrounded.

On the 20th May the British Navy decided to act. Admiral Sir

[2] Churchill: *The Second World War*, Vol. II, p. 53.

Bertram Ramsay, Flag officer commanding at Dover, was put in charge of all cross-Channel shipping. For the first time plans were put in train for the "emergency evacuation across the Channel of very large forces".

But was the perilous situation "obvious" to everyone? On reading the records it seems that the War Office, even on the 20th were not all of one mind, nor were their decisions all of a piece. At 2 a.m. on the 20th, General Ironside arrived at Boulogne on a visit to Lord Gort. He had been sent by the War Cabinet to tell Gort that the only way for the B.E.F. to break out of their growing encirclement was an attack in the direction of Amiens. Gort could not agree. Seven of his nine divisions were in action on the Scheldt. Even if they could be disengaged it would open a gap between his own army and the Belgians. He reluctantly agreed to try to break through towards the Somme with his two remaining divisions.

"I asked Lord Gort," wrote Ironside in his diary, "under whose orders he was acting." The answer was General Billotte (Commander French Army Group 1) who had a headquarters under Vimy Ridge near Lens. Billotte had given the B.E.F. no orders for eight days. . . . "I found Billotte . . . at Lens in a state of complete depression. No plan, no thought of a plan. . . . I lost my temper and shook Billotte by the button of his tunic. The man is completely beaten."[3]

Billotte was persuaded to draw up a plan for an attack south of Arras, twenty-five miles from the Somme. Ironside had lost all confidence in the French Command and feared it might be too late to save the B.E.F. On his way back to London he stayed the night of the 20th May in Calais at the Hotel Excelsior. C. R. Hodgson, the new Town Major, paid him a visit and expressed the fear that Calais was already full of fifth columnists disguised as refugees. This was to prove no exaggeration and many were well-trained snipers. Calais was twice bombed that night, between 11 p.m. and midnight, and just before dawn. Most of the bombs fell in Calais-Nord, and one, bursting against the wall of Ironside's bedroom at the Hotel Excelsior, blew him out of bed.

At 5 a.m. on the 21st May, Ironside left Calais for the aerodrome

[3] *The Ironside Diaries*, p. 321.

at St. Inglevert, west of the town. He was kept waiting for an hour but reached Hendon in forty minutes escorted by six fighters. He was deeply pessimistic. "God help the B.E.F.," he wrote in his diary that night. He now felt that the B.E.F. could not be extricated and that the only hope was a march south-west. But he reported that they were "in good heart" and so far had only about five hundred battle casualties.

Two "fearsome alternatives" now faced the British War Cabinet. Either the B.E.F. must make a new effort to get through to the Somme, which Gort believed to be impossible: or they must fall back on Boulogne, Calais and Dunkirk and evacuate the troops by sea under heavy air attack, with the loss of all their artillery.

At 2 p.m. on the 21st a determined effort was made by British tanks and infantry to break through south of Arras. At first it succeeded, and 400 prisoners were taken, but during the night the British were forced to withdraw by pressure from the Seventh and Eighth Panzer Divisions. This action gained time for the defence of Boulogne and Calais and improved in consequence the prospects of holding Dunkirk. It made "a considerable impression on the staff of Panzer Group von Kleist," wrote Guderian angrily, "which suddenly became remarkably nervous."[4]

This spirited British counter-attack at Arras forced Guderian to abandon his cherished plan to rush the Tenth Panzer Division, which later captured Calais, straight to Dunkirk. It almost unhinged von Rundstedt and Hitler. Guderian's protests that the chance had come to take all three Channel ports were overruled. He was ordered to wait on the Somme. The B.E.F. lay within his grasp but he was powerless to move.

The morning of the 21st May, therefore, saw testy Guderian hamstrung before his prey, the B.E.F. counter-attack a failure and the War Office unable to make up its mind. Ironside was grimly disconsolate about the B.E.F. but Admiral Ramsay was well ahead with the plans which led to the brilliant success of Operation Dynamo. The French Navy were planning to supply their armies in Northern France through the Channel ports.

[4] Guderian: *Panzer Leader*, p. 114.

On the evening of the 21st May, the Third Battalion, Royal Tank Regiment in Hampshire and the First Battalion, Queen Victoria's Rifles in Kent were ordered to France. The Second Battalion, The 60th Rifles and the First Battalion, The Rifle Brigade were to follow them next day. No one had decided what they should do. All would come under Brigadier Nicholson's command. But what would be his orders?

In Paris that Monday evening, the French leaders were more hopeful. Gamelin had been dismissed and General Maxime Weygand, aged seventy-three, had been appointed commander-in-chief of the Allied armies. At the village of Coulogne, four miles from Calais, the mayor, Monsieur Souilleux, assured me that all would now be well: "Weygand", he said, "c'est un homme." But others shook their heads. It would need more than Weygand, who had never commanded troops in battle, to save France.

CHAPTER THREE

The Defence of Orphanage Farm

ON the 21st May, while Guderian was raging at his headquarters on the Somme, I was conscious of my own lack of training and military demeanour. I never supposed that I should be flung into the bloody conflict of the next few days, let alone experience the adventures described in my earlier books.[1] Despite some infantry training, The Territorial Army had prescribed a "non-fighting" role for me, which in the light of events is faintly amusing.

On the 21st May, the village of Coulogne, off the main road from Calais to St. Omer, showed few signs of impending disaster. I had arrived there on the previous day in my capacity as a troop commander in the Second Searchlight Battery. The First and Second Searchlight Batteries, part of the 1st Searchlight Regiment, both took part in the defence of Calais. Each consisted of 330 men divided into four troops under a junior officer. The men were pre-war Territorials with a number of young "militia" called up for anti-aircraft defence in 1939. The Second Battery, in which I served, had a number of regular reservists as staff sergeants from the Royal Engineers. The rest were "gunners", a generic term in the British Army at that time. As in many anti-aircraft units, there was a high proportion of older men with First World War experience. Most were industrial workers with a few clerks and professional men who did not see themselves as front-line soldiers. All were vocal and democratic.

It is no disrespect to the Searchlights to say that they did not seem likely to hold up one of Guderian's Panzer divisions. Their principal task was to operate searchlights in fields around large towns, to dazzle low-flying and divebombing aircraft and to aid anti-aircraft gunners.

[1] *They Have Their Exits* and *Saturday at M.I.9*, Hodder and Stoughton.

They lived on these rural sites in small detachments and rarely met as a single unit. What they lacked in "regimental pride", they made up in willingness to fight. Their non-commissioned Officers were often leaders, who, but for the confused manpower policy of the War Office, would have been in "fighting" units or have held commissions. The performance of the Searchlights and other anti-aircraft units at Calais was remarkable. They had practically no infantry training and indeed did not expect to meet the enemy face to face on land. They had only rifles, which many had never fired, with old Lewis guns, a few Bren guns for anti-aircraft use, and a weapon known as the Boys anti-tank rifle which no one had yet dared to touch.

Despite alarms from refugees on the 21st May, we did not believe that the Germans had broken through. At Coulogne, such rumours were contemptuously assumed to be the work of the fifth column which in various disguises had penetrated the imagination of the B.E.F. and even more of the fevered French. We were confident that, at most, a few armoured cars, a few motor-cyclists or a few light tanks were threatening the Allied lines of communication.

I travelled from Arras to Coulogne in an Austin Seven of the earliest type. My driver Gunner Cooper was ashamed that we were not staying to defend Arras. He despised the Searchlights and thirsted for action. A large man in an overcoat on a warm May morning, he almost filled the Austin Seven, so that, wedged together, we felt ridiculous in the little khaki motor-car. The Searchlight lorries, three-tonners, rumbled slowly after us through Lens and St. Omer. As we approached the medieval town of Ardres, ten miles south of Calais, a woman spat at us and called us cowards. She shook her fist and shouted: "Merde!" This did not impress us in the least and by nightfall my troop was cooking M & V beneath the plane trees of the market place, by the statute of General de St. Just, the former deputy for Ardres.

Coulogne, where we moved next morning was, in 1940, a humble, straggling place. Roads led from it to Pont de Coulogne, over the St. Omer Canal, and past Orphanage Farm, a large building in tall trees, on the way to the main route to Ardres and St. Omer. The visibility along these roads was poor. Coulogne had been a fortified outpost when Calais was occupied by the English in the reign of Henry VIII and a base camp in the First World War, but in 1940 it was difficult to defend. Rising ground to the south-east meant that there was no reasonable field of fire from that corner of the village. Nor was the dead straight road to Pont-de-Briques in the south a pleasant position for a road-block.

The villagers were farm-workers or people from factories in Calais-St. Pierre who cycled to work and spent their evenings in the café de la Mairie. The Mairie, built in 1830, was my headquarters. It has survived the war, and stands, encircled by elm trees, at the cross-roads in the centre of the village. Along the road to Pont de Coulogne in the west were rows of untidy brick villas and bungalows as far as the level-crossing over the Calais-St. Omer railway. The church stands opposite the Mairie, of melancholy design and built in 1870. In its graveyard is buried my cheerful dispatch rider Gunner R. Branton, killed in action at Coulogne at the age of twenty-one.

No bombs were dropped that first night near Calais. On going to bed at the Mairie, I refused to believe that our role in Calais would be other than anti-aircraft defence. I was twenty-four, unmilitary, with opinions of my own.

Next morning, Lieut.-Colonel R. M. Goldney, who had been appointed Air Defence Commander for Calais, moved from Lille to Ardres where he set up his first headquarters. Goldney was a regular gunner officer aged forty-seven, who had seen service in the First World War and, since 1939, had commanded the 1st Searchlight Regiment. He had thirty-four officers and 1,196 men with which to defend the docks at Calais from low-flying attacks by the Luftwaffe who were seeking to prevent the evacuation of the "useless mouths" and the wounded. On the 23rd May, two officers and 230 men joined them from the 2nd Searchlight Regiment at Boulogne.

Goldney organised these troops in support of the infantry when the battle for Calais began, but for the present he had to defend the port. He had particularly counted for help on the 172nd Light A.A. Battery of the 58th Light A.A. Regiment, R.A. This battery had been trained in England on the Bofors gun. But on arrival in France in March, it took over twelve ancient Vickers two-pounder naval guns in position near Lille. These guns were mounted on nine thicknesses of railway sleepers, buried in the ground, and never intended to be mobile. When orders came at 1 a.m. on the 20th May to move to Calais, the gun-mountings had to be left behind owing to lack of transport. The guns were brought to Calais but could not go into action. Their place was taken by transferring four Bren guns each from the five Searchlight batteries.

Manning these Bren guns on the docks became an uncomfortable and hazardous job as the crews were frequently machine-gunned from the air and bombed by day and night, despite little damage to the harbour. Fortunately transport was found to collect the railway sleepers, and the 172nd Light A.A. Battery had eight guns in action within two days. The 6th (Heavy) A.A. Battery had four 3.7-inch guns at Oyez Farm on the road from Calais to Sangatte and three outside Fort Vert on the Gravelines road to the east.

On the afternoon of the 21st May, Paul Reynaud made a dramatic speech in the French Senate. "La Patrie est en danger!" he cried. At once, the roads round Calais were choked with refugees making for the coast. But to the Searchlight men who did not speak French, the "panic" was thought unnecessary, hysterical and ridiculous.

Refugee parties came from east and west, both thinking they were moving away from the enemy. They proved difficult to control at the road-blocks and many fifth columnists and snipers must have entered Calais at this time. They were soon joined by stragglers from the French Army and by Dutch and Belgian units who had been sent to France for training but could go no further.

Coulogne, lying at a central position between the St. Omer Canal and the road from Calais to St. Omer, was a ghastly bottleneck.

On the 22nd May, rumours of a German advance towards Guines began to grow. No one took them seriously except the French civilians who thought the cheerful British soldiers ignorant of war. Many claimed to have seen the Panzers a few miles south of Guines, for the Sixth and Eighth Panzer Divisions were turning north-east to Béthune and St. Omer.

Sceptical though I was about the extent of the German forces, which I still imagined to consist of reconnaissance groups, I was not surprised to receive Colonel Goldney's order that all Searchlight detachments should concentrate at their troop headquarters at dawn on the 23rd May. This meant that sixty or seventy men would now be available to defend Coulogne, with rifles, two Bren guns and one Boys anti-tank rifle which no one had, as yet, been trained to fire. I was ordered to dig trenches to the south and south-east of the village and build road-blocks.

I was not greatly alarmed. I could not believe that, despite all the confusion, the British High Command could be so ill-informed. How was it possible that the whereabouts of Guderian and at least four other Panzer divisions could be unknown?

We know from the First Panzer Division War Diary that they were bombed all day by the R.A.F. Yet the "secret" Situation Map issued by the War Office at 4 a.m. on the 23rd May is devoid of useful information. Calais is not even marked on the map. There is an arrow marked "AFV"[2] in the direction of Boulogne which was attacked and surrounded by the Second Panzer Division at 5 p.m. on the previous afternoon! Another arrow points vaguely to the north-east in the direction of Dunkirk.

Throughout the night of the 22nd May, a stream of weary people flowed through Coulogne and halted at the road-blocks at the entrances to the village. I had orders to prevent them converging on Calais where the bombing had put out of action electricity and water supplies. Food was scarce and many houses and hotels abandoned but still the refugees came in overwhelming numbers. I lay awake in my bedroom at the Mairie and heard the tramp of their feet as they were turned away to sleep in the fields. The red glow of the fires of Calais, started by the Luftwaffe, shone on the ceiling and there was the sharp crack of the anti-aircraft guns.

Towards dawn on the 23rd May, a sergeant woke me. There had been an altercation at the entrance from Pont de Coulogne where some other unit was turning away the people, so that they were sent from pillar to post. Led by a young priest, a column of men, women and children, half a mile long, was standing in the road six of seven

[2] i.e. armoured fighting vehicles.

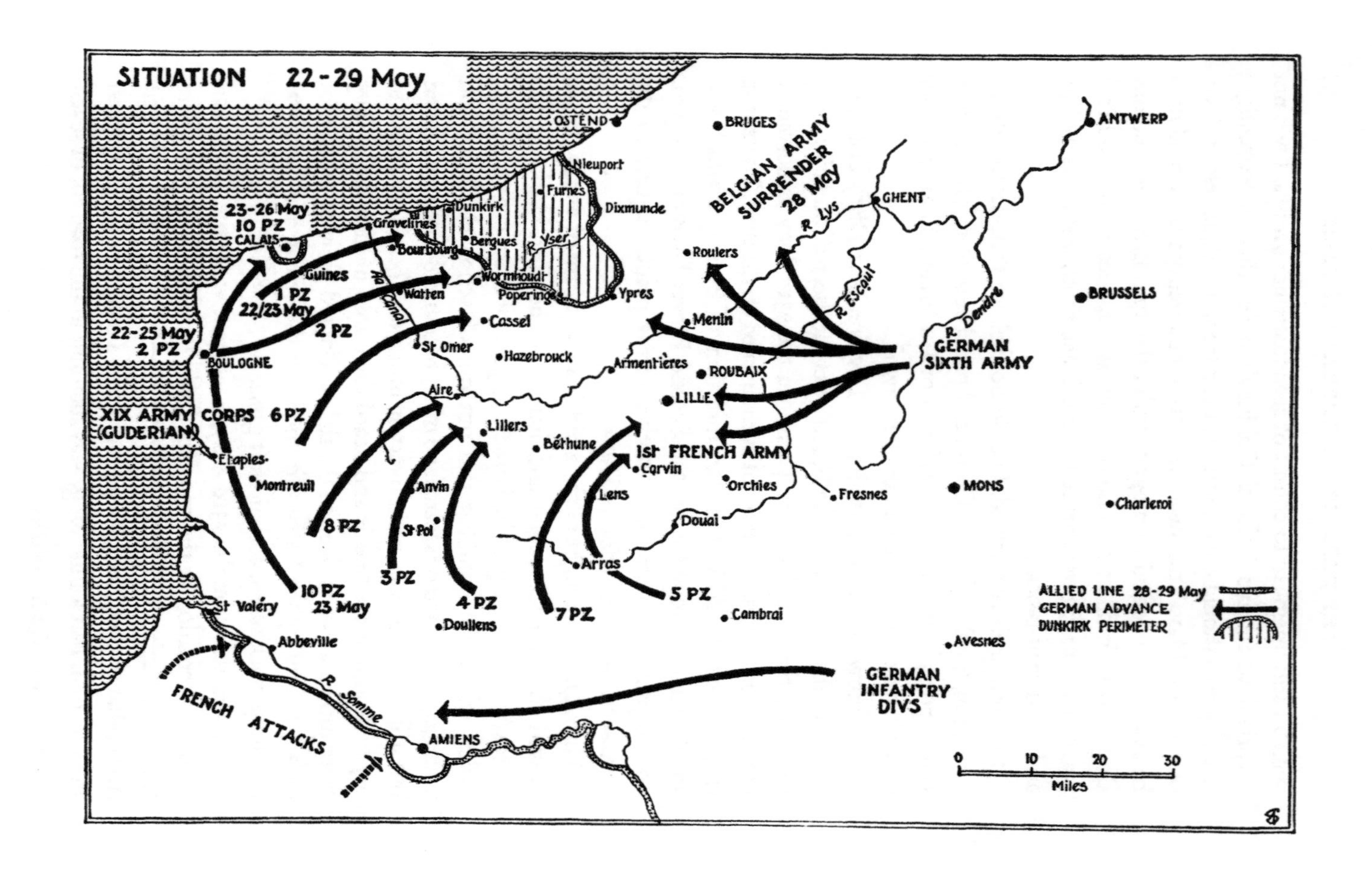
SITUATION 22-29 May
OSTEND
BRUGES
ANTWERP
BELGIAN ARMY SURRENDER 28 May
Nieuport
Furnes
Dixmunde
GHENT
R Lys
23-26 May 10 PZ
CALAIS
Gravelines
Dunkirk
Bergues
R Yser
Bourbourg
Roulers
Guines
1 PZ 22/23 May
Watten
Wormhoudt
Poperinge
Ypres
R Escaut
Aa Canal
22-25 May 2 PZ
2 PZ
Cassel
Menin
R Dendre
BRUSSELS
BOULOGNE
St Omer
Hazebrouck
Armentières
ROUBAIX
GERMAN SIXTH ARMY
LILLE
Aire
XIX ARMY CORPS (GUDERIAN)
6 PZ
Lillers
Béthune
1st FRENCH ARMY
Etaples
Carvin
Montreuil
Anvin
Lens
Orchies
Fresnes
MONS
Charleroi
8 PZ
St Pol
Douai
3 PZ
Arras
10 PZ 23 May
4 PZ
5 PZ
St Valéry
7 PZ
Cambrai
Doullens
ALLIED LINE 28-29 May
GERMAN ADVANCE
DUNKIRK PERIMETER
Abbeville
Avesnes
R Somme
GERMAN INFANTRY DIVS
FRENCH ATTACKS
AMIENS
0
10
20
30
Miles

abreast. The priest, seeing the smoke and flames of Calais against the night sky, had wisely counselled his flock to return to the fields south of Coulogne. This provoked a wild chorus of rage and fear. Women and children sobbed and men cried that the priest was a traitor. He could not be on their side. They could escape the Germans by boat if they reached Calais. They seemed about to rush the road-block, guarded only by the sergeant and a dim militiaman. I drew my .38 Webley revolver of the First World War and asked for silence. "Don't shoot! Don't shoot! mon lieutenant," said several anxious voices.

As the light grew, I could see their pale faces. I explained the situation in Calais and at length they agreed to stay in the fields. As for the young priest, holding out his papers, he seemed serene and unafraid. There was no time to question him further.

These incidents were tiring for British sentries at the road-blocks at all the exits of Calais, who spoke no French. The fear of the Germans was tremendous and at some places people flung themselves at the barriers. Priests were the objects of great suspicion. One was said to have presented papers for twenty tough-looking youths in shorts. Long after they had disappeared, knowledgeable people claimed to have seen "machine-gun parts" in their haversacks.

At this moment, the forward units of the First Panzer Division, and assault group under Oberst Krüger, were only eighteen miles from Calais. They had come up during the night and could have captured the town with little fighting. But Guderian was determined to get to Dunkirk. He did not think Calais important and he ordered the division to press forward south of the town and force bridgeheads over the Aa Canal at Watten.

Krüger was to cross the Guines Canal and cut the Calais–St. Omer road. He was told that there would be a good opportunity to take Calais from the south-east. The town must be taken "by surprise" and "a battle avoided under all circumstances".[3]

These cautious orders had fateful results but the division was at only half strength and the troops were tired from travelling long distances. If the circumstances were favourable, the infantry regiment

[3] First Panzer Division: War Diary.

on Krüger's left was to cross the Marck Canal, circle round and take Calais from the east, while the division pushed on to the Aa Canal and Dunkirk.

Since 10 a.m. on the 23rd May the Tenth Panzer Division under Major-General Schaal had been restored to Guderian's command. Panzer Group Kleist had decided that the crisis at Arras was over and it was no longer in reserve. They were told to hurry to Montreuil, a distance of thirty-five miles. The British were said to be landing fresh troops at the Channel ports as they had already done at Boulogne. So "it seemed most important to the division to follow the rest of the XIXth German Army Corps and gain the Channel ports".[4]

In four hours they covered thirty-two miles and Schaal received the order: "Capture Calais. Details of the enemy there not known."

Krüger's assault group of the First Panzer Division continued their advance eastwards. After he had beaten off an attack by the Third Royal Tank Regiment between Hames Boucres and Guines, his light tanks advanced to the St. Omer Canal at Les Attaques, eight miles due south of Calais on the main road to St. Omer. These tanks were reported to 2/Lieut. R. J. Barr, commander of "C" Troop First Searchlight Battery, at Ferme Vendroux, south of Coulogne, at noon. They were making for the bridge at Les Attaques. With about fifty men, Barr doubled back through Coulogne to hold the bridge and crossroads, where he formed a road-block with a three-ton lorry and a bus. After sending for reinforcements from the Second Searchlight Battery at Pont de Coulogne he waited for the German tanks.

About 2 p.m. they were seen crossing the canal bridge. From the east bank Barr's "C" Troop opened fire with Bren guns, rifles and anti-tank rifles and held the light tanks up for over half an hour. They prevented the Germans from crossing the bridge on six occasions until medium tanks arrived with 2 cm guns and shelled the houses of Les Attaques.

Barr was now forced back to the main road and the larger tanks advanced, pushing aside the road-block. His call for help had been quickly answered by the Second Searchlight Battery. Nothing demonstrates better the youthful enthusiasm and lack of training in

[4] Tenth Panzer Division: War Diary.

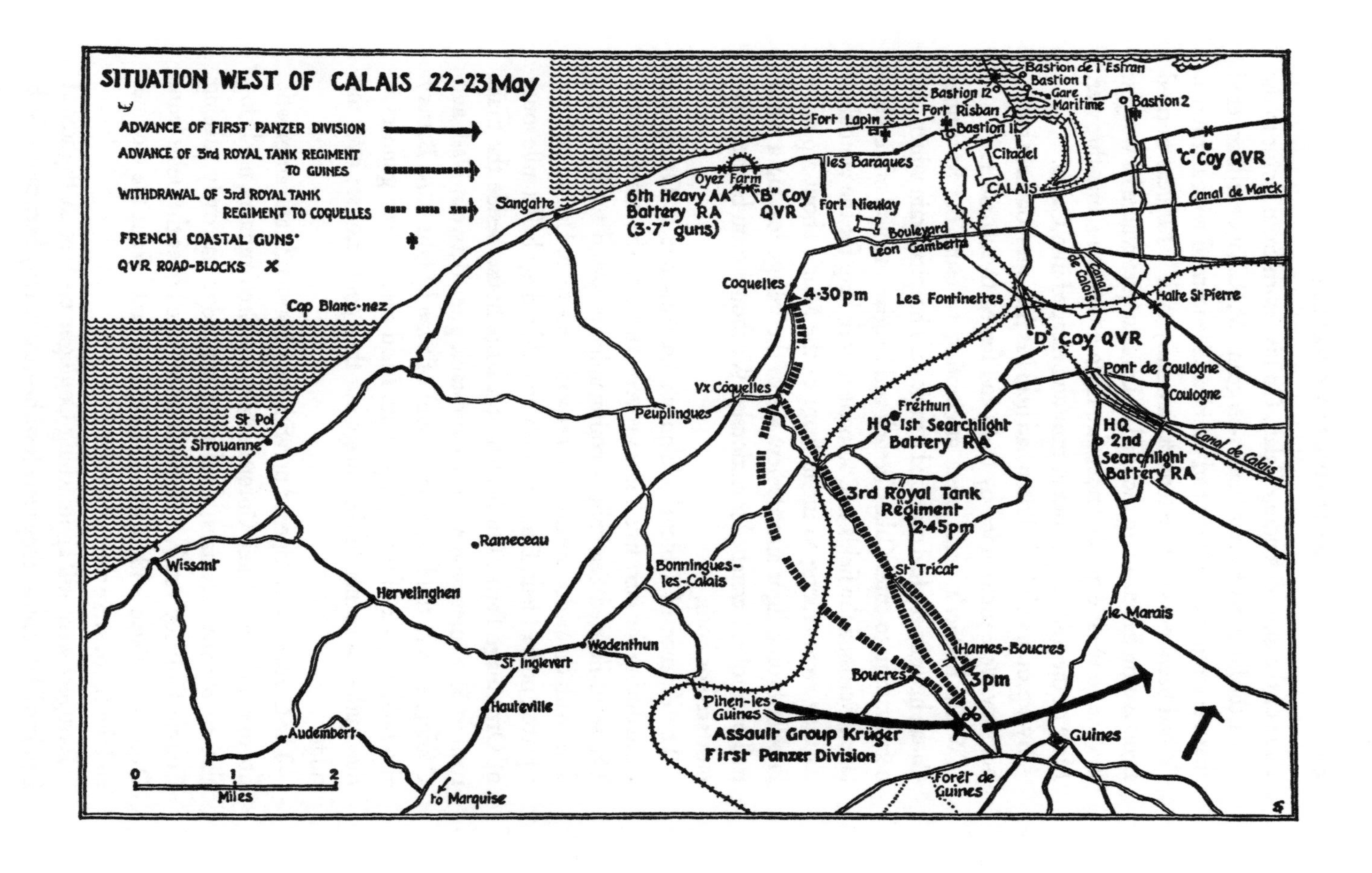

SITUATION WEST OF CALAIS 22-23 May
ADVANCE OF FIRST PANZER DIVISION
ADVANCE OF 3rd ROYAL TANK REGIMENT TO GUINES
WITHDRAWAL OF 3rd ROYAL TANK REGIMENT TO COQUELLES
FRENCH COASTAL GUNS
QVR ROAD-BLOCKS
Bastion de l'Estran
Bastion I
Gare Maritime
Bastion 2
Bastion 12
Fort Risban
Bastion 11
Fort Lapin
Citadel
CALAIS
"C" Coy QVR
Canal de Marck
les Baraques
Oyez Farm
6th Heavy AA Battery RA (3·7" guns)
"B" Coy QVR
Fort Nieulay
Sangatte
Boulevard Léon Gambetta
Canal de Calais
Halte St Pierre
Coquelles
4·30pm
Les Fontinettes
Cap Blanc-nez
"D" Coy QVR
Pont de Coulogne
Coulogne
Vx Coquelles
Fréthun
HQ 1st Searchlight Battery RA
HQ 2nd Searchlight Battery RA
Canal de Calais
St Pol
Strouanne
Peuplingues
3rd Royal Tank Regiment
2·45pm
Rameceau
Wissant
Bonningues-les-Calais
St Tricat
Hervelinghen
le Marais
Wadenthun
Hames-Boucres
St Inglevert
Boucres
3pm
Pihen-les-Guines
Hauteville
Assault Group Krüger
First Panzer Division
Guines
Audembert
Forêt de Guines
0
1
2
Miles
to Marquise

some of the units defending Calais. On his return from a visit to the town, the Battery Quarter-master-sergeant W. R. Kinnear discovered that the ammunition lorry had vanished. He learned with alarm that "it had been sent out to intercept an enemy tank". Kinnear hurried in his Austin Seven along the road to Les Attaques where he was just in time to see it explode under fire from a German flame-thrower. Most of the soldiers got out in time and escaped into Calais.

By 5 p.m. Barr's "C" Troop had held Les Attaques for three hours, but they were surrounded by tanks and forced to surrender.

While Krüger's tanks were attempting to cross the St. Omer Canal, his infantry had captured a stationary hospital train which had been waiting to enter Calais. French and Belgian medical officers had already crossed the fields to Coulogne to seek help for the wounded. As they were talking to me in front of the Mairie about 2 p.m., a Fieseler Storch light aircraft flew across the village leaving a white trail of smoke. I watched it anxiously. We should soon be shelled or mortared or both.

The defence of Colonel Goldney's headquarters at Orphanage Farm during the next five hours proved crucial to the whole battle. The stout-hearted Searchlight commander prepared to defend the farm with the padre, medical officer and a few men. He had ordered a patrol, under Lieut. Duncan Nash, to hold a ridge half a mile south of Orphanage Farm. On his left at a large house beside the main road to St. Omer, was a French anti-tank gun. Between Nash and Coulogne were the headquarters staff of 172nd Light A.A. Battery also holding part of the high ground. I had posted Bren gunners at the south-east corner of the village but they could not see over the ridge.

The Germans now opened up with very heavy rifle and automatic fire to which we replied. Unfortunately, my Bren gunners, not being able to see the Germans, fired over the ridge narrowly missing Colonel Goldney's staff. A dispatch rider roared over the fields from Orphanage Farm with a well-deserved "rocket" from the Colonel and the Brens were moved forward.

Refugees were still approaching Coulogne on foot. A frightened family of Austrians—they were Jewish—reached my barricade which comprised the village hearse and two farm carts. They pleaded with me to let them into Calais but, as we talked, there was a deafening crash. A mortar bomb burst on the roof of the Mairie, showering us with broken tiles and twigs. The village was accurately bombed for fifteen minutes, paving stones were hurled into the air and several houses caught fire.

When the barrage lifted, I walked along the main street. A young girl lay dead at the corner of the road. A soldier gently pulled her tartan skirt over her knees.

At 5 p.m. the party on the ridge came under fire from tanks. They held on gallantly in their exposed position but they were forced to withdraw down the slope to Orphanage Farm. The First Panzer Division War Diary describes the opposition as "stiff". It had already lasted three hours and embarrassed their left flank.

Medium artillery was now brought up and Orphanage Farm shelled for over an hour. I could see the shellbursts in the trees 800 yards away. At 7 p.m. Goldney decided that the place was no longer tenable and after reporting the situation to Colonel Holland in Calais, ordered withdrawal in small parties to a road-block at the Halte St. Pierre, a mile and a half towards Calais.

Orphanage Farm was in flames when I received an order to send the men into Calais by lorry and remain in Coulogne to blow up the "cuckoo". This was the code name for the experimental sound-location equipment which the Searchlights had begun to use and it stood on a trailer in the centre of the village. It was on no account to fall into German hands.

For the next five minutes I was in a delicate position, as with Sergeant Maginis and a sapper with some guncotton, we tried unsuccessfully to blow it up. While German infantry came over the ridge, two huge French aviation tankers appeared. Their drivers ditched them and set the fuel on fire so that a colossal cloud of thick, black smoke covered the village and hid our line of retreat to Calais. The "cuckoo" providentially exploded, and, gasping, we escaped to the main road.

"Battle Group Krüger . . . when darkness fell stood at the gates of Calais. It was reported that the town was strongly held by the enemy and that a surprise attack was out of the question. The capture of Calais was handed over to the Tenth Panzer Division, while the First Panzer Division was ordered to push on towards Gravelines and Dunkirk."[5]

And so a great chance was lost. Guderian's First Panzer Division had been hampered on its left flank, as it advanced to Dunkirk, by British tanks and searchlights.

If Calais had fallen to this division on the afternoon of the 23rd, Guderian would surely have sent his Tenth Panzer Division straight to Dunkirk and captured it before the defences were organised. The German records show that it was Goldney's stand at Orphanage Farm which made him change his plans.

"This little action," wrote Nicholson, "succeeded in delaying the advance of an enemy armoured column by this route by some five hours."[6] It gave a breathing space to the regular British troops who landed from England that afternoon, and with the Territorials held the Tenth Panzer Division at Calais in four days of intense fighting.

[5] First Panzer Division: War Diary for the 23rd May 1940.

[6] Unfinished report.

CHAPTER FOUR

"An Extraordinary Way to go to War"

TWO days before the battle of Orphanage Farm, while Guderian was fuming at Abbeville and Paul Reynaud was addressing the French Senate, the Third Battalion Royal Tank Regiment was at Fordingbridge in Hampshire. This was also the day when the Fourth and Seventh Battalions of the Royal Tank Regiment supported by the Durham Light Infantry began their counter-stroke at Arras which threw the German High Command into confusion.

Earlier in the month, the Third Battalion had been reorganised and had only done a small amount of training. A few days before, about one-third of them had been taken away to form a new unit and were replaced by officers and men from a training regiment. They were thus thrown into the battle when their fighting efficiency was not at its highest.

The Battalion was already under orders to move to France. They were to go to Pacy-sur-Eure in Normandy and complete their training with the rest of the First British Armoured Division. Their tanks and other vehicles had already been loaded on the vehicle ship *City of Christchurch* at Southampton on the 19th May. The men were due to embark on the 23rd May. None of this suggests that any plans existed before the 21st May to land tanks to defend the Channel ports. The difficulties of landing tanks in haste and rushing them into action were certainly not foreseen.

The *City of Christchurch* had been most meticulously loaded in accordance with regulations. These provided that all guns and machine-guns should be packed in thick mineral jelly which took hours to remove. The tanks were at the bottom of the ship with the trucks and light vehicles above them. The petrol tanks were empty, but 7,000 gallons of petrol were stacked on the deck in wooden boxes. At this time the chances of being bombed in the Channel by the Luftwaffe were good. All of this petrol was in four-gallon cans which made fuelling of the tanks a long operation. No doubt the method of packing was suited to a leisurely disembarkation before moving to the training grounds at Pacy-sur-Eure. It proved a disaster when the tanks were badly needed and had to be hurriedly landed in the face of the enemy.

The Battalion had twenty-one light and twenty-seven cruiser tanks at Calais. The light tanks were Mark VI. They had a crew of three with two machine-guns, one a .303-inch and the other .5-inch. They were lightly armoured and easy meat for German anti-tank guns. Visitors to the Tank Museum will see what I mean.

The cruiser tanks were of three varieties. Some were A9s with a crew of six, a 2-pounder gun and three Vickers machine-guns. There were a few A10s which instead of the 2-pounder gun had a 3.7-inch mortar for close support. The remainder were A13s which had a crew of four, a 2-pounder gun and one machine-gun. The thin armour of these tanks made them vulnerable to German anti-tank guns but their 2-pounder guns were effective against German tanks.

At 8 p.m. on the 21st May, Lieut.-Colonel Reginald Keller, the battalion commander, had taken his wife to dine in Bournemouth expecting to leave for Pacy-sur-Eure next day. Keller was a regular tank officer who had seen service in the First World War and had received command of the Third Battalion in October 1939. He was having a drink before dinner, when he was called to the telephone and ordered to return at once to his headquarters at Fordingbridge. When he reached there, he was told to leave with his battalion for Dover at 10 p.m. This was impossible since the men were in widely scattered billets and some were out on passes.

Notices were flashed on cinema screens for the men to return and, by what Keller describes as "gigantic administrative effort", the Battalion was on the train by midnight. Only one officer and twenty-five men were missing as it drew out of Fordingbridge. Nothing whatever had been said about the Battalion's destination and as the train steamed through the night, there was some anxiety concerning the tanks buried in the hold of the *City of Christchurch* at Southampton.

This atmosphere of vagueness and mystery was not dispelled when the train arrived at Dover at 7 a.m. Keller was met by a staff officer who took him to the Lord Warden Hotel. A large bundle of maps was handed over to him with an envelope addressed to the Senior British Officer at Calais. It will not surprise those who experienced the campaign in 1940, to hear that the War Office did not know the name of this officer or where he was to be found in Calais. An eyebrow might possibly be lifted, when it is remembered that Colonel Holland had already been installed as Base Commandant in the Boulevard Léon Gambetta for the past two days and that he was in continuous touch with the War Office by telephone. This method of communication was kept open by the Royal Corps of Signals during most of the battle.

At Dover Keller was told: "The Germans have made a big break to the west but there is no enemy north of St. Pol."

On the day that this statement was made (the morning of the 22nd May) the Sixth and Eighth Panzer Divisions were already *west* of St. Pol and had turned north-east to Béthune and St. Omer. Generally, the War Office were from twenty-four to forty-eight hours behind the Panzers and sometimes more. This is surprising in view of the great R.A.F. activity of which Guderian especially complained.

The War Office Situation Maps do not identify five separate armoured divisions in the Pas de Calais until 5 a.m. on the 25th May when seven were actually in the area. Information given to Keller was further complicated by the mention of "a small German armoured force in the area Boulogne-Calais, numbering 7 light and 4 medium tanks". This suggested no more than an isolated battle group.

At Dover, Keller was given no clear instructions about the role of his tanks. He was led to think that the B.E.F. headquarters, believed to be at Hazebrouck, would issue orders on arrival and he was to be ready for action as soon as possible. The purpose of landing his tanks was presumably to stop the Germans, who had encircled Boulogne, from capturing Calais, but Keller was not told this till Brigadier Nicholson arrived twenty-four hours later.

The Battalion boarded the personnel ship *Maid of Orleans* and left Dover at 11 a.m. in a thick mist, which, slowly clearing, revealed the spire of Notre Dame and the clock tower of the Hôtel de Ville. There was no sign of battle except broken glass on the platform as the ship tied up at the Gare Maritime at 1.15 p.m. There was no news of their vehicle ship *City of Christchurch*. One of their junior officers, Mr. R. W. McAllum, wrote to me:

"All our tanks were left in their own boat. All of the personnel on another. If either had sunk the battalion would have been useless."

The *City of Christchurch* did not appear till 4 p.m. and it was necessary for the tank crews to wait in the sand dunes which formed the shore of the Bassin des Chasses de l'Est, a large artificial water east of the Gare Maritime.

On stepping ashore, Keller found the British embarkation staff nervous. They had been severely bombed and were anxious to get the ships out of the harbour before the next wave of Heinkels appeared. The new arrivals had first to disembark and the "useless mouths" and the wounded to be taken aboard before the ship could leave for England. By now, refugees were besieging the Gare Maritime and men of the Corps of Military Police, who played a splendid part at Calais, were brought in to control the gangways.

On the platform of the Gare Maritime Keller encountered a Full Colonel to whom he reported the arrival of his battalion. The Full Colonel replied that it was nothing to do with him as he was getting out with his kit as soon as the ship sailed. Like many others the Colonel had proper authority to leave for England as part of the evacuation of the non-combatants ordered by the War Office. None the less this was a shock to Keller.

He had no transport and, finding the Full Colonel's staff car, he dumped the luggage from it on the quay, and, with his adjutant, drove into Calais. It was more than an hour before he found Colonel Holland in the cellar of a clinic in the Boulevard Léon Gambetta. First he tried the Hôtel de Ville but the gendarmes refused to let him enter, since none of his battalion had been given the military identity cards issued to the B.E.F. A maddening discussion ensued outside the entrance from which it emerged that "some sort of British H.Q."

existed 600 yards east of the Pont Jourdan, a railway bridge at the Boulogne end of the Boulevard Léon Gambetta. Here he found Holland, harassed by many visitors, but aided by No. 1 H.Q. Signals section of the B.E.F., under Captain F. R. B. Bucknall and Lieutenant C. A. Atkinson. A telephone line to London had been fixed through the Post Office at the eastern end of the Boulevard. Holland's request for air cover for the landings had, as a result, been met by the arrival of two Spitfires which kept off the Heinkels during the afternoon.

No. 12 Wireless section under Lieutenant A. Evitts was already in the town. They had landed on the 21st May but the bombing led to their ship leaving before their wireless sets and trucks were unloaded. They did not get them for another two days.

Colonel Holland was tired from the two nights of bombing since he arrived in Calais. But he was as helpful as he could be. After reading the War Office letter in the dim light of the cellar, he said to Keller: "You will get your orders direct from G.H.Q. at Hazebrouck, but please get unloaded at once."

Keller explained that the vehicle ship had not arrived and it would take a long time to unload. He could not forecast when the tanks would be ready. When he returned to the Gare Maritime, the *City of Christchurch* was coming into the harbour. A Dock Company of the Royal Engineers had accompanied Keller on the *Maid of Orleans* to help with the unloading. They now told him that the fighting vehicles were at the bottom of the ship with the light transport on top. Nor did anyone know when the *City of Christchurch* berthed whether the gun and machine-gun ammunition for the tanks was on it or not.

During these anxious moments, Lieut.-General Sir Douglas Brownrigg, the Adjutant-General of the B.E.F., appeared. Brownrigg had left the Rear H.Q. of the B.E.F. which had moved to Wimereux, three miles from Boulogne, and was about to depart from Calais by destroyer. His orders to Keller reveal with grim clarity how ill-informed was the British Higher Command. He said that the German breakthrough would soon expend itself as it consisted of only light armoured fighting vehicles. "As soon as you are unloaded," said

4

Brownrigg, "move into harbour at the Forêt de Boulogne and get in touch with 20th Guards Brigade at Boulogne."

At the moment this conversation took place, about 5 p.m. on the 22nd May, the Second Panzer Division attacked Boulogne from the south. Within three hours, Assault Group Krüger of the First Panzer Division would be taking up night positions in the Forêt de Boulogne. It was fortunate for Keller and his battalion that he was quite unable to obey this order.

At 10.30 p.m. that night Mr. Horniblow, the Assistant Editor of the *Daily Mail*, rang the Admiralty. A "private listener" had picked up a radio message from Colonel Holland to the *City of Christchurch* that German tanks were only a mile from Calais. This was thought to be a "false enemy report".

It was soon discovered that not only were all the Battalion's guns in mineral jelly but several machine-gun barrels had not been packed. Some of the machine-guns had no shoulder pieces and the radio sets lacked parts. Keller realised that he could not be ready before 1 p.m. the next day. But he made plans to concentrate the tanks at Coquelles on the Boulogne road four miles due west of Calais and eight miles from Boulogne.

The unloading of the *City of Christchurch* went very slowly throughout the night. At 9 p.m., the ship's crew and the stevedores refused to continue to work owing to the visits of the Luftwaffe. Keller's second-in-command even had to place some of the crew under guard. Unloading did not begin again until 1.30 a.m. next day. At 9 p.m. all electric power was cut off so that the cranes on the quay could not be used and unloading had to be continued by means of the ship's derricks.

Officers and men worked throughout the hours of darkness without sleep to clean the guns and prepare them for action. Mr. P. A. Howe, who drove a cruiser tank, remembers that there were not enough H.E. shells for the close support guns. The Germans were surprised to be fired on with smoke shells.

Major Quentin Carpendale, then a second lieutenant wrote:

"I remember the crews sitting on the sands thumbing rounds of ammunition into belts and thinking this was the most extraordinary way to go to war."

In was not the only extraordinary event of the evening. At dusk, Major Bailey, a liaison officer at Gort's H.Q. at Hazebrouck, forty miles away, arrived in Calais by car. He brought verbal orders for the Tank Battalion to go immediately to St. Omer, twenty-five miles south-east of Calais, and "seize crossings over the Aa Canal at St. Omer and Watten". The purpose of this move was to extricate Gort's headquarters from encirclement by the Eighth Panzer Division now on its way to St. Omer.

This order not only flatly contradicted Brownrigg's but meant that the enemy was in the opposite direction. Keller took the new arrival to be interviewed by Colonel Holland who decided that the order was genuine. A patrol of light tanks left along the Ardres road to St. Omer. They found the town in flames but no one there and returned to Calais early next morning. On the way back they met 2/Lieut. G. R. G. Anderson of the Second Searchlight Battery with fifty men who had also patrolled St. Omer and found it empty. At 3 a.m. on the 23rd May, Keller received a cipher message from Brownrigg, now at Dover, confirming the order to go to Boulogne!

At dawn, Major Bailey continued to urge that tanks should be sent to St. Omer, in accordance with his orders from Gort's headquarters. He evidently did not know, like everyone else, that several Panzer divisions were exceedingly near at hand. Keller was very reluctant to send the tanks but he was persuaded to do so by Colonel Holland. A fresh patrol of three light tanks to escort Bailey in his car, set out at 6.30 a.m. under 2/Lieut. Eastman but they lost touch with him in the town, crammed with refugees and stragglers. Three miles south of Ardres, the patrol found an R.A.S.C. convoy of twenty-five supply lorries under fire from German infantry of the Eighth Panzer Division. Eastman forced them to withdraw, and put two armoured cars out of action.

He tried to escort the convoy back to Calais, but German heavy tanks and anti-tank guns had blocked the main road to Ardres. This was the left flank of the Eighth Panzer Division and only one of Eastman's tanks survived to report back to Calais. At noon, Bailey reached Coquelles after being wounded near Ardres, where he had run into a German motor-cycle patrol. He still maintained that tanks should be sent to St. Omer.

Throughout the morning, agitated messages reached Keller that a German column was advancing from Marquise, twelve miles south-west of Calais on the road to Boulogne. Oberst Krüger was indeed in this area. But difficulties in unloading, made it impossible for British tanks to attack. At 12.30 p.m. Keller was still not ready but decided "very much against my better judgment"[1] that he must make another effort with all the tanks available to get through to St. Omer. He wrote in his report:

"I was very concerned how I was to get there. It appeared from Major Bailey's report that the Germans were already enveloping Calais from the south-east. A column from Marquise to the south-west must be coming up rapidly and my only chance was to try and pass ahead of it—trusting that the column already south-east of Calais were only advanced guards."

The "column south-east of Calais" which had attacked Eastman and blocked the Ardres road were from the Eighth Panzer Division. They were only about ten miles from Calais and moving eastwards. There were now five Panzer divisions within a radius of twenty-five miles, with Krüger's Assault Group not far from Guines.

Keller decided to advance south from Coquelles and moved off at 2.15 p.m. through a dense crowd of refugees. After about a mile, his advanced guard saw an armoured column halted under some trees. It was raining and misty and they could not see whether it was French or German. What happened next is described by Carpendale.

"I moved my troop across country to investigate and thought they must be French because I had never been led to believe that there was any chance of meeting Germans in force. We came upon the column which was stationary and resting and they were as surprised to see us as we them—There was only twenty yards between us when I realised they were Germans—An officer fired a revolver at my head as I was looking out of the turret."

Hastily, the tanks moved to firing positions. The country was difficult with sunken roads jammed with refugees and French

[1] Keller: Report to War Office, June 1940.

transport. The Germans quickly removed their anti-tank guns from lorries and a sharp engagement followed, lasting three-quarters of an hour, but it was inconclusive. The German tanks had a crew of three with a 2-cm. gun and a heavy machine-gun but their armour was similar in thickness to the British cruisers. Three medium German tanks, two light tanks and three anti-tank guns were knocked out, but the British shooting, though accurate, made little impression on their heavy tanks, with a crew of five and a 7.5-cm. gun.

It was field artillery which forced Keller to break off the engagement and retire north. The shelling was precise, Keller's command tank was hit and the gun put out of action but he still hoped, by retiring behind the railway to attack again from Pihen-lès-Guines.

Mr. Alan Wollaston heard a crash and thought the turret of his cruiser tank had been hit. It transpired that the gun had hit a tree, while traversing. The driver was conscientiously driving on the right-hand side of the road on his first visit to France.

Captain O'Sullivan's A9 tank had to be left isolated in a field. It was twice hit by shells which smashed one of the tracks. The machine-gun would not fit properly, so O'Sullivan had to fire it from the turret while the tank was stationary. He was soon forced to abandon this dangerous position and shortly afterwards the tank was struck again, killing two of the crew. O'Sullivan was forced to make his way north on foot but was later captured with some of the First Searchlight Battery. Under interrogation, he cleverly told the Germans that the whole of the First British Armoured Division was to be landed at Calais. Was this another reason for Guderian's cautious advance on the town?

When it was clear that the enemy was too strong for him, Keller moved the Battalion back to high ground south-west of Coquelles. On the way, he received an indistinct message on his wireless that a Brigadier Nicholson wanted to meet him. Keller was still under shell-fire and replied: "Get off the air, I am trying to fight a bloody battle."

The message was repeated half an hour later when Nicholson himself came on the air saying he had urgent orders for the Battalion. He was coming out to see them at Coquelles. Keller, who had already received contradictory orders before from senior officers, from

Brownrigg, Holland and Bailey, did not know who Nicholson was, and did not know that he was the newly appointed Commander at Calais. He was not aware that his tanks came under Nicholson's command. He had no orders from the B.E.F. to this effect and it was not until 8 p.m. when Nicholson actually arrived, that this was sorted out.

Before their meeting at Coquelles, Nicholson had ordered two cruiser and two light tanks which had not been ready to take part in the advance on Guines to patrol the St. Omer road at 5 p.m. This patrol, commanded by Captain R. H. Howe, ran into German motor-cyclists four miles south of Calais. The motor-cyclists suffered casualties but, two miles further on, Howe found an anti-tank gun covering the former Searchlight road-block at Les Attaques where fighting had taken place earlier in the afternoon. From the far side, a field-gun fired at him at point-blank range. As he was unable to advance, he withdrew into Calais.

Before leaving Coquelles, Nicholson told Keller that he should not move his remaining tanks into Calais until dark. He was then to fill up with petrol and await orders under the trees of the Parc St. Pierre opposite the Hôtel de Ville. His plan, Nicholson explained, was to break out east to Dunkirk with part of the First Battalion, The Rifle Brigade, supported by tanks.

I had now reached the Hôtel de Ville after a weary march from Coulogne, half expecting the Germans from Orphanage Farm to pursue me. At 9 p.m., Keller's tanks were gathering in the shadows. The tracks rattled and jingled in the darkness—were they ours or theirs? The long whine of the shells from a German battery in the south promised a night of fear.

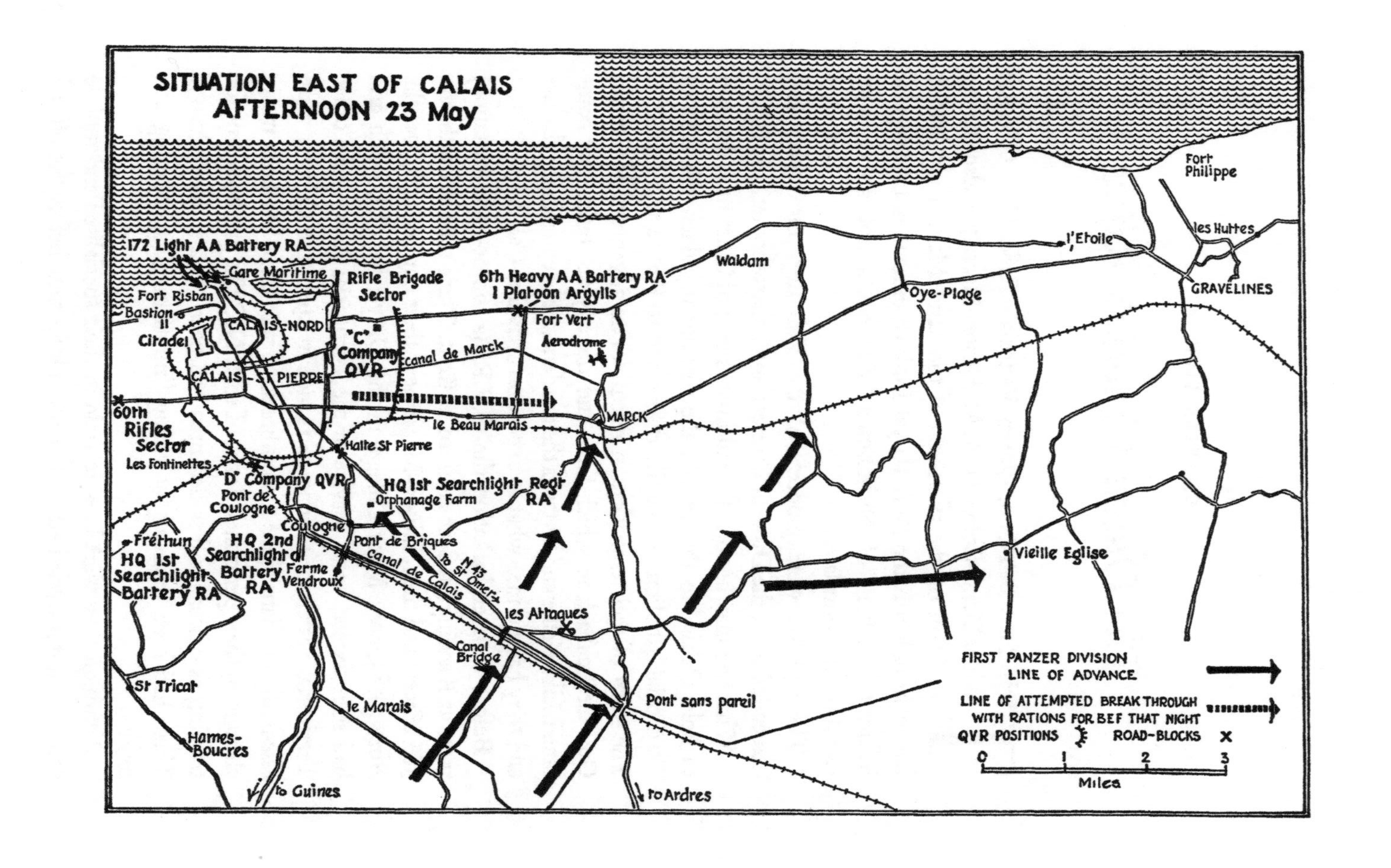
SITUATION EAST OF CALAIS
AFTERNOON 23 May
172 Light AA Battery RA
Gare Maritime
Fort Risban
Bastion II
Citadel
CALAIS-NORD
CALAIS-ST PIERRE
Rifle Brigade Sector
"C" Company QVR
canal de Marck
6th Heavy AA Battery RA
1 Platoon Argylls
Fort Vert
Aerodrome
Waldam
Oye-Plage
l'Etoile
Fort Philippe
les Huttes
GRAVELINES
60th Rifles Sector
Les Fontinettes
le Beau Marais
MARCK
Halte St Pierre
"D" Company QVR
HQ 1st Searchlight Regt RA
Orphanage Farm
Pont de Coulogne
Coulogne
Pont de Briques
to N 43 to St Omer
Canal de Calais
Fréthun
HQ 1st Searchlight Battery RA
HQ 2nd Searchlight Battery RA
Ferme Vendroux
les Attaques
Canal Bridge
Vieille Eglise
St Tricat
le Marais
Pont sans pareil
Hames-Boucres
to Guines
to Ardres
FIRST PANZER DIVISION LINE OF ADVANCE
LINE OF ATTEMPTED BREAK THROUGH WITH RATIONS FOR BEF THAT NIGHT
QVR POSITIONS
ROAD-BLOCKS X
0 1 2 3
Miles

CHAPTER FIVE

The Queen Victoria's Rifles

THE First Battalion, Queen Victoria's Rifles (The Q.V.R.) under Lieut.-Colonel J. A. M. Ellison-Macartney also arrived in Calais on the afternoon of the 22nd May. They landed half an hour before the Third Royal Tank Regiment, but the regular infantry battalions of Nicholson's brigade did not arrive until twenty-four hours later.

The Q.V.R. were pioneers of the Volunteer movement and descended from the Duke of Cumberland's sharpshooters of 1803.

Whatever may be said of the ultimate merit of Churchill's decision to hold Calais "to the death", the manner in which this famous Territorial battalion was hastily dispatched to France was shameful. The story of their embarkation resembles an adventure of Captain Guy Crouchback in which farce and tragedy are intimately combined. Like Keller and his tanks their orders were depressingly obscure and they had no idea what to expect on arrival at Calais.

Before their embarkation the Q.V.R. (a motor-cycle battalion) were at Kennington near Ashford in Kent. Their total strength was 566 officers and men. Ellison-Macartney, their commander, was the Bursar of Queen Mary College in the University of London and had seen sixteen years' service in the Territorial Army. Like other Territorial battalions serving in France in 1940, the Q.V.R. were essentially civilian. Since the outbreak of war there had been many changes in their personnel. Some of their N.C.O.s had been sent for training as officers, and skilled men had been released for industry. These had been replaced by young "militiamen" numbering 200 in all.

Although they were keen to train in their specialised and mobile role as a motor-cycle battalion, it was a long time before the official

War Department vehicles were ready. During the winter at Paddock Wood near Tonbridge in Kent, they were obliged to use hired civilian motor-cycles and tradesmen's vans. It was not until the early part of 1940 that they were slowly equipped with motor-cycles and motor-cycle combinations.

On paper, the First Q.V.R. were part of the 30th Infantry Brigade commanded by Brigadier Nicholson. In practice, they were a motor-cycle reconnaissance battalion, trained as "Divisional Cavalry" to the 1st London Motor Division at Tonbridge in Kent. They had not trained with Nicholson's brigade, with whom they were destined to fight at Calais, though in April they had got ready to embark with it to Norway. Within a week of the British withdrawal from Norway, they were returned to the 1st London Motor Division for Home Defence duties. This was a disappointment for they had regarded it as a compliment, as Territorials, to serve in Nicholson's brigade.

By the middle of May, the Q.V.R. had 238 vehicles. On the 18th May, they were suddenly deprived by the War Office of their twenty-two scout cars, their only offensive vehicles, which were handed over to the 1st Armoured Division. They were given to the Third Royal Tank Regiment and next seen standing on the quay at Calais without any drivers. This was a distressing conclusion to their training, for when the War Office sent them into action on the 22nd May, they sailed without any transport whatever, even their motor cycles and wireless trucks being left behind in Kent.

As Ellison-Macartney wrote afterwards:

"The battalion left for Calais, shorn of its mobility and customary means of communication. It fought in a role divorced from its training and practice: it dived straight into battle."

Motor-cycle battalions in 1940 had substantially less firepower than regular motor battalions like the 60th Rifles and the Rifle Brigade. A motor-cycle battalion had three rifle companies. Each was armed with only ten Bren guns and five Boys anti-tank rifles each. One-third of the men had only revolvers and were not issued with rifles since they were classified as "cavalry". On the 22nd May, the officers of the 1st Q.V.R. had not even been issued with revolvers. The Waugh-ish nature of the operation was demonstrated by their need to acquire weapons and transport abandoned on the quay by the "useless mouths".

When they left for Calais the majority of the Q.V.R. had, "owing to the absence of facilities", only once fired the Bren gun annual course. Selected riflemen had fired the Boys anti-tank rifle but only *five* rounds. Though one-third of the Battalion had only pistols, there had been *no* pistol practice. In view of experience gained by other units in Norway, plans had been made for them to carry 3-inch instead of 2-inch mortars. "These weapons were *borrowed* with difficulty," wrote Ellison-Macartney, "but live ammunition could not be obtained." In any case, the 3-inch mortars disappeared to some other unit before the Q.V.R. embarked for Calais. There were no bombs for their 2-inch mortars. They had only smoke bombs at Calais, but each man had fired fifty rounds on the ranges through the rifle.

Why was this fine Territorial battalion launched so badly equipped into the bitter street-fighting of Calais against tanks, artillery and well-armed German infantry? The answer lies in the scandalous neglect of Britain's defences in the 1930s so glaringly revealed in the documents now available in the Public Record Office. In them can be seen those craven official attitudes which brought the United Kingdom to the very brink of invasion by Hitler.

In the hurry and confusion of the moment, the War Office selected the Q.V.R. for a role which bore no relation to military facts. They were not the only Territorial battalion destroyed in the campaign of 1940, but seldom has any volunteer unit been compelled to fight on such unequal terms. That they kept fighting to the end, says much for their sense of duty, and their pride.

The first indication that the Q.V.R. were about to leave the villages round Kennington, where the cricket season was in full swing, for the front line, came at 7 p.m. on the evening of Tuesday the 21st May. Ellison-Macartney, on a visit to 1st London Motor Division was told that his battalion now came under War Office orders and should be prepared to go overseas. The move was not expected for forty-eight hours, but he warned his company commanders, and a "feeling of expectancy" spread through the Battalion.

The usual rumours grew, significant conversations were overheard and private plans were made.

About 9.45 p.m. Mr. A. R. Jabez-Smith, then a second-lieutenant and second-in-command of "D" Company, was informed that a Red Air Raid warning was imminent. Such an alert involved stopping all movement of troops and a "scheme of preparedness" on which it was his duty to report. When he arrived at battalion headquarters on his motor-cycle, he received a telephone call from Eastern Command, Hounslow. A voice asked: "Is Paddock Wood your nearest station?"

"No we left there two weeks ago. Ashford is our station."

"Here is a message for you. Eastern Command to 1 Q.V.R. Battalion will move in two parties to Port Vic[1] for embarkation. First Party will leave by train from Ashford at 0515 hours and 2nd party at 0545 hours tomorrow morning. Load all equipment in trucks at Ashford."

"Are we expected to load our motor transport or drive it to Port Vic?"

"I am afraid you will have to leave it behind."

Jabez-Smith was told that seats on the train had been arranged for 800. It was evidently believed that the Q.V.R. were a rifle battalion and not a motor-cycle battalion of under 600 men. This staff blunder had serious consequences. There was room for the motor-cycles aboard the personnel ship, *City of Canterbury*, at Dover. And they could have been ridden there from Kennington with the result that some of the Q.V.R.s own transport would have been at Calais. As it was, they had to march for miles with all their equipment.

A few minutes later, Ellison-Macartney and Major T. L. Timpson, the second-in-command, arrived. There was another telephone call and the order was confirmed. On this occasion the Battalion was told to leave all vehicles and one of its signal sections behind at Ashford.

There was little time to get ready. The men who were not on duty had to be roused, a meal cooked and eaten before departure, billets cleared and documents sorted and destroyed. Those who were able to, telephoned their families. It was many weeks before their fate became known. Those who were taken prisoner-of-war received no

[1] Dover—though security was so strict that the Q.V.R. did not know this.

letters till the following October. Since no one had been told the situation in France, many packed their full kit, expecting to go to an organised reception camp. The loading at Ashford was a nightmare and the station yard was strewn with the trucks and motor-cycles which had to be left behind.

The trains were late in arriving—despite Jabez-Smith, they were inevitably sent to Paddock Wood. It took some time to direct them to Ashford. While waiting for them the men lay down and slept in the yard. The trains pulled out at 5.30 a.m. and 6 a.m. and reached Dover in an hour and a half. Their arrival there was described by Timpson:

"As the trains halted by the seashore on a still, misty morning, the steady boom of gunfire could be heard coming over the water from France. Rain was falling at Dover in a light drizzle. A patrol of three British fighters circled at frequent intervals over the harbour and disappeared into the low cloud."[2]

The railway station was empty. On the quay were a number of smartly-dressed staff officers who appeared to know nothing, and were not prepared to give orders. Military police prevented anyone from crossing the railway tracks making it much more difficult to reach the quays. The baggage was manhandled from the station in rain which now began to pour down on the troops as they staggered up the gangways of the personnel ship S.S. *City of Canterbury*.

When the loading was done, they were herded into a large shed and issued with one sausage-roll, chocolates and tea. Some ate at a canteen which was full of troops just returned from France. Here a staff officer remarked, idiotically, to Ellison-Macartney: "Most of the movement today seems to be in the opposite direction to yours."

This remark is constantly remembered more than thirty years after the defence of Calais by those who were left to spend the next five years in a prisoner-of-war camp.

At Dover, Ellison-Macartney opened on the quay, a sealed envelope from the War Office with the familiar statement that, "a few German tanks have broken through towards the Channel ports". The remainder of the 30th Infantry Brigade, then in East Anglia, would

[2] Timpson: Prisoner-of-War Diary.

"disembark next day either at Calais or Dunkirk according to the situation". The Q.V.R. were to proceed to Calais in any event, and take "necessary steps to secure the town". Timpson, in an account which he wrote from a prisoner-of-war camp added dryly:

"It was surmised from these orders that the battalion *once more* formed part of the 30th Infantry Brigade, though this could not be confirmed until after that Brigade had landed at Calais next day."

When he received his sealed orders stating that "a few German tanks" had broken through, Ellison-Macartney realised that without his motor-cycles and wireless trucks he would have no means of communication. The mistake by Eastern Command concerning the total numbers was now significant. There was also room aboard the ship. He telephoned Ashford for as many motor-cycles as possible to be ridden to Dover, but when the *City of Canterbury* sailed at 11 a.m., they had not arrived.

Escorted by destroyers and fighters, the ship moved out of the harbour in the wake of the *Maid of Orleans* which carried the personnel of Keller's tank battalion. The sea was calm and soon the rain and mist vanished. On deck it became quite warm as Jabez-Smith sat next to the Reverend R. G. Heard, the Battalion Chaplain. Jabez-Smith had a copy of Shakespeare's *King Richard II* in the Temple Classics. He opened it at random "for an omen". The passage which he read was that of the banishment of Thomas Mowbray, Duke of Norfolk:

> "The hopeless word of 'never to return' breathe I against thee, upon pain of life."[3]

He changed the conversation. Both officers were taken prisoner and not released till the end of the war.

In his cabin aboard the *City of Canterbury*, Ellison-Macartney issued orders to company commanders. "C" Company (Major J. Austin-Brown) was to disembark first and secure the landing place, covered by "B" Company (Captain G. P. Bowring) from the ship, while "D" Company (Lieut. H. V. E. Jessop) found the anti-aircraft defence.

[3] *King Richard II*, Act I, sc. 2. Richard to Norfolk.

The *City of Canterbury* steamed on until a cloud of dark smoke could be seen to starboard. Gradually the familiar outline of Calais with the clock tower above it became more distinct. It was then possible to see that the Germans did not occupy the harbour.

As the *Maid of Orleans* berthed at the Gare Maritime and the *City of Canterbury* abaft her, there were shouts of welcome from the French sailors and soldiers in Bastion 1 and Fort Risban on either side of the Avant Port. But there were signs of the bombing. A coaster had been sunk alongside the Quai Paul Devot. There was a large hole in the roof of the Gare Maritime, houses were burning in the Courgain and round the lighthouse at the Place de Russie. Timpson noted that the wall of a house at the south end of the Gare Maritime had collapsed, leaving the rooms and their furniture exposed. To the south, he could see two large fires burning.

An agitated embarkation staff officer told Timpson that they must clear harbour as quickly as possible in case the bombers returned, and the crew of the *City of Canterbury* earnestly expressed the same opinion. The ship must be unloaded at once and the quay divested of riflemen and baggage. The haunting note of the air-raid siren and the sound of the 3.7-inch anti-aircraft guns added point to their entreaties. But they were not easy to comply with. A French train blocked the whole length of the railway siding, so that all baggage had to be carried round it to the roadway along the western shore of the Bassin des Chasses.

Unlike Keller, the Q.V.R. had no vehicle ship to wait for, and they were able to unload. There were three powered cranes at the Gare Maritime, and one hand-operated. The former were out of action in the absence of the drivers, so that despite help from the ship's derricks equipment had to be manhandled down the gangways. As the unloading continued during the afternoon, German bombers were driven off by the anti-aircraft guns and the two Spitfires requested by Holland. One bomber was shot down into the sea. The young soldiers of the Q.V.R., busy as they were, stared anxiously at British and French wounded who were lifted aboard the *City of Canterbury* even before it was unloaded.

When Ellison-Macartney reached Holland's headquarters at the clinic in the Boulevard Léon Gambetta, he was told that German "light armoured vehicles" had been reported that afternoon at the Forêt de Guines. They were also reported near St. Omer. Civilians were still passing between Calais and Guines, some of them children on bicycles, who claimed to have seen fifty armoured vehicles including troop carriers and two tanks.

Colonel Holland (though astounded that a motor-cycle battalion should be told to leave all its transport in England) directed the Q.V.R. to block the six principal roads into Calais. They should relieve the platoon of the Argylls on the Fort Vert road east of the town: guard the submarine cable terminal at Sangatte on the coast road to the west: reconnoitre the beaches to "prevent German aircraft landing at low tide" and establish battalion headquarters at Les Fontinettes, a railway suburb outside the Fortifications in the south-west.

It was 5 p.m. before Ellison-Macartney returned by car to the docks, his men having already "impressed" several British and French cars and motor-cycles.

The "front" which the Q.V.R. were ordered to defend was an enormous one for a battalion without transport and only two-thirds of whom were armed with rifles. All equipment and ammunition had to be carried on foot over long distances and speed or movement was essential. No reconnaissance was possible that evening, positions beyond the outer perimeter of bastions were hastily picked from a small-scale map. Nor were the men equipped to dig trenches, for their picks and shovels had been left behind as part of their vehicle equipment.

Austin-Brown's company which had been the first to disembark covered the main bridges dividing Old Calais or Calais-Nord from Calais-St. Pierre while the others unloaded and sought to control a gathering swarm of refugees who tried to board the ship.

Austin-Brown was next ordered to block all roads leading to Dunkirk and Gravelines and patrol the eastern shore. He established his company headquarters at a farm, a mile east of the Porte de Gravelines and to the north of the Marck Canal. The Argylls at Fort Vert were relieved by one of his platoons next morning.

Jessop's "D" Company had to march three and a half miles from the docks to block the roads leading south to Fréthun, Guines and Ardres. At dusk, he had one platoon at the road and rail bridges over the Canal de La Rivière Neuve, a mile along the road to Fréthun. A second platoon was at the crossroads formed by the Route de Coulogne and the rue du Grand Voyeu, using a ten-ton supply lorry as a road-block.

Jessop's third platoon marched out along the Boulevard Victor Hugo and was stopped by a "British Major" who said that German tanks, advancing from St. Omer, were three miles away. On the road to Ardres this platoon took up a position not far from the French anti-tank gun on the left of the line held by Colonel Goldney and the First Searchlight Regiment at Orphanage Farm.

"B" Company under Captain Bowring had the longest march to block the coast road to the west to Sangatte and to cover the shore for a distance of three miles. Already short of sleep, they had six and a half miles to reach Oyez Farm about a mile and a half east of Sangatte. A platoon was sent forward under 2/Lieut. Dizer, the youngest officer, to Sangatte itself to secure the submarine cable to London. The Q.V.R. positions on the evening of the 22nd May are shown on the map on page 41.

Late in the evening, reports that the Germans were approaching along the Guines road led Captain Munby (the scout platoon commander of the Battalion who had been deprived of all his vehicles on the 18th May) to take a party to investigate. About two miles from Guines he met a convoy of ten-ton lorries belonging to No. 2 (L of C) Railhead Company R.A.S.C. and an ambulance company who had been ambushed in the Forêt de Guines. Three lorries had been destroyed and the rest had narrowly escaped. When darkness fell with no sign of the enemy, Munby returned to the Gare Maritime.

Finding Les Fontinettes a maze of waterways and rail tracks, Ellison-Macartney changed his battalion headquarters to the Porte de Dunkerque at the eastern end of the Boulevard de l'Egalité. At dawn, he was for the first time able to communicate with his companies and improve his road-blocks some of which had been sited overnight in unsuitable positions. For twenty-four hours these Volunteer soldiers at their improvised defences were all that stood between Guderian and the capture of Calais.

When the outlying battles fought by the Third Royal Tank Regiment and the Searchlight took place on the 23rd May, the Q.V.R. did not encounter the First Panzer Division as it by-passed the town to the east. It was not till dawn on the 24th May that they were in action against the Tenth Panzer Division which first attacked "D" Company at Les Fontinettes followed by Fort Nieulay on the road to Boulogne. By that time, Brigadier Nicholson had taken over from Colonel Holland. His brigade, consisting of the Q.V.R. with the Second Battalion, 60th Rifles and First Battalion, The Rifle Brigade, were all in position at the outer fortifications of Calais.

Searchlight and Anti-aircraft troops under Colonel Goldney became a reserve to the Green Jackets. I was ordered to join the Rifle Brigade and, with a party of gunners, set off along the bleak Rue Mollien which led to the eastern ramparts. On this tense march, I thought of others who had moved up into the line. This was it. Everything before was of no consequence. But would I pass the test? Such was my chief anxiety as I plodded down the Rue Mollien.

CHAPTER SIX

Claude Nicholson

CLAUDE NICHOLSON who took over command from Colonel Holland on the afternoon of the 23rd May, was forty-two at the time of the battle. He was tall, dark-haired and military. He had been a regular soldier since he was nineteen, when he passed out at Sandhurst to the 16th/5th The Queen's Royal Lancers and served with them in France until 1918. During the 1920s, he was in Palestine, India and Egypt, returning to pass the Staff College at Camberley in 1928. He later returned to the Staff College as an instructor and by 1938 was in command of his regiment. He became a Brigadier when the 30th Infantry Brigade was formed on the 20th April 1940, for service in Norway. Like Guderian and Major-General Schaal commanding the Tenth Panzer Division—his chief opponents at Calais—Nicholson was a true professional. He worked hard and was widely read. His ability was well known and he was apparently destined, had he not been taken prisoner at Calais, for higher command. He had been an admirer of Churchill and a student of his political career, which brings a special irony to this story.

Afterwards, Churchill found it painful to speak of the sacrifice which Nicholson and his troops were called upon to make. His reference to Nicholson's refusal to surrender in the great speech of the 5th June, 1940, moved the crowded House of Commons to genuine emotion.

Churchill's audience knew who he meant by "the British Brigadier" who had led this "memorable resistance", for Nicholson's brother Godfrey was an M.P. His wife Ursula was in the Strangers' Gallery to hear the speech. She sat next to Mrs. Neville Chamberlain, who took her hand in hers as she listened to the challenge to "fight on the beaches". Churchill wrote that he could feel the "pent-up, passionate emotion" at this time. These famous words moved many to tears in a country loth to expose its feelings. Afterwards I heard them on a secret radio at the makeshift hospital of the Pensionnat St. Pierre in Calais. A defenceless prisoner across the Channel, I felt in my desolation that I was near to home and not forgotten.

By temperament, Nicholson was a perfectionist. Outwardly, he was the trained cavalry officer and good horseman which he had dreamed of being as a boy. He was sympathetic and courteous. He was also sensitive, modest and very intelligent. There were some who thought him formal and orthodox but to the rapidly changing situation at Calais, he reacted with great swiftness of mind. He must have been deeply troubled by the conflicting orders which he received, but he was not a man to lose his head. All my researches show that, in the disappointment and frustration of that hopeless battle, he remained splendidly calm. He inspired confidence in those nearest to him, especially the French.

Nicholson received his first orders at Southampton at 6 p.m. on the 22nd May before the ships carrying the rest of his brigade had sailed. Although many hours had passed since Guderian started his drive to the coast, the information available was still largely inaccurate.

"Some German tanks, with artillery, were moving in the direction of Boulogne from the east. The general situation was obscure. . . . The 30th Infantry Brigade would land either at Calais or Dunkirk and would then be used, probably with Third Royal Tank Regiment —to act offensively against the German columns. 229th Anti-Tank Battery R.A. would join the Brigade at Calais."[1]

Nicholson then embarked, with the rest of his brigade, at Dover. After breakfast on board, Nicholson and his Brigade Major Dennis Talbot went ashore to Dover Castle, now General Brownrigg's headquarters, and a conference was held at which Admiral Ramsay was present. Brownrigg had little more to add except that the Rifle Brigade, the 60th Rifles and the Third Royal Tank Regiment were to proceed "by the Marquise road to the relief of Boulogne as soon as possible". Marquise, about twelve miles south-west of Calais was on the left flank of the First Panzer Division now advancing on Guines.

[1] Nicholson: unfinished report.

On his return on board the *Archangel*, Nicholson held a brigade conference, at which he gave more detailed orders.

"The situation was obscure but undoubtedly very serious. Boulogne was being heavily attacked by armoured troops—1 Q.V.R. holding Calais . . . 30th Infantry Brigade to land at Calais as soon as possible and operate with or without 3rd Royal Tanks offensively in direction of Boulogne. . . . As soon as battalions were complete with transport they were to move to concentration areas south-west of the town astride the Boulogne road."[2]

Brownrigg was still thinking in terms of a battle outside Calais to relieve Boulogne. He was in ignorance of the strength and composition of Guderian's forces or he would not have given such orders. Nor have I been able to find any indication that the movements of First Panzer Division which, when Nicholson landed, was advancing to Guines and Les Attaques, was known at Dover. There was certainly no mention of the Tenth Panzer Division. During the whole of the 23rd May it was moving at high speed towards Calais, and that afternoon would be on the Marquise–Calais road.

At 1 p.m. the *Archangel* reached Calais, but the prospect of operating "offensively in the direction of Boulogne" depended on the arrival of the motor battalion's vehicles, and these were on the *Kohistan* and the *City of Canterbury* which had not yet arrived from Southampton so the troops had to wait in the sand dunes for several hours. In the meantime, all chance of intercepting the enemy on the Marquise road was lost.

As soon as he was able to assess the situation, Nicholson realised that Brownrigg's orders were impossible. The defence of Calais itself was becoming hourly more urgent, as during the afternoon the firing got steadily closer. From Colonel Holland's headquarters in the Boulevard Léon Gambetta, he could hear the sound of the tank battle near Guines and knew that Calais would soon be attacked.

While the First Panzer Division were in action against Keller's tank battalion during the afternoon, the Tenth Panzers under General Schaal had received orders to take their place when they moved on Gravelines. At 4 p.m., Schaal, who was at Guderian's command post

[2] Nicholson: unfinished report.

at Recques, heard that the Second Panzer Division were fighting inside Boulogne. He was ordered to move up along the Marquise road and take Calais as soon as possible. He decided that the bulk of his division should advance to the high ground at Coquelles where observation would be good. He ordered his tank regiment, the 90th, to move along the main road, supported by the 86th German Rifle Regiment and a battalion of medium artillery. On their right an assault group led by the 69th German Rifle Regiment, was to advance from Guines to the centre of Calais.

Until the early hours of the 24th May, Schaal was planning to take Calais by "coup de main". He was to be greatly disappointed.

Had Nicholson been in a position to carry out Brownrigg's orders to advance west towards Boulogne with the Third Royal Tank Regiment and his two motor battalions, he must inevitably have collided with an overwhelming force, and, lacking any field artillery, have been destroyed. In that event, the way to Calais would have been open, and the defenders of Dunkirk would have faced an additional Panzer division before Admiral Ramsay's rescue operation had begun. The consequences for the B.E.F. are easy to imagine.

The division which Schaal commanded had already suffered losses and breakdowns on its long journey from Sedan. When it reached Calais it was at a little over half its strength. Despite a day's rest on the 22nd May, the troops were tired. During the 24th May, Schaal reported from his battle headquarters near the Boulogne road that since the 10th May he had lost one-third of his motor transport and more than half his armoured vehicles including tanks. At this stage of the war, the Tenth Panzer Division had two tank battalions of 100 tanks and a similar number of armoured fighting vehicles at full strength.[3] These losses and the exhaustion of the men partly account for his failure to press home the attack earlier. Another reason was "the constant and very heavy air attacks".[4] The R.A.F. flew too high for the division's light anti-aircraft guns.

[3] First and Second Panzer Divisions, however, had three tank battalions, about 150 tanks per division.

[4] Tenth Panzer Division: War Diary.

Throughout the 23rd and 24th May, Schaal was demanding heavy anti-aircraft protection and referring to British "air superiority". Guderian himself was evidently perturbed and anxious to avoid casualties. He was afraid of further British landings higher up the coast towards Dunkirk.

At 5 p.m. on the 24th, when the main attack on Calais had been going some hours Guderian told Schaal that:

"If there are heavy losses during the attack on Calais, it should only be continued with support from dive-bombers and when heavy artillery can be brought up after the surrender of Boulogne. *There must be no unnecessary losses.*"[5]

As he discussed the situation in Colonel Holland's cellar headquarters at the Boulevard Léon Gambetta, Nicholson could know nothing of his opponents' problems. His own anxieties were the vast extent of the fortifications which had to be held and the absence of any field artillery. The same problems were worrying de Lambertye, the French naval commander, and the senior French army officer, Commandant Le Tellier, who had arrived from Dunkirk.

Le Tellier made his headquarters at the Citadel and was next day placed under Nicholson by order of General Fagalde of the 16th French Corps at Dunkirk, under whose overall command the Calais garrison had now come. Hitherto there had been little co-operation between the French and the British forces and there were to be many misunderstandings but both Le Tellier and de Lambertye proved good Allies. Le Tellier had only the company and a half of the 265th Infantry Regiment, four sections of the 202nd Machine-gun Company, a few armed customs officers, some pioneers and firemen. These had been stationed there for some days. His artillery were two French "75s" of the First World War of the 11th Artillery Regiment. These were the only field guns at the Citadel though one more arrived next day. Another was in an anti-tank position at Coquelles on the Boulogne road.

Carlos de Lambertye remained in command of the naval forces on the seafront. He was an elderly and ailing reserve officer who had served throughout the First World War, but who showed the greatest

[5] Tenth Panzer Division: War Diary.

courage in the next few days. His coastal guns were at Fort Lapin on the Sangatte road, at Bastion 12 adjoining Fort Risban, where they were commanded by Enseigne de Vaisseau Georges Wiart who had a remarkable adventure on the 25th May. East of Calais there were batteries at the Bastion de L'Estran and Bastion 2. These naval defences were also equipped with machine-guns and searchlights. But both the heavy and medium coastal guns were designed to fire out to sea. They were practically useless in a land battle, though on the 24th May, the guns at Fort Lapin and the Bastion de l'Estran were able to fire on the Germans' advance from Coquelles. Those at Bastion 2 were also in action for several hours, firing with good effect.

On his arrival at Calais, Nicholson assumed command of all British troops, including the tanks. Most of the Anti-aircraft and Searchlights were still outside the main fortifications and it was not yet known whether they were to be evacuated as "non-fighting" personnel. The Q.V.R. also formed a second line of defence beyond the bastions of the outer perimeter. Before he could issue orders to the two regular infantry battalions, Nicholson had to decide how it was possible to defend Calais with so few troops.

On 11th September 1914, Churchill had noted in a memorandum to the Asquith cabinet:

"Calais is simply an enceinte rather larger in extent than that of Dunkirk and protected by a few well-executed outlying field works . . . it could certainly not be counted on to hold out for more than a few days against a determined attack."[6]

Churchill had inspected the defences on this occasion. His assessment was made before the days of panzers, self-propelled guns and dive-bombers. But he must have been aware that despite the strength of the fortifications, no garrison could resist for long without artillery and air support.

The most formidable and ancient of these defences was the Citadel on the west side of the town. Begun in 1560, it replaced the château captured by French troops under the Duc de Guise in 1558. This victory ended over 200 years of English occupation which had begun with capture of Calais by Edward III on the 3rd August 1347. It was

[6] Quoted in *The World Crisis*, p. 321.

rebuilt by Cardinal Richelieu in 1636 after a siege by the Spaniards and enlarged by Vauban in 1680. From 1660 to 1940 it housed the Calais garrison.

The walls of the Citadel, breached in several places and overgrown, are of formidable thickness and still stand today. A quadrilateral with four main bastions, they now enclose a sports ground. From north to south the Citadel measured 450 yards and from east to west 300 yards. Beneath the bastions are vaulted cellars which, throughout the last war, withstood the heaviest bombardments. On the east side ran the Canal de Calais, crossed by a bridge into the town. On the south side, a similar bridge leading to a seventeenth-century gateway crossed a moat.

The Germans concentrated much of their fire on the Citadel and considered its capture of the first importance. There are strange and ironic parallels with its defence by Lord Wentworth in 1558. The Government of Mary Tudor failed to strengthen the garrison and neglected the fortifications. During 1557 the French sent spies into Calais like the "fifth column" of 1940. They were undetected and reported to the Duc de Guise, the French commander, that Wentworth had only 500 men and was unprepared for any major assault. De Guise advanced from Boulogne, with 30,000 men and, like Guderian, attacked from the high ground at Coquelle on the 2nd January 1558. Like Nicholson, Wentworth found his pleas for reinforcements rejected and he was abandoned to his fate. At that time Calais was on its western side surrounded by water. De Guise began a long cannonade of the Citadel. Its walls were breached and, under cover of darkness, the French attackers crossed the west side of the harbour at low tide. They assaulted the Citadel on the 7th January. The town was surrendered the next day, which, according to tradition, broke Queen Mary's heart.

During the next 400 years the basic pattern of fortifications remained unchanged. It was, said *The Times* of the 26th June 1940, in an article entitled "The Epic of Calais", "a curious instance of the essential immutability of military science".

Fear of attacks by the Spaniards led to the original fortifications built by Henry VIII of England being strengthened in the east. Strong bastions, eight in all, with a complex system of advanced outworks were erected during the seventeenth century, for the defence of the old town, or Calais-Nord. Nothing remained of these inner battlements in 1940 except the Citadel. They were dismantled between 1843 and 1895. After the Franco-Prussian War of 1870 fear of another German invasion led to the enclosure of the whole of the southern industrial suburb of Calais-St. Pierre with twelve bastions. These were linked by ramparts and earthworks constructed between 1880 and 1900. The seafront defences dated from the same period.

This was the "enceinte", surrounded by a deep ditch on which Churchill reported to Asquith in 1914. By 1940, though eight bastions survived, some ramparts, especially in the south, had been removed to make way for railway tracks. On the east or Dunkirk side they were practically intact. On the west and south-west, where the German attack in 1940 was strongest, Bastions 7 and 8 had disappeared. The danger points were at the railway junction of Les Fontinettes and facing the Chemin du Grand Voyeu (not Voyeur as it was called in 1940).

Looking at the unhelpful map provided by the War Office, Nicholson could see that if the Germans advanced with tanks, very strong road-blocks would be needed on the Boulogne road, especially at the Pont Jourdan railway bridge. Bastion 11 where the coast road from Sangatte entered Calais was a key point, as were the Porte des Fontinettes, and the Halte St. Pierre on the St. Omer road. On the afternoon of the 23rd May he had no accurate information about the strength of the expected attack, nor was he warned that the town might be encircled from the east. He still hoped to be able to keep the Dunkirk road open as a supply line to the B.E.F. This had now become part of his orders and he expected that he might be told to withdraw his brigade to Dunkirk. It was the object of preventing his escape that Guderian had already ordered the First Panzer Division to push north-east from Guines that afternoon and cut the road at Marck.

For the time being, Nicholson's task was to prevent the Germans entering the town from the west or Boulogne side. Despite the maze of canals and waterways in the south which might hinder the tanks, there was little in the way of fortified outposts to stop them. On the Boulogne road, a mile east of Coquelles, was Fort Nieulay, known as Newnham Bridge under English occupation. It was rebuilt by order of Louis XIV in 1680 and was the work of Vauban. In 1940, this fort was a large ruin with walls thirty feet high enclosing about five acres. It was about a mile from the Pont Jourdan, the railway bridge at the west end of the Boulevard Léon Gambetta. In between these points was a row of shabby houses and gardens. Holding the Pont Jourdan would be vital, since the Boulevard Léon Gambetta led straight to the heart of Calais-St. Pierre.

At Sangatte on the coast road was the terminal for the submarine cable to England which had to be guarded, and, if necessary, destroyed. Further to the east was Fort Lapin, built in 1690 and restored during the eighteenth and nineteenth centuries, where de Lambertye had four coastal guns manned by the French Navy. On the road to Calais was the group of buildings known as Oyez Farm. Here, in addition to the 3.7-guns of the 6th Heavy A.A. Battery was "B" Company of the Q.V.R. who had arrived the previous night.

A glance at this situation showed Nicholson that there was no purpose in putting his regular troops in advance of the outer perimeter of ramparts and bastions. Apart from the remains of Fort Vert on the Gravelines road, where the Argylls had been stationed, and the farm held by "C" Company of the Q.V.R., there was little cover east of the town. The large artificial lake bordered by sandhills, known as the Bassin des Chasses de l'Est, east of the Gare Maritime, presented a danger (see photograph facing page 129). To prevent the capture of the Bastion de l'Estran and its French guns, the route along the northern shore would have to be effectively blocked. Otherwise the Gare Maritime itself would be in peril.

How could so small a force defend a perimeter at least 3,000 yards square? Nicholson realised that the Q.V.R. and the Anti-aircraft troops could only fight a short delaying action to enable his brigade to organise the defence of the outer perimeter. But how long could the ramparts be held?

In several places, these ramparts were cut by main roads which might be forced by tanks. Once tanks had broken into Calais-St. Pierre they would be impossible to stop in the network of mean streets off the Boulevard Léon Gambetta and the Boulevard Lafayette. Nicholson did not yet know how severe Keller's losses had been in the tank battle near Guines which took place shortly after he landed. There were not many tanks left to support the infantry. Withdrawal into Calais-Nord to defend the docks, which were bombed several times that day, might soon become inevitable. Nicholson studied the street plan of Calais and decided that it might be necessary to hold the three bridges over the canal separating Calais-Nord from the south. This canal, part of the Canal de Calais, comprised the Bassin de Batellerie and Port de Navigation Intérieure. If these bridges could be blown, there was a chance of holding out on the line of this canal.

East of the Hôtel de Ville and its giant clock tower was the Pont Mollien, a vital bridge, linking the port with Calais-St. Pierre. Opposite the Hôtel de Ville and south of the canal, was the leafy Parc St. Pierre where Keller's tanks had been harboured on the previous night. Among tall trees in another park off the Place Richelieu, stood Rodin's monument to the Burghers of Calais.[7] Otherwise there was little cover for tanks and transport from air attack.

Calais-Nord as it appeared to Nicholson has long vanished. Near the watch tower, which still stands, stood the old Hôtel de Ville with a belfry whose chimes played "Gentille Annette" every hour. In the Rue Royale, Beau Brummel, in exile, existed above a bookseller's shop. And in the Rue Française died Emma, Lady Hamilton in 1815. These links with the tragic past were swept away in the flames and dust.

His conference with Colonel Holland finished, Nicholson returned to the docks. At his headquarters near Bastion 1 he issued orders to the Rifle Brigade and the 60th. He made it clear to the two battalion commanders that the situation was serious and that the Brigade could not carry out the role proposed by General Brownrigg at Dover. Nicholson therefore ordered them to hold the outer perimeter formed by the ramparts and ditches, a front estimated by Miller at six or seven miles. They were also to block all roads, railways and other approaches.

[7] It now stands opposite the Hôtel de Ville.

The 60th was to hold the western and southern and the Rifle Brigade (with two companies in reserve) the south-eastern and eastern faces. The boundary between the battalions would be the Canal de Calais running south from the Pont Mollien. The Q.V.R. outside the perimeter would come under their command according to the sector they were holding. As the battalion commanders moved off to give orders to their companies, the sound of firing to the west and south drew closer.

CHAPTER SEVEN

The Green Jackets

IN 1940, The King's Royal Rifle Corps (The 60th Rifles) and The Rifle Brigade were two of the finest regiments in the British Army. The Second Battalion, the 60th, and the First Battalion, The Rifle Brigade who served at Calais had famous histories. The 60th won seven V.C.s and led the assault on Delhi during the Indian Mutiny. It was the First Battalion, The Rifle Brigade, who formed the rear-guard in the retreat from Corunna in 1809 and held the crossroads at La Haye Sainte all day at Waterloo on the 18th June 1815. Besides their fighting traditions, they had a reputation for trust and respect between officers and men. Today, their descendants, the Royal Green Jackets, wear the battle honour "Calais 1940". It was the most important action they fought in the Second World War.

Eden knew that, when he appealed, as he did in the later stages of the battle, to their past, they would not fail to respond. And even if many ordinary riflemen never read his messages, they knew instinctively what to do. It may be fashionable today to sneer at regimental loyalty. Calais could not have been held for so long without it.

Both regiments at Calais were motor battalions, each about 750 strong. A proportion were experienced reservists which in 1940 the British Army could ill afford to lose. "These," wrote Churchill sadly, "were the splendid trained troops of which we had so few."

Great battles are fought by the few and the last stand of the 60th and The Rifle Brigade at Calais was no exception. The sight of these smart soldiers with their black buttons, chevrons and badges, edged with scarlet for the 60th and rifle green for the Rifle Brigade, had an electric effect on the defence.

Both regiments were commanded at Calais by officers of exceptional ability and prestige. The Second Battalion of the 60th was commanded by Lieut.-Colonel Euan Miller. He had taken over five months before the battle, after being a General Staff officer at the headquarters of the B.E.F. A regular, he joined the 60th in 1915 and served in France and Salonika, winning the M.C.[1] His shrewd and expert handling of his battalion, especially in the final stages of the defence, postponed to the last possible moment the fall of Calais-Nord. He was supported by officers and men who were to give Guderian the toughest fight since he crossed the Luxembourg frontier.

The First Battalion, The Rifle Brigade, was commanded by Lieut.-Colonel Chandos Hoskyns, another splendid soldier who was mortally wounded at Calais and died at Winchester on the 18th June 1940. He had joined the Rifle Brigade on the 15th August 1914 before he was nineteen. He was wounded in France in 1915 and later served in Salonika. After the First World War, he was in India and Malta, and on the 27th August 1938 was appointed to command the First Battalion at Tidworth. His ability was well known and his death symbolised the sacrifice of military talent among the 204 riflemen who died at Calais.

His second-in-command, Major Alexander Allan took over in the desperate fighting round the harbour on the 25th May. He kept the Battalion in action for another twenty-four hours, in the face of hopeless odds, and postponed the fall of the Gare Maritime. His professional skill and courage made a great contribution to those last tragic moments of the battle.

On the 23rd May, the first ship to berth was the *Royal Daffodil* with the 60th. Two days before, the Battalion had been under canvas at Fornham Park near Bury St. Edmunds. The 30th Infantry Brigade (less the Q.V.R.) had moved to East Anglia on the 11th May to "meet an expected invasion on the east coast". About 6.30 p.m. on the 21st May, Miller received orders to be ready to move by road at 11 p.m. complete with war equipment. There were the usual difficulties—a number of men had gone into Bury on pass and the tents and stores had to be collected—but there were no absentees and the Battalion was ready at 11 p.m. But they went to France without some

[1] Despite being taken prisoner, he became a Lieut.-General and Military Secretary of State for War. He retired in 1955.

of their scout cars which had been removed to other units. Each of their motor platoons had a 2-inch mortar but even these first-line troops had only smoke bombs! There was an "inadequate" supply of H.E. bombs for the 3-inch mortars.

The route to Southampton was Newmarket–North Circular Road –Staines–Winchester. The 60th were behind the Rifle Brigade who had received the same orders. It was, wrote Miller, "a long, weary, and generally uneventful drive. . . ."

While they were passing through London, it rained heavily and the men in their open vehicles were soaked to the skin. After refuelling on the Great West Road, a halt was made—it was still raining—for breakfast at Hartfordbridge Flats. This lasted for an hour and a quarter, then the Battalion continued to Southampton, arriving about 1 p.m.

After breakfast, Miller had gone ahead to Southampton. He did not yet know, and he was not told till that evening, where he was being sent. His account of what happened when the transport arrived at the docks demonstrates, in his restrained way, the officiousness of the embarkation staff:

As the vehicles drove up, most of our maps were collected and the vehicles were at once seized by somewhat excited staff officers. . . . The C.O. was not allowed to arrange anything. The result was considerable muddle and confusion: weapons and kit wanted by officers and men on the personnel ship were loaded on to the vehicle ship. Vehicles and personnel of different companies were all mixed up.

At the docks the same mistakes were repeated by staff officers, entirely ignorant of the composition or functions of a motor battalion. Among others, all Brens and Bren equipment were removed from the Scout carriers and placed on the *Royal Daffodil*, the personnel ship, in spite of protests from our officers on the spot. The result was that some 70 to 80 Bren guns with all equipment and much small arms ammunition were put on the *Royal Daffodil* where they were not wanted and where there was so little room. . . .[2]

[2] Miller: report dated June 1940.

Miller agrees that these zealous staff officers had to embark a large mechanised unit in record time. They also had to get Nicholson, his brigade headquarters and the Rifle Brigade aboard the *Archangel*. The confusion in which riflemen, equipment and vehicles were loaded led to very great difficulties next day when they disembarked at Calais, with the enemy no more than two or three miles away. Readers of this story who have not experienced a military embarkation in wartime, may wonder how the 60th managed to cross the Channel, let alone fight a heroic defence a few hours after landing.

The truth is that, like the Rifle Brigade, and to a lesser degree the Territorials who, being civilians, had their first taste of it, they were trained to put up with situations of this kind. Such muddles were (and no doubt still are) an integral part of the history of the British Army. In 1940, the terms "shambles", "balls-up" and stronger words, expressed the resignation of those who knew for certain that embarkations took place in no other way.

While the loading continued, officers and men of the 60th were eating meat and vegetable stew at a rest camp three miles from the docks. Corporal J. E. Howell found time to write a last letter on toilet paper to a girl-friend at Sturminster Newton. Many other letters were collected and posted that afternoon before the men paraded and marched down Southampton High Street at 5 p.m. Five days later, the writers were either dead or would not emerge from German prison camps for another five years.

It was 6 p.m. when the 60th started to embark on *Royal Daffodil* a very much smaller steamer than the *Archangel*. The staff officers took charge again and marched the men on board the ship in a hurry without allotting any part to individual companies, so that they became "mixed and disorganised". In cramped and uncomfortable conditions, they set sail for Dover in convoy with their two vehicle ships *Kohistan* and *City of Canterbury* at 7.30 p.m. Sleep was impossible on the closely crowded decks of *Royal Daffodil* and they got very little to eat.

The Rifle Brigade had been, since the 11th May, at Needham Market in Suffolk and in surrounding villages. They had a tiring day on the 21st May constructing road-blocks and digging trenches against the invasion. Like the 60th they received their orders at 6 p.m. and at 11 p.m. they led the convoy to Southampton. The rain had now stopped and it was a warm May evening as they marched to the docks. They passed a cricket match on their way. This peaceful scene remained in the thoughts of those who survived the grim years in the prisoner-of-war camps. As they reached the *Archangel*, a rifleman was heard to say: "The only crack regiment left in England will be the A.T.S."

The Rifle Brigade experienced the same muddle and confusion as the 60th when their transport was taken from them and loaded on the *City of Canterbury*. They arrived at Dover at 6 a.m. Apart from Miller, who had received a copy of the orders at Southampton in case the ships became separated, the men of both battalions could only guess at their destination.

The personnel ships sailed from Dover with the "Autocarrier" carrying the 229th Anti-Tank Battery at 10.40 a.m. This battery left Sheffield, where it was stationed, at 4.45 a.m. on the 21st May and did not reach Dover till 1.10 p.m. next day. They had been expected to sail at 10.30 a.m. but the "Autocarrier" had six wireless trucks on board destined for another unit. In consequence there was no room for the whole of the Battery. Their commander, Captain Woodley, was ordered to embark only two of his Troops and his Battery staff. The remaining men were to follow "within twelve hours". Only eight of their twelve guns were loaded on the ship. The rest never arrived at Calais.

When the convoy sailed, it was not only unclear what the role of the two motor battalions would be, but their vehicle ships sailed separately and no one knew when they would arrive at Calais. On *Royal Daffodil* all ranks were crammed below decks except the machine-gunners on air alarm stations. As they neared Calais, a Heinkel dropped two bombs near the *Archangel*. Anti-aircraft guns on the single escorting destroyer opened fire and drove the aircraft off. The sound of gunfire which had been audible all day drew closer. It seemed to come from the coast between Calais and Boulogne. Shortly before the ships entered the harbour the destroyer dropped a number of depth charges.

During the crossing, Nicholson issued orders which were not altered in principle. The Battalions were to concentrate right and left of the Calais–Boulogne road, the first unit to disembark to take the right. This order had the effect of determining the tasks of the 60th and the Rifle Brigade. Throughout the fighting, the 60th were on the west and south-west of Calais.

As they left the ship, the 60th were marched by companies along the south edge of the Bassin des Chasses de l'Est to their "hide" area, a small wood east of Bastion 2. They reached it at 2.30 p.m. and the trees gave them some cover from air attack as well as shelter from a steady downpour of rain. There they waited for their transport to arrive, armed with the eight Brens and two anti-tank rifles per company which they had brought with them in *Royal Daffodil*.

The Rifle Brigade were in the sandhills between the north side of the Bassin des Chasses and the seashore, looking out to sea for a sign of the vehicle ships. Allan, the second-in-command, wrote a vivid account of the Rifle Brigade's arrival at the Gare Maritime.

> Broken glass from the station and hotel buildings littered the quay and platforms in which many bomb craters were visible besides overturned and bombed trucks on the lines . . . the men gazed curiously at the piles of abandoned kit lying on the quays jettisoned by crowds of soldiers and airmen who were being shephered on to the *Maid of Orleans* recently vacated by the 3rd Royal Tank Regiment, homeward bound. These troops were in the main non-combatant personnel, R.A.F. ground staff, H.Q. clerks, etc., who suffered a severe battering by the Luftwaffe on their travels to the coast. They bore every sign of this and made a far from cheerful welcome to the theatre of war.[3]

While they were waiting in the sand dunes the Rifle Brigade watched the first shells burst on the far side of the harbour. German artillery had now got the range of the Gare Maritime and on to the quays swarmed a hysterical mob of French people crying in terror: "Les Allemands! Les Allemands!"

[3] *Rifle Brigade Chronicle, 1945.*

There was nothing the riflemen could do until their vehicles and weapons—apart from eight Brens per company which they brought with them—arrived. Those who were not on duty lay in the sand and talked and smoked and made tea. Their calm impressed a gunner officer who was reminded of "Hyde Park on Sunday".

The *City of Canterbury* with the 60th vehicles and the *Kohistan* with those of the Rifle Brigade arrived at 3.30 p.m. at low tide. There were no tugs to tow them into the Avant Port for unloading and they continued to "churn up mud for an hour and a half".

About this time, as the Searchlights were defending Orphanage Farm, the First Panzer Division moved up a battery to the Forêt de Guines. Their first shells landed in the water without damaging the Gare Maritime but they caused panic among the dock staff. This had already diminished in numbers since the Tanks and the Q.V.R. arrived twenty-four hours before. The stevedores and crane hands who remained were exhausted.

The *City of Canterbury* was the first to tie up but unloading did not begin till 5 p.m. Thirty tons of petrol in wooden boxes had first to be moved from the deck of each ship! In consequence, when Nicholson returned from the Boulevard Léon Gambetta at 4 p.m. to give orders to Miller and Hoskyns, there was no transport available for either battalion. They had to reach their company positions on foot.

Miller allotted the sectors to the 60th companies on the western and southern faces. He made his battalion headquarters in the Boulevard Léon Gambetta. "C" Company (Captain M. A. Johnson) had the longest march. They were to hold from the seafront west of the Citadel to a point on the railway at Bastion 10. When they reached Fort Risban, they found it occupied by the French Navy and, marching along the Sangatte road, they came to the Porte des Baraques south of Bastion 11. Here they set up a road-block and manned an embankment overlooking the cemetery to their left. In the centre, blocking the Route de Boulogne, west of the Pont Jourdan railway bridge was "B" Company (Major J. S. Poole), holding the western face as far as Bastion 9. The southern face was held by "D" Company (Major Lord Cromwell). "A" Company (Major F. L. Trotter) was to be in reserve on the eastern bastions until the arrival of the Rifle Brigade. Later the Canal de Calais became the boundary between the two battalions, the Rifle Brigade facing Dunkirk and south along the Canal de Marck.

There had been little reconnaissance owing to the slow unloading of the vehicle ships. The scout platoons with their Bren carriers did not join their companies until after dark. Many platoons had no transport till next morning. They had little time to do more than block the approaches. Had General Schaal pressed home his attack with the Tenth Panzer Division during the night, he might have saved the Germans time and many casualties.

On the Rifle Brigade front, Hoskyns had established his headquarters at Bastion 2. He began by reinforcing the Q.V.R. post on the perimeter. He sent platoons to the Halte St. Pierre on the St. Omer road, to the Porte de Dunkerque and two platoons to the north-east of the Bassin des Chasses de l'Est. These were to cover a possible assembly area for the Battalion if they withdrew to Dunkirk. The remainder dug in on the sand dunes in front of the Bastion de l'Estran and at the north-east corner of the Bassin des Chasses.

An hour before the vehicle ships had berthed, Nicholson received an order from the War Office which could only be executed with motor transport. This was to escort a column of ten-ton lorries to Dunkirk with rations for the B.E.F. The Rifle Brigade were to accompany them with their Bren gun carriers "half way" there. The task was to be given priority "overriding all other considerations". Three hundred and fifty thousand rations which had been sitting on the docks for a day, were loaded on to the lorries. The only chance of carrying out the plan was for them to leave at once, with carriers and tanks to clear a path for them along the Dunkirk road. But the First Panzer Division was already moving up to block the road at Marck. It was many hours before the ration column was ready and by then it was no longer possible to break through.

At 10 p.m., I arrived at the Porte de Marck, shaken by the bombing of Coulogne and my narrow escape. After the long journey on foot up the Route de St. Omer, I had been able to find some of my own troop. I was nervous and footsore but I tried to appear unbowed.

How could I, a dilettante, compete with the brave traditions of the Rifle Brigade? They received me as if there was nothing unusual afoot. I could see the outline of the ramparts against the fierce red glare over Dunkirk.

Any supposition that I was part of a "non-fighting" unit had been dispelled by the defence of Orphanage Farm and Coulogne. I now found myself, with several weary gunners, under the command of "A" Company of the Rifle Brigade (Major John Taylor), lying on the ramparts with a rifle pointing towards Gravelines. The shells whined and crashed on the docks behind us.

The Rifle Brigade trucks and carriers were an interminable time in unloading. Three cranes were still working when the 60th vehicles were taken off the *City of Canterbury* but the Rifle Brigade ship, last in, had only one to aid it. British stevedores who had unloaded the rations into the ten-ton lorries for the B.E.F. at Dunkirk had worked for thirty-six hours and were, wrote Allan, "too tired to stand". After the Rifle Brigade landed, he had remained at the Gare Maritime to act as liaison between Nicholson and Brownrigg and a number of visiting British and French commanders.

When the shelling of the docks started in earnest, the stevedores, wrote Allan, "showed an inclination to leave work". Surely the most masterly of understatements. All unloading was stopped for some hours. Both stevedores and crane hands went away at about 10 p.m. and were, with great difficulty, persuaded to resume work at 3 a.m. Nearly all the weapons of both battalions, the ammunition and other equipment, were packed in vehicles still on the ships. The situation was so urgent that a Rifle Brigade officer, Captain T. R. Gordon-Duff, spent several hours in search of the "various holes and corners" where the stevedores were sleeping and induced them to return.

By 4 a.m. all the brigade headquarters and 60th vehicles had been unloaded from the *Kohistan*. The *City of Canterbury* took longer. At 7.30 a.m. a Sea Transport Officer, who said he had Nicholson's permission, gave orders that the holds were to be closed down although the ship was still full of vehicles, weapons and ammunition. Wounded were loaded from a second hospital train. Rifle Brigade drivers whose vehicles had not appeared, carried them aboard, leaving on the platform some twenty bodies of men who had died as a result of the delay in getting them to hospital.

Meanwhile, preparations were made by the Rifle Brigade for the column of ten-ton ration lorries and their escort to break through to Dunkirk. As the vehicles were unloaded, a composite company was made up under Major G. L. Hamilton-Russell. They moved in trucks along the Dunkirk road to await the tanks which were due to accompany them. The column was to leave the Porte de Dunkerque at 2 a.m. on the 24th May. But Keller was anxious to leave at first light and the column was therefore delayed until 4 a.m.

By the evening of the 23rd May, Guderian was anxious. In the race for the Aa Canal, he had left Calais exposed on his left flank. The brush with the Third Royal Tank Regiment and the Searchlights in the afternoon seems to have upset his staff. These small battle, some distance from the walls of Calais, convinced him that the British would land more troops. Reluctantly, he committed the Tenth Panzer Division to the capture of the town instead of sending it in the wake of the First Panzer Division to attack Dunkirk.

Despite all the information at their disposal which included telephone conversations between Ironside and Nicholson, the War Office was still uncertain whether to evacuate or defend Calais. The 30th Infantry Brigade and the Third Royal Tank Regiment had been shipped over to the port before it was decided what they should do. Much equipment had been left behind and throughout the night of the 23rd, Nicholson received a baffling flow of contradictory orders.

By dawn on the 24th, German infantry and artillery were in position to launch a general attack on Calais from the west.

PART II
THE OUTER PERIMETER

Principal events covered by Part II

24th May 1940	3 a.m.	War Office order evacuation of Calais "in principle"
	8.30 a.m.	The *City of Canterbury* leaves for Dover
	11.42 a.m.	Hitler orders the Panzers to halt on the Aa Canal and leave Dunkirk to the Luftwaffe
	4.30 p.m.	Capture of Fort Nieulay
	9 p.m.	Withdrawal of the 60th and Q.V.R. to the inner perimeter
	11.23 p.m.	War Office order Nicholson to fight on for the sake of "Allied solidarity"

CHAPTER EIGHT

Evacuation in Principle

THROUGHOUT the night of the 23rd May, Nicholson received a series of messages from the War Office which did little to clarify the situation at Calais. At midnight, General McNaughton, the commander of the First Canadian Division, arrived at the Gare Maritime by destroyer. Nicholson was away from his headquarters which had been moved to the Boulevard Léon Gambetta, and he had left Colonel Miller of the 60th in charge of the defence of the town. McNaughton spent three hours in Calais but his visit brought little news and no fresh orders. There had been talk of landing the Canadian Division at one of the Channel ports to help the tired B.E.F. but, the situation at Calais appearing far from propitious, McNaughton sailed at 3 a.m. for Dunkirk.[1]

While Nicholson was visiting the Rifle Brigade east of the town, Miller remained in touch with the War Office. One of the most absurd messages which he received was that Péronne, Albert, and Amiens had been "officially" recaptured on the previous day. This was entirely untrue.

During the night hours, Miller spoke to Ironside on the telephone, and to the staff of Admiral Ramsay at Dover. He was promised the support of the Navy who would shell the tanks. But it was all too clear that the War Office still believed that these were "few in number". Their attitude was no doubt influenced by their decision in the early hours of the 24th May to evacuate Nicholson's brigade from Calais.

On the previous afternoon, Nicholson had spoken by telephone to Major-General R. H. Dewing, Director of Military Operations at the War Office and there had been no mention of evacuation by sea.

[1] Advance units of the Canadian Division embarked for Dunkirk on the 24th but the order was countermanded.

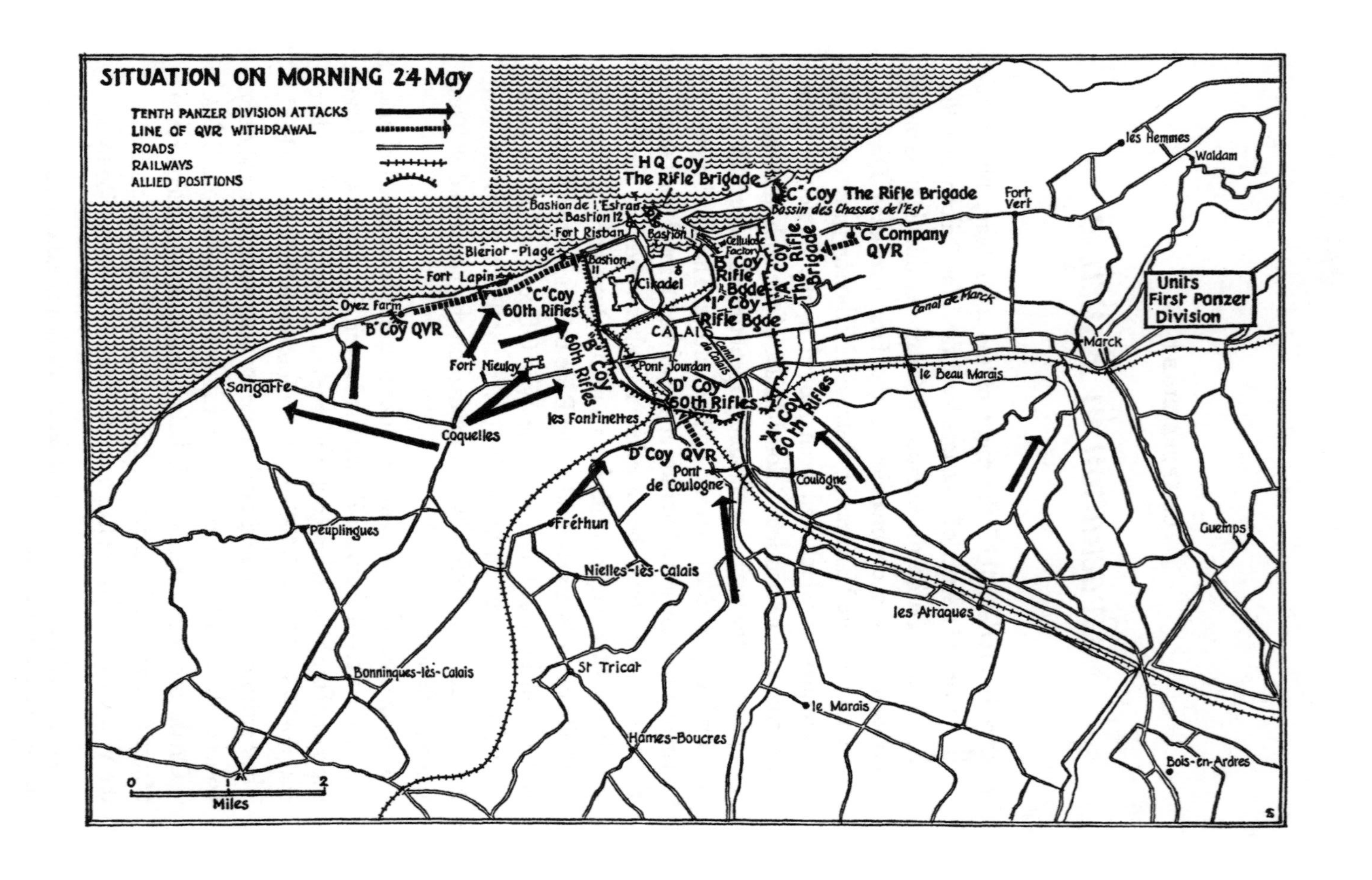
SITUATION ON MORNING 24 May
TENTH PANZER DIVISION ATTACKS
LINE OF QVR WITHDRAWAL
ROADS
RAILWAYS
ALLIED POSITIONS
HQ Coy
The Rifle Brigade
'C' Coy The Rifle Brigade
Bassin des Chasses de l'Est
'C' Company
QVR
Bastion de l'Estran
Bastion 12
Fort Risban
Bastion 1
Bastion 11
Cellulose Factory
Blériot-Plage
Fort Lapin
Oyez Farm
'B' Coy QVR
'C' Coy
60th Rifles
Citadel
'B' Coy
Rifle Bgde
½ 'I' Coy
Rifle Bgde
'A' Coy
The Rifle Brigade
CALAIS
Canal de Calais
Canal de Marck
Fort Vert
Units
First Panzer
Division
les Hemmes
Waldam
Marck
Fort Nieulay
'B' Coy
60th Rifles
Pont Jourdan
'D' Coy
60th Rifles
'A' Coy
60th Rifles
le Beau Marais
Sangatte
Coquelles
les Fontinettes
'D' Coy QVR
Pont de Coulogne
Coulogne
Fréthun
Peuplingues
Nielles-lès-Calais
Guemps
les Attaques
Bonningues-lès-Calais
St Tricat
le Marais
Hames-Boucres
Bois-en-Ardres
0
1
2
Miles

Nicholson was told that he was at liberty to withdraw to cover Dunkirk if the "situation warrants it". He was to move as many troops there as possible, the remainder "to form and hold a defensive position at Calais". It was difficult to know what this meant. If a "defensive position" at Calais was to be held, it could not be done by splitting his small force.

On the same evening, the War Office decided to evacuate the 20th Guards Brigade which had been holding Boulogne for the past two days. By 9 p.m. destroyers had already withdrawn 1,000 men from the harbour. A thousand were disembarked early on the morning of the 24th May, leaving French troops to hold on for another twenty-four hours.

The War Office decided that it was hopeless to attempt to hold Calais and that Nicholson's brigade with its highly trained regular soldiers must be re-embarked. They foresaw the loss of most of the B.E.F. and the need to save what forces they could for the defence of England against invasion. In the event, it was Nicholson's brigade who were sacrificed and the B.E.F. who were saved.

At 3 a.m. General Dewing telegraphed:

"Evacuation decided in principle. When you finished unloading your two M.T. ships commence embarkation of all personnel except fighting personnel who remain to cover final evacuation."

When this message was received, Nicholson was with Colonel Hoskyns on the Dunkirk road waiting for the Rifle Brigade and the tanks to move off as escort to the 350,000 rations. The B.E.F. were already on half-rations as they began to withdraw to the coast. On reading the War Office message, Nicholson ordered his Brigade Major, Captain Dennis Talbot, to prepare an operation order for withdrawal to the Gare Maritime by stages. Though this first message did not say when the evacuation was to take place, it was known by 7 a.m. that it was planned for the evening of the following day, that is to say the 25th May.

Nicholson did not yet know that he was already surrounded, but the First Panzer Division failed to take advantage of his position. During the evening, the Rifle Brigade sent a section of Bren gun carriers under one of their best young officers, 2/Lieut. A. P. R. Rolt as far as Fort Vert on the Gravelines road. As darkness fell, he found himself ringed by bonfires lit by the Germans to show the Luftwaffe the limit of their advance. At dawn, he managed to extricate the carriers and return to Calais.

The First Panzer Division had lost interest in Calais—their thoughts were on Dunkirk, and Calais was the problem of the Tenth Panzer Division. As they rested for the night astride the Calais–Gravelines road, an amazing incident occurred. A patrol of one cruiser and three light tanks of "B" Squadron, Third Royal Tank Regiment, set off under a full moon to see if the road was clear. They had only moved a short distance when they lost wireless touch with Colonel Keller and the remaining tanks who were to follow them. There was no turning back. They continued through three unguarded enemy road-blocks and lines of German troops who took them for their own tanks. A German motor-cyclist rode up to one tank, examined the number plate with a torch and beat a hasty retreat. The squadron reached Gravelines in safety. They fought in the town next morning, knocking out five German tanks and two troop carriers. Their commander, Major W. R. Reeves, received the immediate award of the D.S.O.[2] This was a splendid exploit but there were now four tanks less to defend Calais.

The composite force under Major Hamilton-Russell, commander of "B" Company of the Rifle Brigade, had been ready since midnight. After vainly waiting for news of Major Reeves and his tanks, they moved off at 4 a.m. along the Dunkirk road, accompanied by Nicholson himself. Hamilton-Russell had five tanks in front, followed by three carriers, three platoons in trucks and two platoons in the rear. After two miles, a point was reached between Le Beau Marais and Marck, where the column found a strong German road-block with anti-tank guns among the houses and allotments on either side. The British tanks were forced to stop, but platoons of the Rifle Brigade worked their way round the German flanks. A spirited action followed which lasted till daylight, but when it became clear that Hamilton-Russell would be surrounded, he reluctantly withdrew, losing two riflemen killed and several wounded.

[2] Liddell Hart: *The Tanks*, Vol. II, p. 22.

"B" Company of the Rifle Brigade now went into reserve at the Cellulose Factory (see map on page 90) and the rest of Hamilton-Russell's party rejoined their own companies. The riflemen were in excellent spirits but some of their officers thought the operation a waste of effort. This was the end of the abortive attempt to get the rations through to B.E.F. and it was now time to concentrate on the defence of Calais.

At the Gare Maritime, the vehicle ships were being unloaded under shellfire and in darkness. When the 60th vehicles had been unloaded, the first group of wounded were put aboard the *Kohistan*. A second hospital train arrived during the night which had been three days on the way to the coast and had already tried to get in to Dunkirk and Boulogne. Many of the wounded were in terrible distress and several lives were lost through the delay. After waiting for hours outside Calais, the French engine driver refused to proceed to the docks without an official signal. He protested that he was under military law and could be shot. He was told by the Rifle Brigade that he would be shot if he did not move his train immediately and it drew in to the Gare Maritime at 7 a.m. It was the wounded from this train, who were carried aboard the *City of Canterbury* which was half unloaded.

By 7.30 a.m. the news that evacuation had been decided "in principle" had become known to most British troops in Calais and many breathed a sigh of relief. When the Sea Transport Officer at the Gare Maritime ordered the holds of the *City of Canterbury* to be closed down, the crew announced that the ship would leave for England in an hour. More than half the Rifle Brigade vehicles and much ammunition and other equipment were still on board. Unloading stopped and the Movement Control and quay staff said they had orders from the War Office to return to England. Major Allan, the second-in-command of the Rifle Brigade, was horrified. The War Office message clearly meant that there would be no "final" evacuation for thirty-six hours. Early that morning, Hoskyns visited the Q.V.R. headquarters at the Porte de Dunkerque and told Ellison-Macartney that it was intended to evacuate the town on the evening of Saturday the 25th May but that "everything must be done to prevent the enemy becoming aware of this intention". The Rifle

Brigade would need train transport and ammunition to cover the withdrawal.

Nicholson confirmed this order to the garrison. The embarkation of "non-fighting personnel" on the *City of Canterbury* had already begun, as Allan protested that the Rifle Brigade could not fight with only half their transport and ammunition. But shells were now falling round the Gare Maritime and exploding near the *City of Canterbury*. No one who considered himself authorised to depart—and some were not so authorised—was anxious to remain any longer. At 8.30 a.m., its decks covered with wounded, the *City of Canterbury* left the harbour.

Afterwards, many stories were told in prisoner-of-war camps about this incident which was damaging to the fighting efficiency of the Rifle Brigade. It was even said that a fifth-columnist in British uniform had given false orders to the *City of Canterbury*. The ship's departure had nothing sinister about it. Ironside himself confirmed General Dewing's instructions that "non-fighting" personnel and the wounded should be sent back as soon as possible. Indeed no other course made sense if a final evacuation of the fighting troops was to take place. But the return to England of half the Rifle Brigade transport was a blunder understandable only in the conditions of heavy shellfire.

In the Official History of the War, Major L. F. Ellis takes a more lenient view of the *City of Canterbury* episode:

"It may be that further unloading was considered unnecessary, for, early that morning, Brigadier Nicholson was informed by the War Office that evacuation had been decided 'in principle' and that, while fighting personnel must stay to cover the evacuation, non-fighting personnel should begin embarking at once."[3]

Throughout the morning of the 24th May, "non-fighting" men were released to the docks to join the wounded on the *Kohistan*, the last ship to leave. There was some confusion as to the definition of "non-fighting". Nicholson told Keller to send back all men not required for tank crews and the "B" echelon of the Third Royal Tank Regiment marched to the Gare Maritime where they set fire to their

[3] *The War in France and Flanders*, p. 174.

transport. Colonel Goldney, the Air Defence Commander, organised a reserve of anti-aircraft troops to the 60th. He allowed about 200 to leave but ordered the rest to remain and fight. Some had been sent as far as the ship and ordered back at the gangway. There was little panic and, as the *Kohistan* left at noon under shellfire, men of the Rifle Brigade stood on the quay waving goodbye. No one expected the "final" evacuation to be cancelled.

With the *Kohistan* went the remaining stevedores and quay staff and a number of administrative soldiers including a brigadier who had escaped from Brownrigg's former headquarters at Wimereux. Allan tried to persuade the Sea Transport Officer and quay staff to remain. One officer was found trying to cut the telephone to London. When asked what he was doing, he replied: "There is no further use for this. We are all going home and I advise you to do the same."

At the Rifle Brigade positions near the Porte de Marck on the east I had watched the dawn rise over Dunkirk. Save for the occasional shell which landed in the harbour area, the night had been quiet. But it had been impossible to sleep so strong was the sense of danger. By now, I knew that Calais would soon be surrounded. I realised that there would be a bloody battle. And yet, throughout the night, rumours of evacuation grew, passed on from man to man in the darkness.

With the departure of the *Kohistan*, several hundred "non-fighting" soldiers, some unarmed, were left behind. They lay silently on the banks of the Bassin des Chasses de l'Est. Many had been stopped at the entrance to the Gare Maritime and were beginning to realise their predicament. Among them was my small party of Searchlight men.

During the morning, I received permission to withdraw the men from the Porte de Marck and was told to wait in the sand dunes. Calais had become a city of doom and I was not in the least anxious to remain. I did not feel heroic. Leaving the men, sleepless and anxious, I walked to the Gare Maritime in time to see the *Kohistan* leave harbour. The quay was now deserted save for the twenty dead on the platform.

The scene remains vivid. It was a clear day and I could see the cliffs of Dover. The sad corpses, covered in grey blankets, had begun to stink. Shells burst among the cranes or landed in the sea. A mile out, the destroyer *Wessex*, struck by Luftwaffe bombs, was sinking. Black smoke from the blazing oil refinery billowed across the harbour and, to the west and south of the town, there came the growing noise of rifle and anti-tank fire. The real battle was about to begin.

After the action on the Dunkirk road, Brigadier Nicholson returned to the Boulevard Léon Gambetta at 9 a.m. and Colonel Miller was restored to the command of the 60th. A number of shells had landed in the street without doing much damage. Stray rifle shots from the roofs and windows inside the town showed that fifth-column snipers were already active.

Nicholson, faced with the failure to break out of the east and with evacuation in mind, now issued fresh orders. The "outer perimeter", of modern fortifications, as well as the Citadel Bastion 11 and Fort Nieulay were to be held. An inner line, behind the waterways of Calais-Nord as far as the harbour, would be taken up if the length of the "outer perimeter" proved too great to defend, or evacuation by sea was finally decided. Hoskyns gave more details to the Q.V.R.

> In order to prevent the enemy from concentrating for an attack, the R.A.F. would that day start extensive bombing on an arc stretching from Sangatte to Gravelines. On the arrival of the order to withdraw, the Q.V.R. would return to the Gare Maritime and embark first. A shortened line would be taken up by the Rifle Brigade and 60th. This would be the line of the canal dividing Calais-Nord from Calais-St. Pierre, running from Fort Risban in the west to the Porte de Marck in the east. The boundary between battalions would be the Canal de Calais.[4]

The defence of the "outer perimeter" began at dawn on the 24th May when the Germans attacked in the west and south-west under cover of heavy and accurate mortar fire. It was the Q.V.R. who took the brunt of this attack since they remained at their advanced positions which they had occupied all the previous day.

The Q.V.R. platoon under 2/Lieut. R. Snowden blocking the

[4] Timpson: Prisoner-of-War Diary.

. Brigadier Claude Nicholson.

. Lieut.-Colonel Euan Miller.

3. Lieut.-Colonel Chandos Hoskyns.

4. Lieut.-Colonel J. A. M. Ellison-Macartney.

5. Major Alexander Allan.

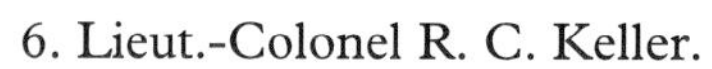

6. Lieut.-Colonel R. C. Keller.

7. Lieut.-Colonel R. M. Goldney.

8. Capitaine de Frégate Carlos de Lambertye.

9. André Gershell.

10. Colonel-General Heinz Guderian.

11. Major-General Ferdinand Schaal, Commander Tenth Panzer Division.

. Enseigne de Vaisseau Georges Wiart at Bastion I.

13. Brigadier Nicholson in a prisoner-of-war camp.

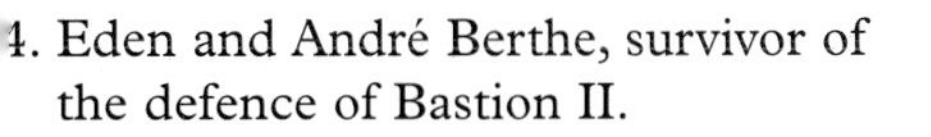

4. Eden and André Berthe, survivor of the defence of Bastion II.

15. The harbour from Calais-Nord before World War II.

16. Calais-Nord after the battle.

17. The west side of the Citadel before the battle.

18. The tunnel under Bastion I, today.

19. View today from Bastion I.

20. The Bassin des Chasses de l'Est, today.

21. Boulevard Léon Gambetta, today.

22. Fort Nieulay, today.

23. The Hôpital Militaire after the battle.

24. Pont Georges Cinq, today.

25. Pont Freycinet, today.

26. Calais from a German aircraft during the bombardment.

27. The Bassin Carnot after the battle.

28. Street scene after the battle.

29. Calais-Nord looking towards the clock tower, after the battle.

30. Corner of Rue Edison, 1940.

31. Corner of Rue Edison, today.

To Commanding CALAIS
From War Office

Secretary of State to Brigadier
NICHOLSON ⊙ Defence of CALAIS to the utmost
is of highest importance to our country
as symbolising our continued co-operation
with France ⊙ The eyes of the empire
are upon the defence of CALAIS and
H.M. Government are confident you and
your gallant regiments will perform an
exploit worthy of the British name.

System in	Time in	Recorded
W	16.26	A. Jordan

Staff Captain
Copy of a message received – for
information of all ranks

C.N.
1345 hrs 25/4

32. Eden's message to Nicholson, 25th May. Found in Colonel Hoskyns' battledress after he was mortally wounded.

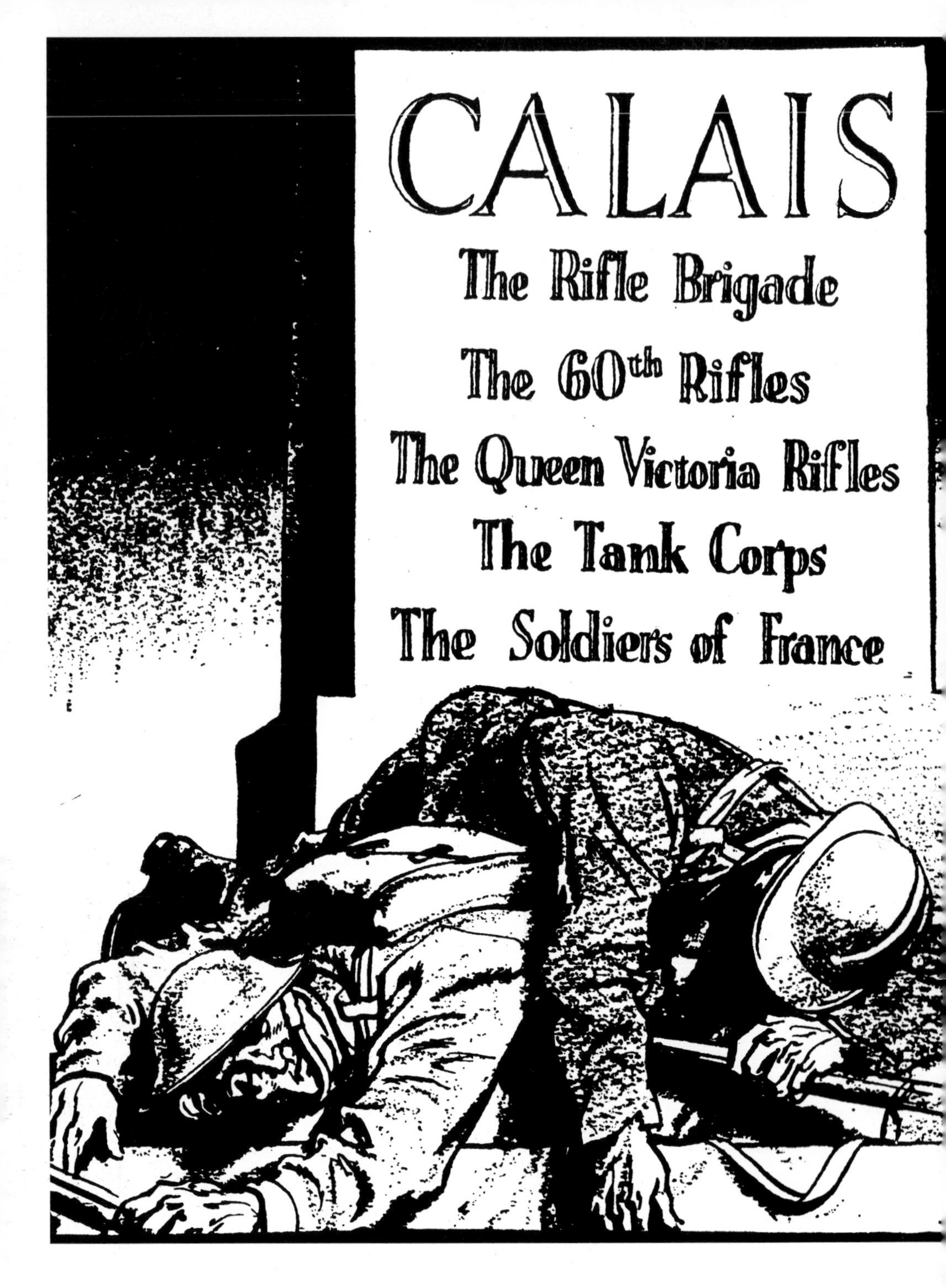

33. The *Daily Mirror* cartoon at the time of the battle. The caption reads: "Their Name Liveth for Evermore!"

34. German troops in Calais, after the battle.

35. French and British prisoners-of-war.

36. British dead at a road-block in Calais.

37. British graves in the Citadel.

Chemin de Fréthun and the railway at Les Fontinettes had passed the night strengthening their defences. In the half-light, they saw twenty figures approaching who were at first taken for "refugees or unarmed Allied soldiers". They moved slowly along the Chemin de Fréthun and the cluster of railway tracks. The Q.V.R. opened fire, and they dropped to the ground. Nothing happened for half an hour until there came the whistle of mortar bombs which exploded on the road-block killing two riflemen and wounding two others.

The mortar fire continued for ten minutes, but Snowden, observing from the control cabin, was unable to see the Germans. At 7 a.m., to their disappointment, his platoon and another of Lieutenant Jessop's company at a road-block on the Route de Coulogne were withdrawn to strengthen the line held by the 60th. This was a series of posts from Bastion 9 eastwards to Bastion 6 which formed the southern ramparts of Calais. They were defended by companies of the 60th commanded by Lord Cromwell and Major Trotter. Gaps in this precarious line were filled by the Q.V.R., by French troops and by sixty men of the Second Searchlight Battery.

The Q.V.R. platoons had no sooner joined the 60th than the Germans opened fire from the houses opposite them. Infantry advanced from a factory south of the Chemin du Grand Voyeu and more were seen leaving lorries on the road. Anti-tank rifle fire put two of these lorries out of action and Bren guns prevented the infantry from making progress. The Germans replied with mortar bombs.

The Q.V.R. platoon at Bastion 7[5] (2/Lieut. Brewester and Sergeant Tonge) who were in advance of the railway embankment had a particularly unpleasant time and were pinned down for several hours by machine-gun fire. Plans were made to move them back behind the railway embankment and give them covering fire but this provoked even heavier retaliation from the Germans. It was at this time that Corporal Burlton was killed in a gallant attempt to recover a Bren gun. For the moment the platoon were unable to move.

In addition to shelling which forced several units off the ramparts, the defenders were sniped at in the rear by the fifth column from

[5] See map on p. 132.

houses off the Boulevard Curie. Moving them into new positions brought a hail of mortar bombs as the Germans were able to observe their movements from the air.

The Tenth Panzer Division were surprised at their hot reception. The 69th Rifle Regiment had moved up during the morning from Guines and captured Pont de Coulogne at 10.15 a.m. In the advance to Calais-St. Pierre, one company had six men killed and the same number seriously wounded in the fighting in front of the bastions. Four light tanks were lost, two being burned out. But, at noon, the regimental commander reported that: "Despite MG nests and barricades the regiment has reached the inner town at three points."

This was being optimistic. He had not reached the "inner town" but in places breached the "outer perimeter". It was not till a general withdrawal to Calais-Nord began several hours later, that the Germans got a footing in Calais-St. Pierre.

On the western front, the 86th Rifle Regiment and supporting tanks took Coquelles before dawn and awaited the arrival of their artillery. From the old windmill, still a landmark today, a battery shelled the harbour, the French coastal guns and the Q.V.R. positions at Oyez Farm and Fort Nieulay.

The defence of Fort Nieulay standing on the Boulogne road between the Germans and Calais was to be of critical importance in the next few hours.

CHAPTER NINE

"Allied Solidarity"

ON the morning of the 24th when the Tenth Panzer Division began their attack, crucial decisions were made which were to influence not only the fate of Calais but the whole conduct of the war. British and French leaders now took refuge in the expression "Allied solidarity" which appears in numerous directives and telegrams. It meant very little to the troops or their commanders and it was differently interpreted by the two governments. The British were on the verge of deciding not to stay in France and to disembark their army at Dunkirk. Should they show "solidarity" by cancelling the order to evacuate Calais, while withdrawing the B.E.F. to the coast? The French, in their turn, were furious at the British evacuation of Boulogne, where their own troops were still holding out, and determined that Calais and Dunkirk should be defended.

Though the War Office wavered to the end about the "final" evacuation of the Calais garrison, Churchill still had faith in Weygand's plan for a large bridgehead in northern France to be supplied by sea. This involved holding Boulogne, Calais, and Dunkirk as long as possible. The French Navy were also preparing the evacuation of "certain units". Weygand had made a good impression on Churchill in Paris on the 22nd May. "He was brisk, buoyant and incisive," wrote Churchill. He presented a major new plan with great enthusiasm.[1] The plan for the "large bridgehead" was, for the time being, secondary.

Weygand proposed that the British and the French First Army should attack south-west towards Bapaume and Cambrai with about eight divisions supported by the R.A.F. The French Seventh Army concentrating along the Somme, should attack northwards and join

[1] Churchill: *The Second World War*, Vol. II, p. 57.

the B.E.F. at Bapaume. The left of this army should push forward to Amiens. "The Panzer divisions must not," said Weygand, "be allowed to keep the initiative."

While the conference was taking place, the news came of the death of General Billotte in a car accident. Billotte was the only Frenchman who knew Weygand's plan, but Churchill felt he had no choice except to welcome it. He informed Gort by telegram of his agreement.

On his return to London, Churchill was in good spirits. Privately he had complained to Reynaud of the days which had passed without Gort receiving orders. But he still retained a romantic faith in the French Army and memories of the "Miracle of the Marne".[2]

Ironside was not reassured. Disillusioned by his unfortunate visit to Billotte, he felt that Weygand's plan was merely a series of *projets*. After the War Cabinet meeting on Churchill's return to London at 6.30 p.m. on the 22nd May, he wrote in his diary:

"The B.E.F. has lost a chance of extricating itself and is very short of food and ammunition. I am trying to square up this end to clear the Channel ports for Gort."

Within a few hours events took shape which were to shake Churchill's faith in the Weygand plan. When Gort received the directive to attack south-west with the French on the 23rd May, he was very despondent. Such an attack was impossible. Since the death of Billotte there was no one, until the appointment of his successor, General Blanchard, three days later, to co-ordinate the B.E.F. with the French and Belgian Armies.

Gort had already decided that the French would never attack and it must have been reassuring to him to receive this telegram from Eden on the 23rd May:

"Should, however, situation on your communications make this (Weygand Plan) at any time impossible you should inform us so that we can inform French and make naval and air arrangements to assist you should you have to withdraw on northern coast."

In effect he was to act according to his own judgment. At 7 a.m. on the 23rd to the consternation of Churchill and the French he had already ordered General Franklyn to withdraw and give up Arras. It

[2] Alistair Horne: *To Lose a Battle.*

was an action which aroused great bitterness between the Allies. But in any case it was too late to attack. The German infantry divisions had come up to protect the Panzer divisions from an Allied breakout to the south.

The Panzers had had an anxious time for the past three days. Schaal, the Commander of the Tenth Panzer Division reported that his troops were covering the western end of the flank along the Somme over a distance of sixty miles. But many officers close to Gort felt, like Ironside, that it was too late to save the B.E.F. "Only a miracle" could prevent catastrophe. Despite violent French recriminations, Gort continued to withdraw northwards.

Gort was about to make the most vital decision of the entire campaign for on the 25th he was to withdraw his army to the north. As Alistair Horne writes in *To Lose a Battle*:

"Had the B.E.F. been wiped out in northern France, it is difficult to see how Britain could have continued to fight; and with Britain out of the battle, it is even more difficult to see what combination of circumstances could have aligned America and Stalin's Russia to challenge Hitler."

By abandoning an attack southwards and ordering a withdrawal to the north, Gort, on his own initiative, saved the B.E.F. and much beside it. But he made it essential to hold Calais to keep open Dunkirk and this now became the main purpose in landing Nicholson's brigade.[8]

The scene was changing hour by hour. To understand the complex process by which the orders and decisions of the 24th and 25th May were made it may be useful to review them before describing the battle itself.

Eden telegraphed Gort on the 23rd that the choice rested with him —a choice which Gort had already taken. Major-General Dewing said much the same thing to Nicholson on the telephone that evening about the withdrawal of his brigade from Calais to Dunkirk.

On the 24th May the decision to evacuate Calais "in principle" was influenced by the impending loss of Boulogne. General Dewing was later called upon by an angry Churchill to explain his telegram. This he

[8] Eden: *The Reckoning*, p. 109.

did in a minute dated the 27th May after Calais had fallen. He wrote:

"About 6 a.m. on the 24th I spoke to C.I.G.S.[4] in his room. He agreed with the principle. I then spoke to Nicholson by telephone making it quite clear that evacuation was approved in principle but that final evacuation would not be for at least 24 hours; that is at the earliest the morning of Saturday 25th."

On the 25th Churchill had written to Ironside:

"Pray find out who was the officer responsible for sending the order to evacuate Calais yesterday and by whom this very lukewarm telegram I saw this morning was drafted in which mention is made of 'for the sake of Allied Solidarity'. This is no way to encourage men to fight to the end. Are you sure there is no streak of defeatist opinion on the General Staff?"

The "lukewarm telegram" which annoyed Churchill, reached Nicholson late on the 24th May. It read:

"In spite of policy of evacuation given you this morning fact that British forces in your area now under Fagalde who has ordered no repeat no evacuation means that you must comply for the sake of Allied Solidarity. Your role is therefore to hold on, harbour being at present of no importance to B.E.F. Brigade Group 48 Div started marching to your assistance this morning. No reinforcements but ammunition being sent by sea. Should this fail R.A.F. will drop ammunition. You will select best position and fight on."

This unhappy telegram signed by a junior officer was the outcome of sharp exchanges between the French and British commands about Calais which continued during the 24th May.

General Dewing's minute is given in full as an appendix to this book.

At 9.33 a.m. the Admiralty sent this signal to H.M.S. *Gulzar* and H.M.S. *Wessex* off Calais to be passed to Nicholson:

"Confirm that evacuation is not repetition not to take place except for non-essential non-fighting troops."

By this time the *City of Canterbury* had left, watched by the French with considerable annoyance. Colonel Holland had told Capitaine

[4] Ironside.

de Frégate Loïs Petit, who was acting as second-in-command to Le Tellier at the Citadel, of the contents of Dewing's first telegram ordering evacuation "in principle". This was freely discussed by the troops on the ramparts and led to a coolness, not to say hostility, between the Allies in Calais.

An even more serious incident for Anglo-French relations occurred at 9 a.m. when Colonel Keller was told by Nicholson that men not required for tank crews could leave on the *Kohistan*.

"Orders were issued," wrote Colonel Holland after the war, "that tanks and transport likely to fall intact into enemy hands were to be destroyed. Owing to a misunderstanding some tanks were prematurely destroyed."[5] Five cruiser tanks were set on fire. The sight of them, blazing on a sandy space near the Gare Maritime, created a deplorable impression. Many believed that evacuation was actually about to take place. The noise of their exploding ammunition led the Rifle Brigade to think that the fifth column were attacking the Gare Maritime behind them.

On the same morning General Fagalde, commanding, the XVIth French Corps, took over the land defence of Dunkirk under the naval commander-in-chief in the north, Admiral Abrial. According to French sources, Loïs Petit made a violent protest by telephone to Fagalde about the British evacuation plans and described the burning tanks. Fagalde alerted Weygand, who spoke to the War Office himself and demanded that the evacuation be cancelled. Throughout the 24th, there was strong pressure from the French that the British should stay in Calais.[6]

In the afternoon Weygand issued orders to General Blanchard, the successor to Billotte:

"Every effort should be made to hold the area of the ports of Boulogne, Calais and Dunkirk and to maintain a large bridgehead supplied by sea and which can be held for a long time."

It was this proposal, secondary to the more grandiose "Weygand plan", which had almost gone by the board, that Churchill felt bound to support by the defence of Calais.

[5] Report to War Office, 17th May 1945.

[6] Robert Chaussois: Article in *La Voix du Nord*, 20th May 1965.

In a telephone conversation with Blanchard, Weygand said of the defence of the ports: "Il va falloir se battre comme des chiens!"

When General Fagalde assumed command at Dunkirk he was made responsible for the defence of Calais. His first action was to confirm Nicholson in command of the Allied defence and Le Tellier as second-in-command. He ordered "no evacuation" and since they had agreed that Nicholson was under him, the War Office had no alternative but to comply.

The French had evolved a respectable military reason for defending Calais to maintain supplies by sea: to the Allied Armies in the North. The War Office, however, were keen to withdraw the British Army from France. They had already decided that Calais was of "no value to the B.E.F."

It was not till next day that any mention was made of saving the B.E.F. by holding Calais. Brigadier Nicholson could hardly have received a less inspiring telegram than that dispatched by the War Office at 11.23 p.m. on the 24th May. It is easy to understand Churchill's annoyance. "Allied solidarity" was not repeated as a reason for asking the British troops to fight to the death. Henceforward the appeal would be to regimental tradition and the "eyes of the Empire". On the 24th, the War Office regarded the decision to cancel evacuation with dismay. They knew it would mean the loss of the only two trained regular battalions for Home Defence if the B.E.F. were lost.[7]

Was Calais a sop to the French? Was it decided to pacify them when Gort started to withdraw? There is no simple answer.

Throughout the 25th May, the British authorities, leaving Nicholson to "fight on", were feverishly debating how the B.E.F. could be disembarked. The plans made by Admiral Ramsay for the flow of personnel ships to Dunkirk involved the holding of a defensive perimeter to cover the evacuation. By the evening of the 25th, the time had come to put both these plans into action and the first troops were due to be taken off from Dunkirk on the evening of the 26th. It was only then realised that every hour that the Tenth Panzer Division could be kept from crossing the Aa Canal would count.

[7] Information from Lord Avon.

Though some in London seem to have wavered in their resolution to hold Calais and were sickened by the deliberate sacrifice, it was clear that the deed had to be done. At 9 p.m. Churchill, Eden and Ironside drafted the telegram which read:

"Every hour you continue to exist is of greatest help to B.E.F. Government has therefore decided you must continue to fight. Have greatest possible admiration for your splendid stand."

This makes it clear that in spite of previous telegrams the possibility of evacuation had been in mind to the last moment.

The destroyers which had stood off Calais all day within sight of the garrison were then withdrawn to Dover but there was still some confusion as to the true intention. Admiral Ramsay refused to give up hope of rescuing some of the men. On the night of the 25th a force of yachts, trawlers and drifters with some small craft was sent over in case there was a last-minute change of plan.[8]

The Germans too, were by their decisions on the 24th May to shape the story of Calais. As General Fagalde and the British Third Corps were hastily organising a defensive line on the Aa Canal, the German High Command dealt a fatal blow to Guderian's ambition. Although the First Panzer Division had secured four bridgeheads over the canal and an S.S. division,[9] placed under his command, was advancing on Watten, both were ordered to halt. At 11.42 a.m. when the attack on the "outer perimeter" of Calais had hardly begun, Guderian was astounded to receive the order:

"Dunkirk is to be left to the Luftwaffe. Should the capture of Calais prove difficult, this port too is to be left to the Luftwaffe."

This order had come from Hitler himself and it could not be questioned.

"We were utterly speechless," wrote Guderian, "but since we were not informed of the reasons for this order it was difficult to argue against it."[10]

He issued the order to the First Panzer Division:

[8] David Divine: *The Nine Days of Dunkirk.*

[9] The *Leibstandarte* of Adolf Hitler.

[10] Guderian: *Panzer Leader*, p. 117.

"Hold the line of the canal. Make use of the period of rest for general recuperation."

What had led Hitler to deprive Guderian and the other Panzer commanders of this glittering prize? Guderian has tried to shift responsibility on to Goering who persuaded Hitler to leave Dunkirk to the Luftwaffe. There are other explanations, each part of a complex chain of events.

Hitler saw von Rundstedt at Army Group "A" headquarters at Charlesville at 10.30 a.m. on the 24th. Von Rundstedt was cautious. He made much of the possibility that the B.E.F. would attempt to break through from the north and join up with the French Seventh Army south of the Somme. He told Hitler of von Kleist's "nervousness" about Arras and that fifty per cent of the tanks of the Panzer Group were out of action.[11] Von Runstedt and Hitler had both served in Flanders in the First World War and they remembered the "marshy" ground with its many ditches and canals which could impede the tanks. Guderian later declared this explanation to be a "poor one". Finally, von Rundstedt argued that the tanks should be preserved for the coming fight with the French forces south of the Somme and other parts of France. Hitler expressed agreement and the order to halt was sent out in his name. Goering had already boasted that the Luftwaffe "could finish the job single-handed". Fortunately for the B.E.F., bad weather and a superb performance by R.A.F. fighters and bombers stood in Goering's way. On the morning of the 3rd June, the last British troops were embarked from Dunkirk. Of the total of 337,000 men brought back to England, 110,000 were French. Sadly, a rearguard of 30,000 Frenchmen, who were holding up the Germans, had to be left behind.

It is in the context of what in fact happened that the true meaning of the defence of Calais must be judged. When Guderian turned north with the First and Second Panzer Divisions at 8 a.m. on the 22nd May, intent on capturing the Channel ports, the decision to land British tanks and infantry at Calais had been belatedly taken, but had not yet assumed a critical importance. It was not till later that, as Churchill put it: "The defence of Boulogne, but still more of Calais,

[11] The larger part were repaired in a few days.

to the latest hour, stood forth upon the confused scene. . . ."[12] Churchill wrote afterwards that he had in mind the barrier of the "Gravelines waterline" or the Aa Canal.

"This region," he wrote, "was lighted in my mind from the previous war when I had maintained the mobile Marine Brigade operating from Dunkirk against the flanks and rear of the German armies marching on Paris. I did not therefore have to learn about the inundation system between Calais and Dunkirk and the significance of the Gravelines waterline. The sluices had already been opened, and with every day the floods were spreading, thus giving southerly protection to our line of retreat."

The flooding would not, in the event, have stopped Guderian from reaching Dunkirk. When Hitler stopped the advance on the 24th, the First Panzer Division was already across the Aa Canal at Watten. What would have happened had Calais fallen earlier, which might easily have happened? What would have happened if Boulogne had not been defended?

Mr. David Divine comments:[13]

"There would have been instead of the somewhat attenuated First Panzer Division, three armoured divisions[14] on the canal line, flushed with victory. It seems inconceivable in the circumstances that Guderian would not have gone straight through to Dunkirk, his avowed objective."

Had this happened there would have been no need for Hitler's intervention which lost Guderian the historic chance of winning the Second World War almost in a morning. The decision to land troops at Calais was momentous since it led him to falter in his thrust for Dunkirk.

At noon on the 24th, Paul Reynaud the French Prime Minister telegraphed Churchill, urging that the B.E.F. should "join hands with the French forces which are marching from south to north in an attempt to debouch from the Somme and in particular from Amiens."

[12] Churchill: *The Second World War*, Vol. II, p. 70.

[13] *The Nine Days of Dunkirk*.

[14] i.e. The First, the Second, which attacked Boulogne, and the Tenth, which attacked Calais.

The telegram continued:

"It is urgent to supply Gort's Army, which is protected by Fagalde's two divisions at Dunkirk. It is very desirable that you send troops to the harbours as you did yesterday to Calais."

So the French motive in demanding the defence of Calais was to keep Gort supplied and fighting at their side. General Fagalde, a staunch friend of Britain, in ordering "no evacuation" was following Weygand in believing that Calais could still be used to supply the B.E.F. and the Northern French Armies. He was forty-eight hours too late. But not as late as Churchill, who, on the 27th May, telegraphed Gort:

"At this solemn moment I cannot help sending you my good wishes. No one can tell how it will go. . . . Very likely the enemy tanks attacking Calais are tired, and, anyhow, busy on Calais. A column directed upon Calais while it is still holding out might have a good chance. Perhaps they will be less formidable when attacked themselves."

When this telegram was sent Calais had been in German hands for over twelve hours.

CHAPTER TEN

The Honour of France

ON the 24th, Calais was crowded with demoralised Allied troops, many of them unarmed, who, until the fighting began, thronged the main streets. At the Gare des Fontinettes, the Q.V.R. discovered a large Belgian contingent sitting in railway carriages parked in a siding and destined for a training area at Boulogne. They refused to move and remained there until the Germans advanced along the railway line from Fréthun. Thousands of French soldiers hid in the cellars and air-raid shelters and were captured there. Yet there were the few who fought for the honour of France.

Early in the morning an artillery duel began between the Tenth Panzer Division's guns on the high ground at Coquelles and the coastal guns—or those which would fire inland—of Fort Lapin, the Bastion de l'Estran and Bastion 2. These batteries were enthusiastic and prodigal of ammunition. By 10 a.m. the Bastion de l'Estran had fired 683 rounds out of a stock of 895. A Rifle Brigade officer observed that the main idea of the French gunners "was to get rid of their ammunition as quickly as possible". There was too much truth in this remark for comfort. As the Germans encircled the town, it became increasingly difficult to bring the coastal guns to bear on enemy targets. Officers gave orders to spike the guns and evacuate the bastions and the naval crews were joined by French soldiers in a march along the beach to the harbour near Fort Risban where some were seen to be sitting on suitcases. The naval tugs came into the harbour during the afternoon and they began to embark.

The departure of the French gunners at the beginning of the battle was hardly in keeping with Weygand's orders "to fight like dogs". It caused consternation in the British ranks. The tugs had been ordered by the French Navy to take the men to Cherbourg. But de Lambertye the French naval commander at Fort Risban was determined to stay and fight.

When it was realised that the War Office were only evacuating "non-fighting" troops that morning, the French had been placated. Colonel Holland and Capitaine de Frégate Loïs Petit shook hands. It was now Nicholson's turn to wonder if the French would make a fight of it. He had spoken to the War Office at 11.30 a.m. on the 24th May, and still expected "final" evacuation on the evening of the following day. Calais would have to be held for at least twenty-four hours. It was still not nearly midnight that the order to fight for the sake of "Allied solidarity" was in his hands.

Carlos de Lambertye was a French naval officer of the old school who believed in duty and discipline. It was clear to him that if Fort Lapin and the other bastions on the seafront were simultaneously abandoned, the Germans could surround and capture the Citadel before the end of the day. He knew of General Fagalde's orders that there was to be no evacuation. He determined to ignore the naval tugs with their orders to go to Cherbourg and keep back as many French sailors and soldiers as possible to defend the bastions. Even though the guns were spiked there were still machine-guns and these fortifications, especially Bastion 11, presented formidable obstacles to the Germans.

Many of the men were already aboard the tugs at 3 p.m. Later in the afternoon, they were joined by gunners who had evacuated Bastion 2 and the Bastion de l'Estran on the east. In a fine display of leadership, de Lambertye addressed the men: "Many of my sailors have already been killed or wounded. I need men to defend the forts. Who will volunteer?"

The German battery at Coquelles and another south of Calais had been shelling the bastions with considerable accuracy and the re-occupation of them if only as infantry positions, would mean further casualties. Bastion 11, a key post in the defence of the Citadel was already occupied by Capitaine Bernard de Metz and fifty Moroccan troops who to their great credit—for most of them were killed in action—refused to follow the rest to the harbour. At the Citadel,

Commandant Le Tellier and the few French infantry with their two 75 mm guns stood firm.

At first, only one man stepped forward at de Lambertye's question —this was Capitaine Michel de la Blanchardière a staff officer of the 21st French Infantry Division. He was badly wounded in a last desperate defence of Bastion 11 with men of the 60th Rifles under Captain Everard Radcliffe. Other French soldiers and sailors who had not embarked, now followed de la Blanchardière's example and remained on shore. De Lambertye told them bluntly: "We must be ready, gentlemen, unless something quite unexpected happens, to fight to the death."

This was the second time on the 24th that men had been marched to the harbour and then told to return and fight. The first had been before the departure of the *City of Canterbury* and the *Kohistan* in the morning. Now it was the turn of these Frenchmen, known today as the "Volunteers of Calais" in recognition of their conscious sacrifice. Among them was a naval reservist André Berthe one of the few survivors of the defence of Bastion 11.[1] On the evening of the 24th, de la Blanchardière and about a hundred volunteers, mainly Bretons, marched away from the tugs which would have taken them to safety, and hoisted the French tricolour at Bastion 12. As they watched the tugs sail from the harbour they felt that, whatever might happen, they were staying to fight for the honour of their country.

When other officers of the 21st French Infantry Division had searched the dunes for volunteers, they were posted in the small wood west of Fort Risban. The total of French soldiers and sailors who remained in Calais to fight was about 800. The rest waited in cellars for the town to fall.

Although relations between the British and French improved during the 24th May as General Fagalde's orders became known in the town, Captain A. N. L. Munby of the Q.V.R. had been hampered by French fears that the British were abandoning Calais. When the Third Royal Tank Regiment withdrew from Coquelles into Calais on the previous evening after their heavy losses near Guines, they left the Boulogne road wide open to the enemy. Munby was ordered to

[1] See photograph with Lord Avon facing p. 96.

block it with three borrowed scout cars. It was a vulnerable position. The road was straight, the ground flat, without cover, and intersected by ditches. Munby had no entrenching tools and a tank attack from Boulogne would make his barricade of a lorry and some farm implements untenable. He was also having a terrible task with refugees. The Germans were reported to be only ten miles away and he had the painful impression that he was turning them back into the arms of the enemy.

On the same road were groups of motorised French infantry who went past "in pretty good order", after their defence of Desvres. In contrast were thousands of exhausted Belgians who had been on the march for days, unarmed, and chased from pillar to post.

Inside Fort Nieulay a mile ahead of Munby's road-block on the north side of the Boulogne road was a French captain named Herremann, a lieutenant, and about forty soldiers. There were also seven French marines armed with rifles, two heavy machine-guns and a 25mm anti-tank gun. It seemed to Munby that joining forces with this party made more sense than crouching behind a farm cart on a long, straight road. He went to Fort Nieulay and tried to persuade Herremann to let him in. After a telephone call to Commandant Le Tellier in Calais, he was allowed to enter the fort with his troops "on condition that they did not retire". This uncomplimentary condition was the result of French bitterness at the "premature" British withdrawal from Boulogne.

Munby returned with fifty-two men of the Q.V.R. and three of the 1st Searchlight Regiment. They had six Bren guns, revolvers, one anti-tank rifle and twenty-five rifles. With this armament, the Q.V.R. and the French held the fort under very heavy fire for most of the 24th May against attacks by tanks and infantry from Coquelles.

The Q.V.R. took up position in the north-west and north-east bastions of Fort Nieulay from which they had a clear view of the road to Coquelles which they covered with Brens and an anti-tank rifle. The ruinous condition of the old fort made it an uncomfortable place to fight in, especially as there were no sanitary arrangements. But the thick walls were thirty feet high and there were a number of tunnels. The defenders were far better protected than at the road-blocks. At the east end, a kitchen and officers' quarters had been built but there was no longer any water supply. The French party were holding the south-west bastion. Here they had two heavy machine-guns and forty soldiers with rifles. At the gateway, facing Coquelles, French marines manned an anti-tank gun.

The Q.V.R. spent an unpleasant night. They had no blankets and very little food. They were short of ammunition. At 3 a.m. on the 24th May, Munby was awakened by a commotion at the main gate. French sentries had opened fire on three men of the First Searchlight Battery who were seeking to enter. He persuaded the French to admit them and found them a place to sleep. They proved to be a corporal and two gunners who took part in the defence later that day.

Munby dozed for another half-hour and then ordered the Q.V.R.s to stand to on Vauban's battlements. As he stared into the darkness, three ominous Very lights went up to the south-west. The defenders waited for the Germans to open fire.

At 4.45 a.m. three carriers of the 60th under 2/Lieut. R. Scott went past the fort towards Coquelles and returned almost immediately. They brought back twenty soldiers of the First Searchlight Battery who had escaped when only a few hundred yards from the enemy. Scott and his carriers returned to Coquelles and this time ran into a German anti-tank gun on the edge of the village. One carrier only returned, driven by Rifleman Wilson with a badly shattered leg, and with the body of another man beside him. Scott's driver was killed and he himself had a bullet-hole in his helmet and a leg wound. An hour later, he reached Fort Nieulay with another rifleman. They had crawled along a ditch full of water for several hundred yards and escaped.

At dawn, a few shells landed around Fort Nieulay and German infantry started to emerge from a wood on the north side of Coquelles. To the Q.V.R. they appeared to be moving in the direction of the coast. They advanced over open ground and Munby was anxious to wait till they got within range. He gave orders to the Q.V.R. to keep quiet, and not open fire until the Germans were within four or five hundred yards of the fort. If his plan had succeeded, there is no doubt that the Germans would have suffered heavy casualties. But the French in the south-west corner, were volubly impatient. They opened fire at 1600 yards with their two machine-guns, revealing that the fort was occupied. The Germans went to ground and then retired to the wood.

German machine-guns soon fired on Fort Nieulay and it was subjected to mortar and artillery fire. The Q.V.R. began to suffer casualties and Munby sent his dispatch rider on a French motor-cycle into Calais with an urgent appeal for food, blankets and ammunition. Two hours later, during a lull in the bombardment, he was amazed to see an R.A.F. lorry approaching from the direction of Coquelles with the supplies for which he had asked. The lorry arrived as a result of a visit by Ellison-Macartney to Oyez Farm where Captain Bowring and "B" Company of the Q.V.R. were dug in astride the Sangatte road. He had ordered a truck with food, water and ammunition for the defenders to be sent along the Boulogne road to Fort Nieulay but it had been unable to get through. Ellison-Macartney therefore drove along the Sangatte road to Oyez Farm, and sent an R.A.F. lorry from there. The lorry drove south along a track from the coast and turned towards Fort Nieulay. It appeared to those in the fort to be driving out of Coquelles and it is surprising that the Germans did not shoot at it. After delivering the supplies, the lorry returned along the same route and was seen to come under fire. A further attempt to supply Munby was later made along the same route by the 60th. The leading carrier got quite close to the fort but there was no sign of any British troops and it was wrongly supposed that they had surrendered. In fact, the fort was held for another five hours.

An intense bombardment of Fort Nieulay began at 2 p.m. and the Boulogne and Sangatte roads were also shelled. At the north-west bastion of the fort, a sergeant was severely wounded by a piece of shrapnel in the right side of the chest and the French too began to suffer casualties. In the midst of the bombardment a German motorcyclist, who had presumably lost his way, appeared on the road from Coquelles. He was fired on and surrendered. Shortly afterwards a van driven by a French civilian appeared at the gate and reported to Munby that a badly wounded British soldier was lying beside the road 300 yards from Coquelles. Two riflemen went down the road and lifted the soldier into the van which escaped into Calais.

At 3.30 p.m. the artillery fire grew heavier and shells and mortar bombs landed inside the fort. In the north-east corner Munby and another officer were nearly killed by a shell which hit the bank a few feet above them. At the gate, the French anti-tank gun was destroyed and their heavy machine-guns received direct hits, killing and wounding several men. Even the massive cellars became unsafe and large cracks appeared in the ceilings. But the Q.V.R. fought on and in the north-west corner, Sergeant Osborne lay in a hollow of the mound calmly firing his Bren gun.

Half an hour later, the Germans, advancing under cover of a tremendous barrage, were within 100 yards of the fort. When it became clear that they were about to assault it, Munby thought the time had come to pay a visit to his French colleague. He found him seated at a table in a cellar where lighted candles flickered with each detonation above. Captain Herremann said that the fort was surrounded and that they must surrender. The white flag was run up and the Germans streamed through the gate, forcing the men to drop their rifles and Bren guns and march dejectedly along the road to Coquelles. As they looked back, the swastika was flying over Fort Nieulay at 4.30 p.m.

The defence of Fort Nieulay inflicted considerable loss on the Germans and blocked the main Boulogne road for several hours. But from early morning, the Germans were threatening the 60th on the western face of Calais. By-passing Fort Nieulay, German tanks and infantry moved across country. By afternoon their infantry occupied the Cimetière Nord opposite the Citadel and opened fire on the 60th across the Canal de la Rivière Neuve. Had this attack succeeded, the Citadel would have been in danger, but with the aid of reserves under Sergeant Dryborough Smith of "C" Company of the 60th, the Germans were enfiladed and forced to withdraw from the cemetery. Although the shell and mortar fire continued, pressure on "C" Company stopped. On the same day, Dryborough Smith drove away an abandoned ambulance under fire and rescued several badly wounded men. The company had fifty casualties during the afternoon.

In the centre, "B" Company of the 60th were fiercely attacked all day. At noon, German tanks appeared north of the Boulogne road. They moved toward the 60th positions but were engaged by three light tanks of the 3rd Royal Tank Regiment and made no progress. An hour later, German light tanks again attacked the 60th in the south-west. Two of them were set on fire with anti-tank rifles and destroyed. The Germans did not continue the attack.

These successes heartened the defenders but soon shells and mortar bombs fell more heavily around the Pont Jourdan railway bridge. Telephone wires, broken glass and paving stones littered the Boulevard Léon Gambetta. Two companies of German infantry on either side of the Boulogne road were seen preparing to attack but they were forced to scatter by accurate shell-fire from French "75"s. They re-formed and with ten tanks advanced along the Boulogne road. But "B" Company with one anti-tank gun of 229 Battery were able to hold them for the time being.

It was about 3 p.m. that I arrived in the Boulevard Léon Gambetta. When the *Kohistan* had vanished, Green Jacket officers asked for reinforcements from the crowd of soldiers and their officers sitting unhappily on the banks of the Bassin des Chasses de l'Est. It was now time to forget evacuation and show what "non-fighting" soldiers could do. Fifty volunteered to go with me to the west of the town. They formed up behind the Gare Maritime and marched along the dock road as far as the Hôtel de Ville. Once under the determined glance of the Green Jackets, not a man faltered. It would never have done to be seen to be afraid even though the shells were now coming in fast over the harbour.

In front of the Hôtel de Ville was Colonel Holland, looking weary, but intent on getting as many men to the support of the 60th as possible. There were threats of a German breakthrough in the south-west where Lord Cromwell's company were hard pressed.

From noon, Colonel Miller was receiving frequent reports that his line was in danger. The Germans made another determined attack in the afternoon near Bastion 9. But they met with tough resistance from the 60th, Q.V.R. and about eighty searchlight personnel so that they were forced to withdraw, although the attack was in battalion strength. Miller and his adjutant, Captain E. A. W. Williams, collected a cruiser tank and bringing up two reserve platoons plugged the holes in the line, but throughout the day there was desperate fighting in the south-west.

My orders were to reinforce "B" Company of the 60th in the centre. From the Hôtel de Ville, a staff officer led my party down the empty shopping streets of Calais—the Boulevard Jacquard. We hurried across the Place Albert Premier at the east end of the Boulevard Léon Gambetta. German tanks and machine-gunners on the Boulogne road were now firing up the whole length of the boulevard.

Breathless and weary in the hot weather, we followed the officer down a long, narrow, way. Reaching the corner of a side street I left the men in the shelter of a doorway and moved gingerly into the boulevard itself. A steady hail of tracer bullets and some tank shells came flying over the hump of the Pont Jourdan railway bridge. They bounced off the paving stones in all directions as I clung for life to the walls of houses on the south side of the boulevard and crept towards the bridge. This was my first experience of street fighting and I was acutely frightened. It was difficult to understand how others could remain so collected under fire. Throughout the battle, the noise was so great that if you were more than ten yards away it was impossible to understand what was said to you.

Fatigue, thirst and the need to do the right thing, made it difficult to think clearly as I reached the railway embankment. A figure, standing below me on the tracks beckoned to me to climb down. It was Major Poole, "B" Company Commander, with several First War decorations for gallantry. Poole was a reserve officer. He was wounded and taken prisoner in the second battle of Ypres in 1915 while serving with the Fourth Battalion 60th Rifles. In October 1916 he escaped from a German prison camp to neutral Holland. He was captured a second time when Calais fell and thus became a prisoner in two wars. He died in 1966.

"I am afraid they may break through," he said. I was very surprised at the anxiety in his voice. "Get your people in the houses on either side of the bridge and fire from the windows. You must fight like bloody hell."

CHAPTER ELEVEN

The Boulevard Léon Gambetta

AS the hail of fire beat down on the Pont Jourdan railway bridge, Brigadier Nicholson's headquarters were still at the Clinic in the Boulevard Léon Gambetta, only 600 yards east of the bridge. During the afternoon, he spoke to the War Office on the telephone. He said that it was impossible to hold the town for very long without reinforcements. He had no reserves to meet any penetration by the Germans. He emphasised the length of the perimeter he was trying to hold with only 3,000 men. But he had no wish to retire from it since "no suitable rear line" existed. In an earlier conversation at 11.30 a.m., he had pointed out that the "inner perimeter" of Calais-Nord, provided no means of observing the enemy at all. The successful defence of Calais-Nord, once the outer perimeter had been abandoned, depended on whether the three bridges over the canal which separated the northern from the southern part of the town could be destroyed.

As Nicholson knew, there was precious little hope that this would be done. On the evening of the 23rd, a naval vessel had berthed alongside the *Kohistan* at the Gare Maritime. Blue Jackets had unloaded some gelignite and anti-tank mines, had dumped them on the quay and sailed away. The Navy had also landed a demolition party who immediately pronounced that the primers which had been sent with the explosive were unsuitable. The shelling of the docks had not yet become serious but the presence on the quay of a ton and a half of gelignite was uncomfortable.

Major Allan, second-in-command of the Rifle Brigade, had fortunately persuaded this demolition party to remove the gelignite to the dunes until the correct primers were found. They never arrived. No bridges were blown by British troops except the small bridge at the Porte de Marck on the Dunkirk side, destroyed by 2/Lieut. T. Prittie at 7 p.m. on the 24th May with the aid of a French officer. It had been agreed with the French command that the blowing of the bridges over the canals, especially those leading to Calais-Nord, should be a French responsibility. But when a crisis arose next day, the French had neither the charges nor the expertise to do it.

Nicholson remained calm and clear-headed throughout these anxious hours. He knew the importance of holding the town as long as he could and yet he still had reason to think that his troops would be evacuated next day.[1] Troubled by the absence of any field artillery, except the two First World War "75"s at the Citadel and another on the St. Omer road, he pleaded for guns to be sent. The War Office at no time complied with his requests. But the Admiralty ordered destroyers to shell German targets with some effect.

Wessex, *Grafton*, *Greyhound*, *Vimiera*, the Polish destroyer *Burza* and the French destroyer *La Bourrasque* were in action off Calais during the 24th May. They were heavily attacked from the air. *Wessex* was sunk and *Burza* and *Vimiera* damaged. Both *Wolfhound* and *Verity* brought reserves of ammunition from Dover and *Verity* the only reinforcements, a party of Royal Marines under Captain Courtice. At 2 p.m. *Wolfhound* berthed on the west side of the harbour to seek information about future naval targets and remained till nightfall. The presence of these ships, on Admiral Ramsay's orders, did much to sustain morale, though they led many to believe in "final evacuation". They remained off Calais till early on the 26th, since Ramsay hoped to bring off the garrison as he had done at Boulogne.

The mistaken destruction of five cruiser tanks at the Gare Maritime did not prevent the Third Royal Tank Regiment from giving excellent service in the next stages of the battle. It is not clear why the orders to set them on fire were anticipated. The destruction was brought to an end by Colonel Keller as soon as the misunderstanding was realised and the incident does nothing to mar the performance of individual squadrons during the remainder of the 24th May.

After their heavy losses in the battle against the First Panzer

[1] At 2.10 p.m. the War Office said that "no further decision had yet been made".

Division near Guines on the previous day, the Battalion was badly handicapped in men and equipment. But they were active on patrol from an early hour. "A" Squadron fought a spirited engagement at the Porte de St. Omer. A troop of medium tanks under Sergeant Stuart knocked out two German tanks. During the day several other actions were fought but many tanks had track trouble. Several had to be left on the streets and the crews were unable to repair them owing to the increasing number of snipers who picked them off from roofs and windows.

At 3 p.m., Keller rallied his remaining tanks at the north-west corner of the Bassin des Chasses de l'Est to await further orders. At his H.Q. in the sand dunes, he received another fantastic message from the extraordinary General Brownrigg, now on a destroyer in mid-Channel. This was to "carry out his orders" and proceed to Boulogne. The hour was 4 p.m. and Boulogne was effectively in German hands. But the delusion that the tanks could break out of Calais and fight outside was not confined to Brownrigg. On 24th May, Churchill was writing to General Ismay[2]:

> I cannot understand the situation around Calais. The Germans are blocking all exits and our regiment of tanks is boxed up in the town because it cannot face the field guns planted on the outskirts. Yet I expect the forces achieving this are very modest. Why then are they not attacked? Why does not Lord Gort attack them from the rear at the same time that we make a sortie from Calais? Surely Gort can spare a brigade or two to clear his communications and to secure supplies vital to his army? Here is a general with nine divisions about to be starved out, and yet he cannot send a force to clear his communications. What else can be so important as this? Where could a reserve be better employed?
>
> This force blockading Calais should be attacked at once by Gort, by the Canadians from Dunkirk, and by a sortie of our boxed-up tanks. Apparently the Germans can go anywhere and do anything, and their tanks can act in twos and threes all over our rear and even when they are located they are not attacked.

[2] General Lord Ismay, War Cabinet Secretariat.

> Also our tanks recoil before their field guns but our field guns do not like to take on their tanks. If their motorised artillery, far from its base, can block us, why cannot we with the artillery of a great army block them? . . . The responsibility for cleansing the communications with Calais and keeping them open rests primarily with the B.E.F.

Later Churchill wrote:

"This did less than justice to our troops. But I print it as I wrote it at the time."[3]

In his impatience, Churchill had not realised the hopeless nature of the British tank position at Calais. The Third Royal Tank Regiment were not "boxed up" through any fault of their own. They had been landed far too late to prevent their encirclement by a Panzer division with three or four times as many tanks. Their strength had been weakened by the order to break out to St. Omer. This led to a useless engagement at Guines on the 23rd. Had this not happened, Nicholson, with the support of a complete tank battalion, might have delayed the Tenth Panzer Division for even longer than he did.

Nor was it in the least fair for Churchill to suggest that Keller's tanks would not attempt a sortie because they "recoiled" from the field guns planted on the outskirts. When it was known that the First Panzer Division had blocked the Marck Road with anti-tank guns during the night of the 23rd May, it was suicidal to attempt to break out with so weak a force.

The same point was to become a subject of controversy between Nicholson and other commanders next day. He ordered the Rifle Brigade and the tanks on the eastern side of Calais to try to break out to the south to relieve the pressure on the 60th. By that time such a plan was quite impracticable. It was better to use patrols of two or three tanks in support of the hard-pressed infantry, fighting in the streets.

Churchill's admonitions to Gort to attack the Tenth Panzer Division when the B.E.F. was separated from Calais by at least four Panzer divisions on the western bank of the Aa Canal, are evidence

[3] *The Second World War*, Vol. II, p. 12.

of the terrifying ignorance of those conducting this campaign from Whitehall.

Of all the commanders at Calais, Colonel Keller received the most baffling orders. His tanks were still the subject of the ridiculous instruction to "proceed to Boulogne". Since the evacuation of that place had already been decided by the War Office, it seems incredible that Brownrigg should still be sending Keller the same orders which he had given him at the Gare Maritime on the evening of the 22nd May.

During much of the 24th, General Brownrigg was actually in a destroyer within sight of Boulogne and Calais. In the evening, Keller went aboard the Royal Naval Yacht *Gulzar* moored in the harbour and used as a wireless station. He replied to Brownrigg that these orders were "impossible". As it grew dark, with two patrols missing, the tank crews crawled into shellholes near the Gare Maritime. The noise of bombs, artillery, automatic weapons and sniping had all made for intense weariness.

After Major Poole had given me his orders to fight like "bloody hell", I returned up the railway embankment. The situation in the Boulevard Léon Gambetta was becoming unpleasant, for the Germans had now switched their fire to the railway bridge itself. Bullets struck it, as I found my party of soldiers, with two sergeants, crouching behind an ivy-covered wall. They had only two Brens and some rifles.

I told the sergeants to enter a house and fire from a first-floor window on either side of the street. It was possible from these houses to see the German positions about half a mile away on the Route de Boulogne. One of the sergeants, followed by other gunners, got safely across the street.

A door opened and a macabre group of civilians appeared. They hurried over to me carrying the corpse of an old woman. It seemed a desperate risk to take. At a café at the end of the bridge the proprietor wore the Croix de Guerre and served cognac to all. He shouted encouragement through his broken front window: "N'ayez pas peur. On les aura!"

Two hundred yards east of the café, houses were burning near

Nicholson's brigade headquarters which, later that evening, were withdrawn to a cellar at the Gare Maritime. A few hours afterwards, he moved to the Citadel to form a joint headquarters with Commandant Le Tellier.

There was the crack of single rifle shots behind us, and a shout of: "Fifth column!"

Since the 23rd, snipers had been active in all parts of Calais, and they had been concealed in the town for some days. Since the effect of a fifth column is partly psychological, it is possible to exaggerate their numbers. But there were many in the old houses of Calais-Nord before the bridges over the canal were occupied on the evening of the 24th. Some were in German uniform, having entered the town in civilian clothes and hidden with Nazi sympathisers. Wounded German parachutists treated at the Hôpital Militaire had French addresses on them. Before he died in hospital at Winchester, Colonel Hoskyns wrote:

"They sprang up behind us in uniform with submachine-guns, grenades and ammunition."[4]

From upper floors or roofs they shot several officers and men in different parts of Calais. They spread false rumours, especially among the dockers who more than once stopped working during the 22nd and 23rd. Some wore Belgian and French uniform. Their operational headquarters were at Gravelines. Each year, veterans of the "German Fifth Column" hold a reunion and visit the graves of those who were caught and executed in different towns of Northern France.[5]

As others have experienced, the sound of a single rifle shot, close at hand, was far more frightening than the stream of heavy machine-gun bullets in the boulevard. The men kept under cover as I crouched in the doorway of the café.

From the house opposite there was the sound of breaking glass as the sergeant smashed a window. In a short time, the Searchlight party were firing towards Boulogne. Their agitation and inexperience—they had to lean out of the windows to fire—brought protests

[4] 11th June 1940.

[5] Guy Bataille to the author, 18th August 1971.

from the 60th on the far side of the railway bridge. I could hear hoarse shouts: "F—ing well look where you're shooting!" And so on. During a lull in the battle, I ran across the boulevard and stood at the corner of a side street by the bridge.

The position of "B" Company of the 60th, on the far side of the railway facing Boulogne, was now critical. Poole was afraid the Germans would break through his main road-block and on his company's left. At this point Lord Cromwell's company front was very extended. It now included Bastion 6 in the south-east as far as the road to St. Omer. From the first, there had been unavoidable gaps in his line. The number of new bridges and level crossings made the ramparts, where they still existed, very difficult to defend. On several occasions, the 60th were forced out of their positions and the gaps widened.

By 4 p.m. the position had been re-established for the moment. But Colonel Miller who now returned to the Boulevard Léon Gambetta, could see that it was impossible to hold the outer perimeter another day. He ordered his companies to hang on where they were until after dark and organised a line of posts across the centre of the town "to prevent any further penetration by the enemy from the south-west".[6]

These posts were made up of two platoons of the Rifle Brigade, parties withdrawn from other companies of the 60th, and some Searchlight troops. A cruiser tank was stationed at the east end of the Boulevard Léon Gambetta and road-blocks facing west were set up on side streets off the Boulevard Jacquard. A Searchlight detachment blocked the Avenue du Président Wilson opposite the main railway station.

Miller ordered his second-in-command, Major O. S. Owen, to hold the three bridges over the canal[7] and the quayside, from the Citadel to the Rifle Brigade boundary at the Pont Mollien over the Canal de Calais. They were blocked by all available vehicles and houses were occupied along the quayside. He moved his battalion headquarters to the back of a house on the waterfront. This line was

[6] Miller: Prisoner-of-War Diary.

[7] The Pont Freycinet, the Pont Georges Cinq and the Pont Faidherbe.

to be defended by the 60th with great determination for the next two days.

At the Pont Jourdan, about 4 p.m., a cruiser tank moved forward to the railway bridge and an officer peered out of the turret. He fired two or three rounds towards Boulogne and then withdrew. The Germans replied with great violence. Tank shells and machine-gun bullets came thick and fast for twenty minutes. Ricochets off the walls and flying glass made my situation in the Rue Edgar Quinet, a side street next to the bridge, rather exposed. The Rue Edgar Quinet was, in normal times, a quiet street with red-brick houses and a girls' school on the west side. It was now without a sign of life, save for a young girl's white face at a cellar grating. The wall which sheltered me had ragged gaps where mortar bombs had flung bricks into the street. I began to look for a safer position.

The enemy seemed dreadfully close though I could see nothing but clouds of dust and smoke. I was conscious that, standing where I was, I could be of little use except to encourage the Searchlight men as they fired bravely, but inexpertly, towards Boulogne. I was concerned for the safety of the 60th on the far side of the bridge as much as for the Germans. A Bren gun in a window, lace curtains flying, fired fitfully then jammed.

As the afternoon wore on, I began to feel my lack of training for battle. The sun shone and the heat from burning buildings led to an intolerable thirst. If only I could get back to the café. I waited for the firing to lift and was about to cross, when I felt a sharp, bruising pain in my left side. I collapsed to the pavement, my rifle clattering. There came a shout of concern from the lace curtains: "Are you all right, sir?"

I did not reply. I was trying to imagine what had happened. Was it a sniper or a machine-gun bullet? Then I realised I could still walk. Doubled up, I hurried painfully across to the café and into the safety of a side street. My immediate fear was that the Germans would break through in the next few minutes, that I should be left behind and captured. It was a fear shared by all. We had a confused but horrific picture of what awaited us if we were taken prisoner by the Nazis. Death in action was something everyone faced, but stories of the ill-treatment of prisoners, of concentration camps, made capture seem the worst of all.

While the café proprietor with the Croix de Guerre brought a large helping of cognac, a medical orderly opened my battledress blouse. He was pale, very cheerful and he squinted. From far away, I heard him say: "You're a lucky one, sir. 'Arf an inch from the 'eart!"

When I came to, I was lying on the pavement, still afraid of being taken prisoner. I urged the medical orderly to get me out of the line but he was inclined to talk professionally about the condition of the wound. He was certain I had been shot through the lung. I swore at him and ordered him to help me into the next street. A Frenchman joined us, young and talkative, and slowly they walked me away.

There was no sign of any regimental aid post. The nearest hospital was a mile away at the north end of the Boulevard Jacquard. The Hôpital Militaire was even more distant in Calais-Nord. A scout car of the 60th came towards us in the command of a young officer who was to become famous in the history of the regiment. This was Michael Sinclair of "A" Company, shot dead in 1944 while trying to escape from Colditz prison camp. He was about to move to the support of Lord Cromwell, where he held on to a very exposed position until dusk.

That evening, Sinclair did much to prevent the Germans from breaking through on the south-west. His success was also due to Sergeant Bennett who led a section of carriers. Bennett went in front of the ramparts and brought in a wounded man, the Germans firing on him at close range. He was himself wounded the same evening. When I think of these fine men, I am able to measure how small was my own contribution to the defence of Calais.

Sinclair, though busy with his battle plans, smilingly drew my attention to a van flying the Red Cross. This was an improvised ambulance smelling strongly of stale vegetables. I was bundled into it and driven at a high speed as far as the centre bridge over the canal—the Pont Georges Cinq—already manned by a mixed group of soldiers, who looked on me with astonishment as I lay on the floor of the van.

I was suffering more from anger than pain. No one seemed to know the way to the 60th regimental aid post. The French driver wanted to go to the Hôpital St. Pierre in the opposite direction, others loudly suggested the Hôpital Militaire in the Rue Leveux not far from the Citadel. My chief interest was in evacuation by sea to England.

The van was driven, bounding along the narrow streets to the Hôpital Militaire, a former convent of the Minimes, in the Rue Leveux. Outside, stood Lieut. A. F. Stallard, medical officer of the 60th, who examined me and diagnosed a "penetrating flank wound" requiring operation. I was determined not to be captured but Stallard observed sympathetically that everyone ran that risk. I was in no condition to be taken down to the docks. I was carried, protesting, into the dark interior of the hospital where grinning French surgeons in white caps, and smoking Gauloise cigarettes, awaited me.

Stallard had established his regimental aid post in cellars not far from the Rue Leveux so that he could transfer the more serious cases to the Hôpital Militaire. Most wounds were from bullets, but some were lacerated by shell or mortar splinters. In his cellar, Stallard worked with devotion, his equipment consisting only of the standard surgical and medical haversacks, and a large bottle of morphine solution which he felt was the most important item of all. The huge pall of black smoke which lay over Calais-Nord from burning oil tanks hid the daylight, as he stitched and dressed the wounds by the light of candles and torches.

CHAPTER TWELVE

Withdrawal to Calais-Nord

ON the 24th May, Brigadier Nicholson's plans for withdrawal to the inner perimeter of Calais-Nord chiefly concerned the 60th, the Q.V.R. and the Searchlights, who had borne the brunt of German attacks during the day. The Rifle Brigade in the east had not yet seen much action and Nicholson hoped to keep at least two of their companies in reserve to cover evacuation from the Gare Maritime. Except for those who took part in the abortive attempt to convoy the rations to Dunkirk during the night, most of them spent the hours of darkness in trenches in the sand dunes.

Colonel Hoskyns had his first headquarters at the Bastion de l'Estran. Next day shellfire forced him to move, first to Bastion 1 and then to the Cellulose Factory off the Quai de la Loire. Both the Rifle Brigade and Q.V.R. had their regimental aid post in the tunnel under Bastion 1 (see photograph facing page 128). This tunnel was to play a part in the fierce battle to hold the harbour area in the next forty-eight hours.

The wounded were treated here by Captain Cameron, medical officer of the Rifle Brigade, and Lieutenant Gartside of the Q.V.R. The casemates off the tunnel were small, dark, and filthy. Soon they were full of wounded, many in a dying condition. A dispatch rider, Rifleman "Cherry" Orchard, collapsed from his motor-cycle. Blast from a shell had taken the flesh from his forearm, leaving the bones bare. Cameron decided to amputate with a knife. There was no way of cutting through the bone, until Sergeant G. L. Baulch (to whom I am indebted for this account) remembered seeing a rusty hacksaw in the tunnel. It was found, sterilised in a bowl of water and Cameron completed the amputation.

During the morning of the 24th, Hoskyns allotted new positions to his companies. They were ordered to hold an enormous front. "I" Company (Major Peter Brush) were from the Pont Mollien, a bridge overlooked by the clock tower of the Hôtel de Ville. Their line extended southwards along the Canal de Calais to its junction with the Canal de Marck. From this point they had to hold 1,000 yards of the latter canal as far as the Porte de Marck. Rifle Brigade positions are shown in detail on the map on page 132.

From the Porte de Marck to Bastion 2 was held by "A" Company (Major John Taylor). This company looked out over the moat from the outer ramparts which were well-preserved. The defensive position here was stronger then in the south and south-west of Calais. The criss-cross ditches lay in low ground confining armoured vehicles to the Dunkirk and Gravelines roads. But on the west and south-west the town was overlooked by the hills at Coquelles and Guines, and was an easy target for General Schaal's artillery. "A" Company were commanded during most of the battle by their second-in-command Capt. Peter Peel and like the others, had a uncomfortably long front to control. "C" Company (Major Knollys) was dug in during the morning on the northern and eastern shores of the Bassin des Chasses. "B" Company (Major Hamilton-Russell) were at the Cellulose Factory where they remained for most of the fighting. The Headquarter Company (Major Coghill) was dug in at the Bastion de l'Estran and never left it until the battle was over.

As the pressure on the 60th grew during the afternoon, more and more platoons of the Rifle Brigade were taken away to the west to plug holes in the line. On the Rifle Brigade front, the Germans contented themselves with unpleasantly accurate artillery fire and did not attack in strength. The emergencies in the 60th sector especially after 4 p.m. led to Knollys' and Hamilton-Russell's companies, who sent in their reserves, becoming split up.

When evening came all companies were still holding their very long fronts. As it turned out, the position of Major Brush's company along the line of the two canals was the most exposed. As the 60th and Q.V.R. withdrew at nightfall to an inner line, the Germans moved up next morning to occupy the whole of Calais-St. Pierre. Brush was therefore in a kind of salient at the Pont Mollien. He was to come under very heavy fire here at dawn.

Despite the loss of much of their transport and equipment on the *City of Canterbury*, the Rifle Brigade remained calm. The 24th May was spent "in manoeuvre" against the 69th German Rifle Regiment which was now replacing units of the First Panzer Division on the Dunkirk side. Some witnesses describe a "holiday spirit". Riflemen shot at the Germans as if it was "glorified rabbit shooting" in which they were engaged. Dispatch riders tested whether streets were under fire by riding up and down and reporting them safe "provided you went fast enough". Many of the men kept these youthful high spirits until, surrounded and outnumbered, they were forced to surrender. But the older men were more serious. They realised what was to come.

Major Allan wrote:

"The 24th had been a day of great tension. Not a great deal of fighting had been done by the Rifle Brigade nor were many casualties incurred, but the noise of bombs, artillery, automatic weapons and sniping: the fantastic stories put about by enemy agents: the abandoning by the French of the forts and above all the fact that no commander ever had a moment to look around him and think and plan for more than the immediate future, all tended to intense fatigue."

By 6 p.m. Brigadier Nicholson had completed his plans for a withdrawal of the 60th and Q.V.R. to the inner perimeter. Ellison-Macartney received orders to bring the Q.V.R. back to the embankment south of the Bassin des Chasses. His orders were not clear. They did not state when the withdrawal was to begin or what the role of the Q.V.R. would be.

Eventually Austin-Brown's "C" Company withdrew through the Rifle Brigade from their advanced positions on the Dunkirk and Gravelines roads. They had not been in contact with the enemy during the day, and the front had been quiet.

"D" Company (Jessop) retired, after a day of severe bombardment of the southern ramparts, northwards to the line of the Boulevard de l'Egalité. Despite mortar bombs and shells, they had stoutly held their posts. With them came 100 Searchlight personnel under Major

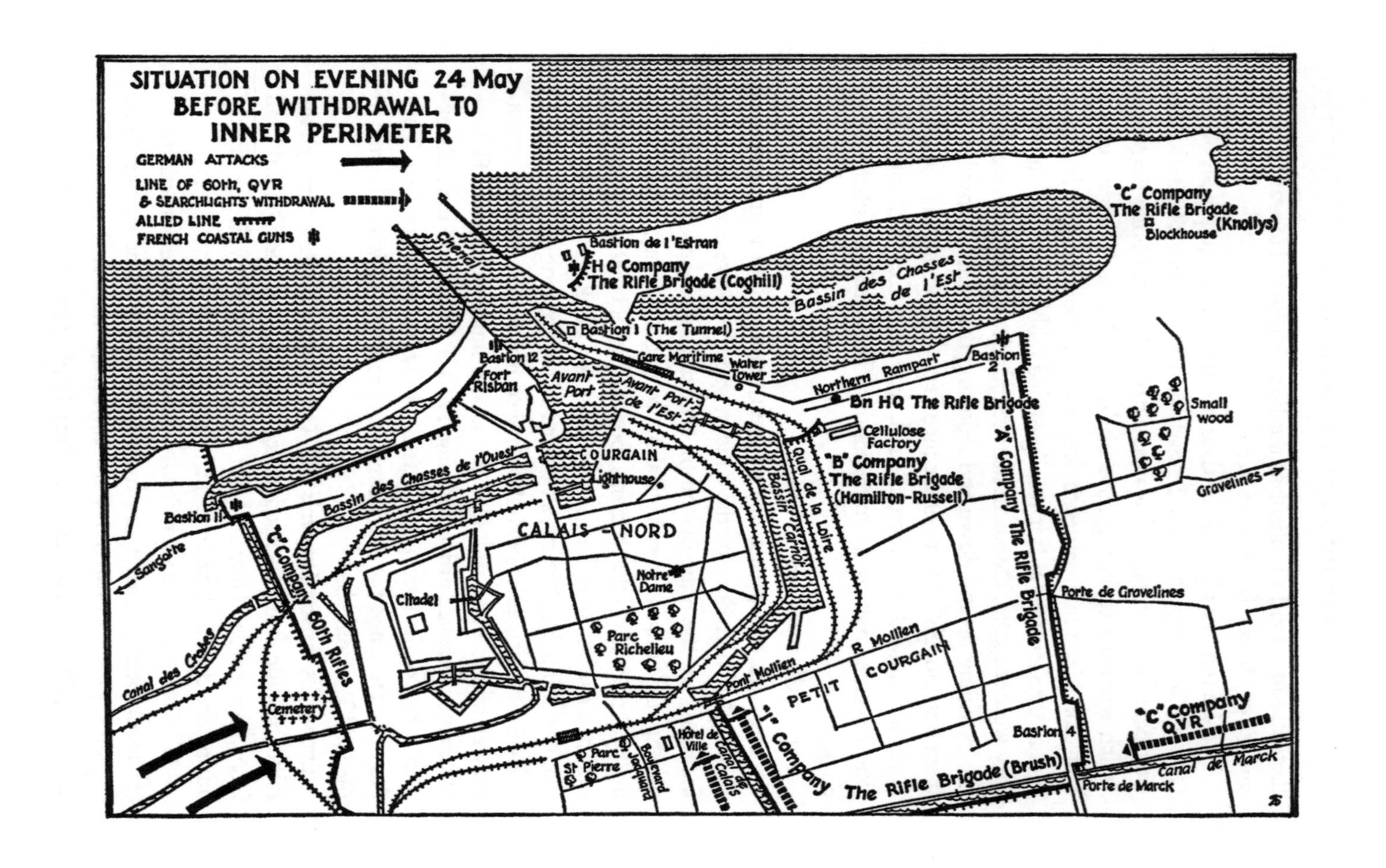
SITUATION ON EVENING 24 May
BEFORE WITHDRAWAL TO
INNER PERIMETER
GERMAN ATTACKS
LINE OF 60th, QVR
& SEARCHLIGHTS' WITHDRAWAL
ALLIED LINE
FRENCH COASTAL GUNS
"C" Company
The Rifle Brigade
Blockhouse (Knollys)
Bastion de l'Estran
H Q Company
The Rifle Brigade (Coghill)
Bassin des Chasses de l'Est
Chenal
Bastion 1 (The Tunnel)
Bastion 12
Fort Risban
Avant Port
Gare Maritime
Water Tower
Avant Port de l'Est
Northern Rampart
Bastion 2
Bn HQ The Rifle Brigade
Cellulose Factory
Small wood
"B" Company
The Rifle Brigade
(Hamilton-Russell)
"A" Company The Rifle Brigade
Gravelines
COURGAIN
Lighthouse
Quai de la Loire
Bassin Carnot
Bassin des Chasses de l'Ouest
Bastion 11
"C" Company 60th Rifles
Sangatte
CALAIS - NORD
Notre Dame
Citadel
Parc Richelieu
Porte de Gravelines
R Mollien
PETIT COURGAIN
Pont Mollien
Canal des Crabes
Cemetery
Parc St Pierre
Boulevard Jacquard
Hôtel de Ville
Canal de Calais
"I" Company
The Rifle Brigade (Brush)
Bastion 4
"C" Company QVR
Canal de Marck
Porte de Marck

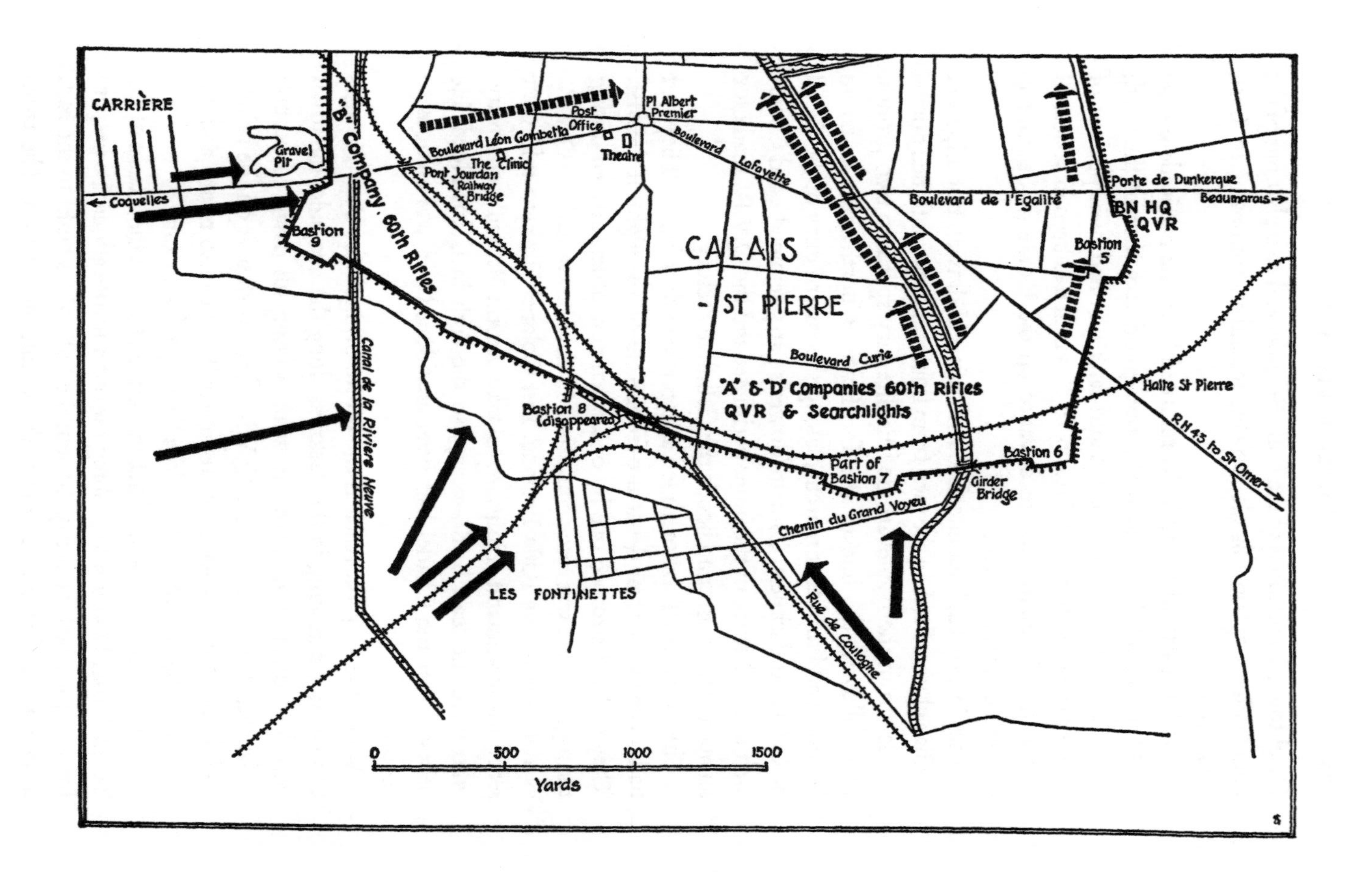
CARRIÈRE
Gravel Pit
← Coquelles
Bastion 9
"B" Company. 60th Rifles
Canal de la Riviere Neuve
Boulevard Léon Gambetta
Post Office
The Clinic
Pont Jourdan Railway Bridge
Theatre
Pl Albert Premier
Boulevard Lafayette
CALAIS
- ST PIERRE
Boulevard Curie
"A" & "D" Companies 60th Rifles
QVR & Searchlights
Bastion 8 (disappeared)
Part of Bastion 7
Bastion 6
Girder Bridge
Chemin du Grand Voyeu
Rue de Coulogne
LES FONTINETTES
Boulevard de l'Egalité
Porte de Dunkerque
Beaumarais →
BN HQ QVR
Bastion 5
Halte St Pierre
RH 43 to St Omer →
0
500
1000
1500
Yards

Deighton, two platoons of the Rifle Brigade, and two platoons of the 60th under Captain Claude Bower, second-in-command to Lord Cromwell.

Another party of the Q.V.R. returned from the barricade on the St. Omer Road. With them was one gun detachment of the 229th Anti-Tank Battery. The second anti-tank gun had been put out of action earlier in the day. A French "75" which had been in action all day as the Germans tried to advance up the Route de St. Omer, covered their retirement.

The Germans did not interfere with this withdrawal. But snipers in civilian clothes fired on the men from houses as they continued northwards. From the Boulevard de l'Egalité they split into two groups. One followed the line of the fortifications northwards as far as Bastion 2 and the other marched along the eastern quay of the Canal de Calais. At darkness, Captain Bower's party rejoined Lord Cromwell in the defence of the inner perimeter and the Q.V.R. made for an open piece of ground beside the Cellulose Factory.

The exhausted Territorials fell asleep where they halted. They had had no rest since their departure from Kent on the night of the 21st. They had to be roused one by one when new orders arrived during the night. There was some confusion. Nicholson wanted the Q.V.R. as a reserve to the Rifle Brigade. But Colonel Hoskyns told their second-in-command Timpson to take Austin-Brown's company, who were the least battle-weary, to the 60th in Calais-Nord. He believed that the Citadel had been abandoned and was anxious to reoccupy it.

When the Q.V.R. reached the centre bridge—the Pont Georges Cinq—after marching in the darkness along the quayside, the town was dead quiet. The Germans were waiting till dawn to occupy Calais-St. Pierre. Luckily the Q.V.R. met a 60th post on the bridge and found that they were not required. They had to return and did not reach the area of the Cellulose Factory till 2.30 a.m.

On the 24th May, General Schaal decided to limit the attacks of the Tenth Panzer Division to probing the outer fortifications. To prepare for a major attack next day, he sent the bulk of his tanks to the east, leaving the infantry to continue the assault on the 25th. The tanks moved through Guines as far as the Dunkirk road and joined up with the First Panzer Division, now halted in front of Gravelines. Schaal's object was to block any attempt by British troops to escape on this side of Calais especially along the beach. He also announced that more of Guderian's corps artillery would be in support of the division and that there would be divebombing attacks on the 25th.

Schaal was quite confident that he would capture Calais in a few hours. But instead of moving into the town as the 60th and Q.V.R. withdrew at nightfall, he waited until after breakfast on the 25th. By that time, Nicholson had fortified the bridges leading to Calais-Nord.

When Schaal had taken Fort Nieulay in the late afternoon he moved tanks up to Sangatte, forcing "B" Company of the Q.V.R. out of Oyez Farm. Second-lieutenant Dizer narrowly escaped after trying to destroy the submarine cable at Sangette with hand grenades. They withdrew along the road to Calais but were bombed by mistake by three Bristol Blenheims of the R.A.F. as they turned for home after attacking German guns at Coquelles. Two riflemen were wounded.

The Q.V.R. had a long and anxious march and it was not till 10 p.m. that they reached the 60th trenches. They now came under the orders of "C" Company of the 60th and helped to hold the line which included the vital Bastion 11, until they were told to withdraw more than thirty-six hours later. They were joined in their retirement from Oyez Farm by gunners of the 6th Heavy A.A. Battery who put their two remaining 3.7-inch guns out of action after hitting several German tanks.

By 8 p.m. German infantry were only 200 yards from the forward posts of the 60th at the Pont Jourdan railway bridge. "B" Company of the 60th (Poole) had now been in action since dawn. Anti-tank rifle ammunition was exhausted and German tanks were working up through the houses in the south-west. As his Bren gun ammunition ran low, Poole was relieved to see the Germans withdraw some distance from his improvised redoubt to the left of the Boulogne road. Half an hour later, on Miller's orders, he began to move back to the inner perimeter overlooking the canal.

During the night the defence of the three bridges over the canal which barred the way to Calais-Nord was organised. Lord Cromwell's company took charge of the right and centre bridges. The first, the Pont Freycinet, with its lock, looked the same as it does today (see photograph facing page 144). The Pont Georges Cinq in the centre has been reconstructed.

When Cromwell was joined by Captain Bower, he brought with him the only anti-tank gun left to the Battalion. The remaining three attached to the 60th had already been destroyed. These two-pounders had little effect on heavy and medium German tanks but they were better than nothing.

At dusk, Major O. S. Owen, the second-in-command of the 60th was seen walking along the canal front pointing out positions to be occupied in houses along the Quai de la Tamise and the Pont Faidherbe or "left-hand bridge". This is little changed today. Houses behind the canal line were fortified with "B" Company under Poole in reserve between the Rue des Marèchaux and the canal. The three bridges were blocked with abandoned vehicles, barricades were constructed across the streets leading off the canal, and houses commanding the bridges were made into firing positions. Miller wrote of the houses along the waterfront:

"The chief difficulty was that most of them could only be entered from the front in full view of the enemy. Work was at once begun on breaking into them from the back and through the side walls for communication. Adequate tools, however, were lacking and though he work went on for twenty-four to thirty-six hours, it was never completed. At the same time all windows in the battalion area were smashed to avoid danger from glass."

The task of occupying these houses at night-time was difficult, for the riflemen had to smash many large plate-glass windows and break open locked doors. They had to remove French civilians and uniformed soldiers from houses in the front line. Within the battalion area, that is to say, between the Citadel and the Pont Faidherbe, ground floors and cellars were crowded with people. Miller, estimated that there were "well over a thousand French and Belgian troops mostly disarmed".

Throughout the 60th defence of Calais-Nord they were fired on by snipers in plain clothes who shot several officers and men. One with a tommy-gun was on the roof of Notre Dame. But the hard-pressed 60th had neither time nor men to hunt them down. The night hours were spent in issuing food and ammunition. Few were able to sleep but they were ready. They knew that what followed on the 25th May would be the decisive battle for Calais.

Despite the telegram ordering him to stay and fight for "Allied solidarity", Nicholson was optimistic. Those who saw him early on the 25th at the Gare Maritime, found him delighted at the news that the British 48th Division was on its way to relieve him. He told everyone that a brigade of this division was "now arriving".

No more preposterously misleading information could have been sent to Nicholson and his hard-pressed troops. The statement in the telegram signed by a junior officer at the War Office at 11.23 p.m. that a "Brigade Group started marching to your assistance this morning" was an outrageous inexactitude. It was one of the unforgivable mistakes in this melancholy story of military hesitation and bad staff work.

The 48th Division was pinned down by several Panzer divisions on the other side of the Aa Canal when this message was sent. Nor was it tactful to tell the commander of a beleaguered force that he was to hold to the death a town "of no importance to the B.E.F."

After midnight a destroyer came into the harbour with Vice-Admiral Sir James Somerville. He landed at the Gare Maritime and visited Nicholson in the cellar. During their conversation Nicholson insisted that he could hold out if only he had artillery. Without it, he could not be sure how long the defence would last. When Somerville was back in Dover he reported on this talk.

"Nicholson is tired but in no way windy. His two chief anxieties are mortar ammunition and the need for artillery."

Somerville then spoke to the War Office on the telephone. The record of this conversation shows the position before the main German bombardment began at dawn.

1. Garrison 3,000 British, 800 French.

2. Tanks 3 remain only but considerable loss inflicted on the enemy.
3. No immediate thought of evacuation.
4. Troops hold line through outskirts of the town.
5. Harbour is under direct fire from battery 5.9″s which makes entry awkward for ships but not impossible.
6. Most urgent need is 2″ and 3″ mortar ammunition (Q (M) 3 is moving in this matter).[1]
7. Artillery also badly needed. Suggest 3.7 Hows. (S.D. is moving in this matter).[2]
8. Our casualties not serious. Destroyer has brought some off.
9. Bombing not severe perhaps owing to smoke from burning oil tanks obscuring view of town.
10. M.O. 4 hold a marked chart shown posn. held by troops.[3]

Admiral Somerville also mentioned the No. 9 W/T set which gave Nicholson communication with Dover, but he had no code. He suggested that Admiral Ramsay should send one by trawler during the day. A trawler with the code did reach Calais and fought its way out of the harbour during the afternoon.

Somerville also saw Eden at his room at the War Office that evening. He described his visit to Calais and said that "if any of the garrison were to be withdrawn we should have to act that evening".[4]

The anonymous staff officers who were "moving" in the matter of mortar ammunition and artillery did not move in the direction of Calais. Neither mortar ammunition nor artillery was sent. Perhaps they could not be spared. Perhaps it was impossible to get a ship into the harbour and unload it. At any rate it was not tried. In his talk with Somerville, Nicholson had "felt confident that given more guns, which were urgently needed, he could hold on for a time". There were now only two light anti-aircraft guns left on the docks.

For the moment, Nicholson could feel that the withdrawal from the outer perimeter had been accomplished remarkably well. A few

[1,2,3] War Office additional notes.

[4] *The Eden Memoirs. The Reckoning*, p. 109.

of the 60th were missing in the streets of Calais-St. Pierre but most of that battalion had taken up their new positions.

Even after the "Allied solidarity" telegram, Nicholson still felt that an evacuation would probably be attempted. The 60th and the Rifle Brigade would hold the inner ring of fortifications to cover the evacuation of the Q.V.R. to the Gare Maritime. The regular battalions would then retire in stages to the quay. A strong feeling prevailed in Calais that as many as possible would be taken off on the night of the 25th. It was a wishful thought. But who with his back to the sea and a Panzer division on three sides, in sight of the cliffs of Dover, would not think of evacuation?

For many of the garrison the constant noise and heat and the need to hold vital positions, at whatever cost, became the first consideration. By the morning of the 25th, lack of sleep had dulled their senses to everything except fighting the Germans. As the struggle raged at the canal front and in the harbour, the men led by their officers became more aggressive and daring. They thought only of killing Germans and by the end of the battle took suicidal risks in the hand-to-hand fighting. Their tenacity and boldness was to stagger General Schaal and the staff of the Tenth Panzer Division. On the 25th May, despite the aid of artillery and dive-bombers, the Germans were decisively repulsed and deprived of a quick result.

On this day, Nicholson twice refused demands to surrender. He was confident that his own brigade and their anti-aircraft supporters would fight whether or not evacuation took place at a later stage. He travelled long distances encouraging the men in the front line. But even he did not yet know what was at stake. No one had explained to him that every hour of delay would help the B.E.F. The lukewarm sentiments about "Allied solidarity", which enraged Churchill, remained his orders at dawn on the 25th.

Nicholson feared that, among the thousands of leaderless soldiers hiding in the cellars and infiltrated by the fifth column, someone might show a white flag with disastrous consequences. He had noticed that German artillery and the Luftwaffe were concentrating on the Citadel, still defended by Commandant Le Tellier, with his infantry and a party of Marines. But it was an enormous place to hold.

At any moment some disaffected person might emerge from its vaults and offer to surrender. He had moved his headquarters to the Gare Maritime on the evening of the 24th in anticipation of withdrawal by sea. He now changed his mind. At 6 a.m. he moved with his staff to the Citadel. He remained there at the north-west bastion with Colonel Holland and Commandant Le Tellier till the Germans forced the south gate on the afternoon of the 26th and took him prisoner.

This decision may seem surprising since it meant that he was further away from the centre of the battle. But Nicholson had good reasons. During the siege of 1558, once the Citadel had fallen, the attackers were able to fight their way into Calais-Nord. The battle of 1940 was different in the complete encirclement of Calais by the Tenth Panzer Division, but the capture of the Citadel would have its psychological impact on both sides.

General Schaal fully realised this. He gave orders to his heavy batteries to concentrate their fire on the Citadel and the docks—the two places of most importance to him. He was not expecting an evacuation by the British but a landing of fresh troops from England and this was the principal anxiety of his corps commander Guderian.[5]

Nicholson believed that his presence at the Citadel with the two most senior British and French officers in Calais, would stiffen the resistance. He therefore endured the most appalling bombardment which shook the old battlements of Richelieu and Vauban for hours on end. He was in constant danger of capture with only "C" Company of the 60th between him and the forward units of the 86th German Rifle regiment who were not yet across the Canal de la Rivière Neuve.

During the night, the Germans got ready their weapons and transport for a full-scale attack and shortly before dawn, as the British stood to, Guderian sent the order to the Tenth Panzer Division:

"Calais will be taken."

[5] Tenth Panzer Division: War Diary.

PART III

THE 25th AND 26th OF MAY

Principal events covered by Part III

25th May 1940	8 a.m.	The swastika flies from the Hôtel de Ville
	11 a.m.	André Gershell, mayor of Calais, is sent by the Germans to Nicholson
	2 p.m.	Eden tells Nicholson that "the eyes of the Empire are on the defence of Calais"
	3 p.m.	Lieutenant Hoffmann sent to demand Nicholson's surrender
	3.30 p.m.	Colonel Hoskyns commanding the Rifle Brigade is mortally wounded
	6.30 p.m.	German artillery bombardment resumed
	9 p.m.	Churchill, Eden and Ironside decide that Nicholson must continue to fight
	9.45 p.m.	Tenth Panzer Division break off the attack
26th May	9.30 a.m.	Stuka bombardment of Calais-Nord
	10.50 a.m.	Germans crossing bridges into Calais-Nord
	11.30 a.m.	Withdrawal of the 60th to centre of Calais-Nord
	1.56 p.m.	Last message to Dover from the Rifle Brigade
	4 p.m.	Fall of the Citadel
	10.30 p.m.	The first troops disembark at Dover from Dunkirk
4th June		Dunkirk evacuation of 330,000 men completed
5th June		Churchill's speech in the House of Commons: "We shall never surrender".

CHAPTER THIRTEEN

The Answer is No

AS I dozed in my ward at the Hôpital Militaire, I could hear distant rifle shots, but the shelling had stopped. Beside me, a young Hurricane pilot with a terrible wound from an aircraft shell was dying. He could still speak and begged me to keep talking to him. As it grew light, his body shuddered and his mouth fell open. With a little French medical orderly, I folded his arms. The orderly saluted and, for a few minutes, the ward was very quiet.

The first shells burst around the Citadel and broke the windows of the Hôpital Militaire. My bed was covered in splintered glass. At dawn, Major Trotter who had been wounded in the throat, got up, dressed and went back to the command of "A" company of the 60th. A French nursing sister opened the door and looked at his empty bed. "Tant mieux," she said tartly and shut the door.

An hour later, a shell landed among the mulberry trees in the hospital garden. Another exploded in the Rue Leveux outside. Splinters struck the walls of the former convent of the Minimes and, in a few minutes, I was taken with the other wounded to the cellar, where I spent the next twenty-four hours.

As the sun rose on the canal front, Calais-St. Pierre was quiet, but the shells were landing at the Citadel, at Fort Risban, and on the docks. Major Owen crossed the Pont Freycinet in a car and drove down the Boulevard Léon Gambetta. With some surprise, he reported to Colonel Miller that he had not been fired on and had seen no Germans. Major Brush of the Rifle Brigade did the same at 5.30 a.m.

Both regiments now sent patrols into Calais-St. Pierre. With two junior officers and a number of riflemen, Brush went down the western bank of the Canal de Calais for a distance of half a mile. He returned up the eastern quay bringing a wounded rifleman who had been lying all night in a garden. He crossed the canal at the Pont Mollien again at 7 a.m. but, this time, there were armed German motor-cyclists in the Boulevard Léon Gambetta. Near the Hôtel de Ville he could see German officers lining up civilians for interrogation. When they were within 150 yards, his patrol opened fire and scattered them. He returned to his headquarters near the Pont Mollien to find that his company was under fire from snipers across the Canal de Calais. At 8 a.m. a bullet struck him in the throat. He refused to go to the regimental aid post until he received a direct order from Colonel Hoskyns.

At dawn, three scout sections of the 60th in Bren carriers were sent over the bridges into Calais-St. Pierre. If no Germans were met, it was Miller's intention to follow them up and hold delaying positions. But the leading section under Michael Sinclair was fired on by an anti-tank gun not far from the Hôtel de Ville. His carrier was knocked out though he and his crew escaped on foot.

Rifle and machine-gun fire from houses off the Boulevard Jacquard showed that the Germans had now moved in and, at 8 a.m., they hoisted the swastika on the clock tower of the Hôtel de Ville, to groans and jeers from the riflemen.

Brigadier Nicholson ordered the 60th to reoccupy the main post office through which telephone communications with London had been kept going till the previous evening. This was at the east end of the Boulevard Léon Gambetta, next to the theatre, which was to become the headquarters of the German 69th Rifle Regiment during the rest of the battle. Miller had to explain that the Germans were already there in force. From now on Nicholson and his brigade headquarters had to depend on the two No. 9 wireless sets operating from the Citadel and the Gare Maritime.

The 60th had with them three parties of Anti-aircraft and Searchlight troops, who had already played their part in the fighting on the previous day. They remained with them to the end. Miller wrote that despite their "inexperience and lack of weapons, they fought bravely". Several, including two of their officers, were killed during the next thirty-six hours.

Despite heavy artillery support, the attack by German infantry on the 25th May moved slowly, but at 10 a.m. they reported to General Schaal that they were making "good progress". A few minutes later, another message was received from the 69th Rifle Regiment that Calais "had been taken". The rejoicing was short-lived. Half an hour later, the regiment reported:

"The quadrangle south-east of Fort Risban, the Citadel and Fort Risban itself are still occupied and are being defended with toughness. The Regiment have decided to send the mayor of Calais as a parlementaire to the English commandant of the Citadel to demand his surrender in view of the civil population still in the town."[1]

Schaal had soon to admit that "the situation had basically changed". It seems that on seeing the swastika flying from the clock tower of the Hôtel de Ville the German infantry commander thought that all was over. He soon discovered that the bridges leading to Calais-Nord were strongly defended by the 60th. A serious misunderstanding had occurred. When they reached the Hôtel de Ville the Germans thought that the whole of Calais had been captured. This is difficult to understand but, according to the Tenth Panzer Division War Diary, they had "insufficient maps".

Monsieur André Gershell, the mayor of Calais, was taken prisoner at the Hôtel de Ville. He was a patriot and in seeking to save the lives of the many civilians stranded in Calais-Nord he was influenced by the best motives.

When Schaal realised that it would be difficult to dislodge the British and French from the Citadel and the line of the canal, he made preparations for an attack with all available artillery and asked for dive-bombers. But first he tried to make Nicholson surrender.

At 11 a.m., the 60th saw an armoured vehicle at the south end of the centre bridge—the Pont Georges Cinq. The vehicle had a large white flag and from it emerged two civilians, André Gershell the mayor, and an interpreter. Both were taken to Lord Cromwell.

André Gershell was respected and courageous. His dilemma in seeking to halt the battle was that of many a civic functionary in war. He knew that if the British held on, the old part of Calais would be destroyed, but he had no reason to sympathise with the Germans. He

[1] Tenth Panzer Division: War Diary.

was Jewish and he had most bravely remained at his post at the Hôtel de Ville, when others had fled. Some months afterwards he was arrested by the Gestapo and died in a concentration camp.

Lord Cromwell and the 60th were in no mood to listen. They had their orders. The mayor and the interpreter were taken to Nicholson at the Citadel. They met in the main courtyard near the wireless truck and Lieutenant Austin Evitts of No. 12 wireless section heard the conversation. "Surrender," said Nicholson brusquely. "If the Germans want Calais they will have to fight for it."

André Gershell and the interpreter were locked in the Post Office at the Place Richelieu until they were released by the Germans next day.

After a lull, the battle continued. Using the theatre and the clock tower of the Hôtel de Ville as observation posts, German artillery opened fire on the Citadel and Fort Risban. Schaal ordered: "The Citadel is to be completely destroyed."

This was easier said than done. Vauban had reinforced the walls and the vaulted cellars withstood the heaviest bombardment. They are more or less intact today after the town was bombed by the R.A.F. in 1944.

It was obvious to Schaal that if the Citadel (which he considered the key to Calais) refused to surrender, he would need even more artillery and Stukas. He had underrated its solid construction and he was evidently unaware of the strength and determination of the defence. These miscalculations were to lead to critical delays in subduing the town.

The shelling continued for half an hour. It was very destructive. The Citadel was constantly hit but the Royal Marines and French infantry were comparatively protected by the huge ramparts. Most of the casualties were on the canal front, where incendiary shells set many houses on fire. The French army barracks adjoining Miller's battalion headquarters in the Rue des Marèchaux were now blazing.

From the clock tower of the Hôtel de Ville, German marksmen commanded most of Calais-Nord. They made it dangerous to cross the Parc Richelieu and the surrounding streets. They were also able to fire on the Rifle Brigade, now preparing for the defence of the harbour and the Gare Maritime. Throughout the rest of the battle, the clock tower was a threat to all movement of Allied troops.

In the houses along the Quai de l'Escaut and the Quai de la Tamise the 60th were subject to tremendous machine-gun fire. They held first and second-floor rooms and barricaded the windows with furniture and bedding. These were the houses of the bourgeoisie who had escaped in their cars. Oak tables, gilt chairs, family portraits and other signs of prosperity were used to shield the Green Jackets from the torrent of bullets.

In the poorer streets, the people unable to leave watched the fighting and during most of the 25th shops and markets were open in Calais-St. Pierre. In Calais-Nord, civilians fought the flames until the battle became so savage that they were forced into cellars while hand-to-hand fighting developed around the bridges.

On the Canal de Calais, Major Brush's company of the Rifle Brigade were mortared unmercifully. They had neither tools, sandbags nor wire and they had to lie on the east side of the canal with little or no cover. Efforts were made to build breastworks by using potato-sacks but the nearest garden where soil could be found was too far away. Houses had to be occupied by breaking in from back yards. Locked front doors caused many casualties in Calais since it was impossible to shelter from the fire. Many locks were so strong that it was impossible to smash them with rifle butts.

At 11 a.m. mortar bombs set fire to the Pont Mollien and a squadron of Stukas screamed down on the Rifle Brigade position killing several riflemen. Major John Taylor, who had taken over "I" company from Brush, was now short of ammunition. Despite the support of light tanks of the Third Royal Tank Regiment, it was obvious that the company front which still extended along the Canal de Marck to the east, would be broken. There was now a real danger that the Germans would force their way through to the Gare Maritime, splitting the Rifle Brigade from the 60th. Leaflets were dropped demanding surrender within an hour or the bombardment would get worse, but few had time to read them.

When he sent the mayor of Calais to negotiate, General Schaal still believed that there was a good chance of taking the Citadel during the

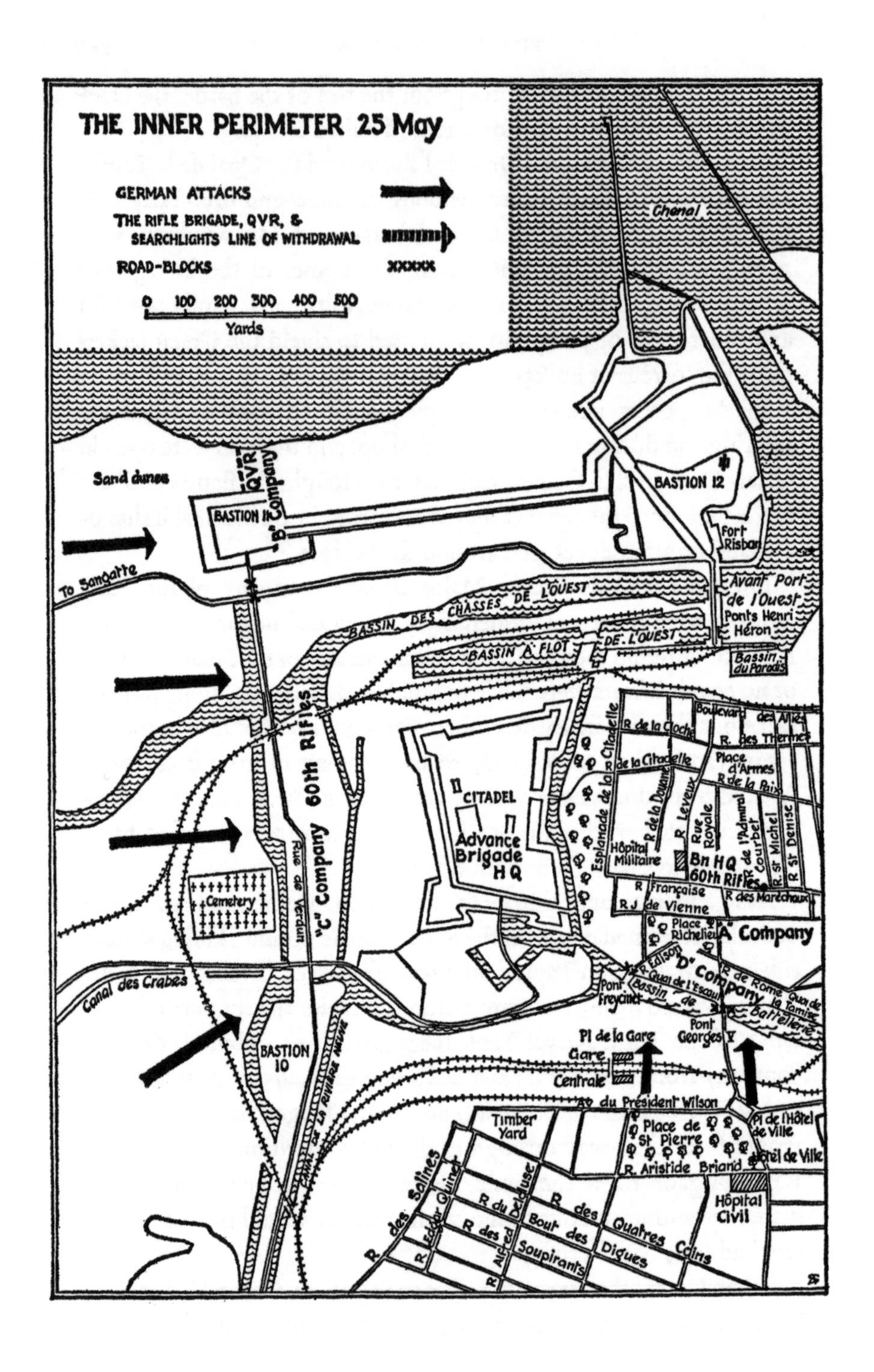

THE INNER PERIMETER 25 May
GERMAN ATTACKS
THE RIFLE BRIGADE, QVR, & SEARCHLIGHTS LINE OF WITHDRAWAL
ROAD-BLOCKS
0 100 200 300 400 500
Yards
Chenal
Sand dunes
QVR
"B" Company
BASTION 11
BASTION 12
Fort Risban
To Sangatte
Avant Port de l'Ouest
Ponts Henri Héron
Bassin du Paradis
BASSIN DES CHASSES DE L'OUEST
BASSIN A FLOT DE L'OUEST
60th Rifles
"C" Company
Rue de Verdun
Cemetery
CITADEL
Advance Brigade HQ
Esplanade de la Citadelle
R de la Cloche
R de la Citadelle
Boulevard des Alliés
R. des Thermes
Place d'Armes
R de la Paix
R de la Douane
R. Leveux
Rue Royale
R de l'Amiral Courbet
R. St Michel
R. St Denise
Hôpital Militaire
Bn HQ 60th Rifles
R Française
R des Maréchaux
R J de Vienne
Place Richelieu
"A" Company
R Edison
"D" Company
R de Rome
Quai de la Tamise
Quai de l'Escaut
Bassin de Batellerie
Pont Freycinet
Canal des Crabes
Pont Georges V
Pl de la Gare
Gare Centrale
BASTION 10
Canal de la Rivière Neuve
Av du Président Wilson
Timber Yard
Place de St Pierre
Pl de l'Hôtel de Ville
Hôtel de Ville
R. Aristide Briand
Hôpital Civil
R des Salines
R Edgar Quinet
R du Bout des Digues
R des Quatres Coins
R des Soupirants
R Alfred

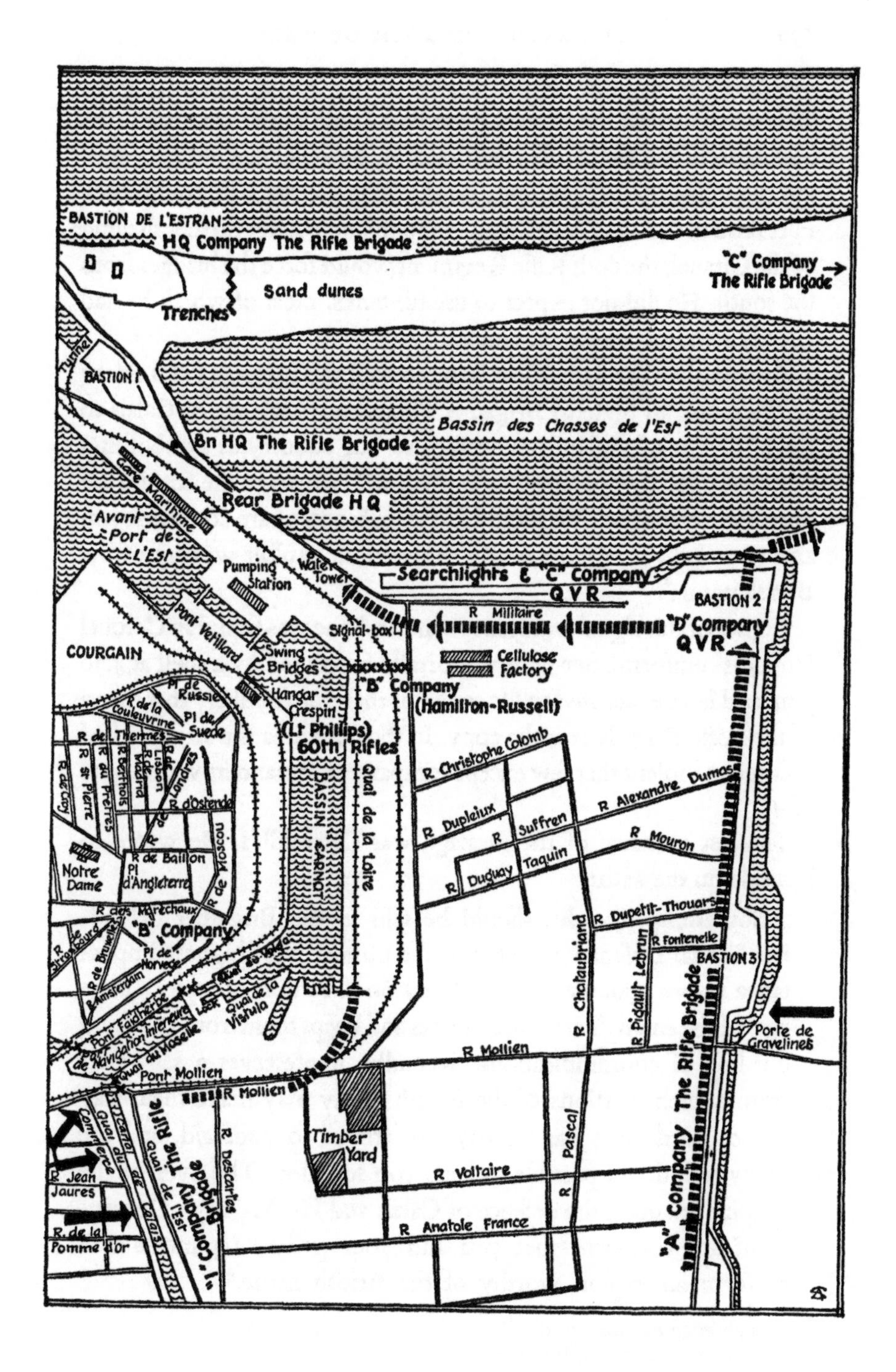

BASTION DE L'ESTRAN
HQ Company The Rifle Brigade
Sand dunes
Trenches
"C" Company The Rifle Brigade
Tunnel
BASTION 1
Bassin des Chasses de l'Est
Bn HQ The Rifle Brigade
Gare Maritime
Rear Brigade HQ
Avant Port de L'Est
Pumping Station
Water Tower
Searchlights & "C" Company
QVR
BASTION 2
R Militaire
Signal-box
"D" Company
QVR
Pont Vetillard
COURGAIN
Swing Bridges
Cellulose Factory
Hangar Crespin
"B" Company (Hamilton-Russell)
Pl de Russie
R de la Couleuvrine
Pl de Suede
(Lt Philips) 60th Rifles
R des Thermes
R de Madrid
Lisbon
R de Londres
R Christophe Colomb
R de Croy
R St Pierre
R du Prêtres
R Berthois
R d'Ostende
BASSIN CARNOT
Quai de la Loire
R Alexandre Dumas
R Dupleix
R Suffren
R Mouron
Notre Dame
R de Baillon
Pl d'Angleterre
R de Moscou
R Duguay Taquin
R des Maréchaux
"B" Company
R de Strasbourg
R de Bruxelles
Pl de Norvege
R Amsterdam
Quai de 1914
Quai de la Vistula
Lock
R Dupetit-Thouars
R Fontenelle
BASTION 3
R Chateaubriand
R Pigault Lebrun
Pont Faidherbe
de Navigation Intérieure
Quai du Moselle
Porte de Gravelines
R Mollien
Pont Mollien
R Mollien
Quai du Commerce
Canal de Calais
Quai de l'Est
The Rifle
"I" Company Brigade
R Descartes
Timber Yard
R Pascal
"A" Company The Rifle Brigade
R Jean Jaures
R Voltaire
R Anatole France
R. de la Pomme d'or

morning of the 25th. He had approved the German infantry plan. This was to attack the Citadel from Fort Lapin in the west with two battalions of the 86th Rifle Regiment. He believed that after occupying the village of Les Baraques on the Sangatte road, he could reach Fort Risban and the Citadel would be enfiladed. After further shelling of the Citadel, the 69th Rifle Regiment would force the bridges from the south. He did not expect to use his tanks, most of which he had already sent into reserve at Guines.

At 2 p.m. on the 25th Nicholson received this message from Eden:

"Secretary of State to Brigadier Nicholson: Defence of Calais to the utmost is of highest importance to our country as symbolising our continued co-operation with France. The eyes of the empire are upon the defence of Calais and H.M. Government are confident you and your gallant regiments will perform an exploit worthy of the British name."

Copies of this signal were sent round and one was found in Colonel Hoskyns' uniform after he was mortally wounded by a shell at 3.30 p.m. and later evacuated to Dover.[2] It is therefore unlikely that many of the Rifle Brigade saw the copy. In the 60th area the struggle had become so violent that few except company commanders were aware of it.

The last sentence of the message was Churchill's. He wrote to Ironside on the 25th:

> Something like this should be said to the Brigadier defending Calais: Defence of Calais to the utmost is of highest importance to our country and our Army now. First, it occupies a large part of the enemy's armoured forces and keeps them from attacking our line of communications. Secondly, it preserves a sally-port from which portions of the British Army may make their way home. Lord Gort has already sent troops to your aid, and the Navy will do all possible to keep you supplied. The eyes of the Empire are upon the defence of Calais and His Majesty's Government are confident that you and your gallant regiments will perform an exploit worthy of the British name.[3]

[2] See photograph facing p. 160.

[3] *The Second World War*, Vol. II, p. 73.

In Eden's telegram the last sentence was kept intact, but the passage describing Calais as a "sally-port" for evacuation of the B.E.F. was omitted. Events had moved fast and the last ship had left the harbour twenty-four hours before, except for the yachts and other small craft which were still collecting the wounded.

Churchill again showed himself to be at least two days behind. The original plan to evacuate the B.E.F. from Calais had been impracticable since the 23rd. The reference in his draft to "portions of the British Army" making "their way home" would hardly have been inspiring to the men on the spot. Nor was it possible for Eden to maintain any longer the pretence that Gort now imprisoned behind the Aa Canal, could do anything to save Calais. The words "Lord Gort has already sent troops to your aid" were also left out. But it is not clear why the reference to occupying "a large part of the enemy's forces" was deleted. Perhaps it would have been mere guesswork. In fact more and more elements of Guderian's corps, especially artillery, were being brought in to reduce Calais.

When the mayor did not return, Schaal decided to make one more attempt to compel Nicholson to surrender before the attack began. He sent Lieutenant Hoffmann of the Second Battalion, 69th Rifle Regiment with a French captain and a Belgian soldier at 3 p.m. They arrived at the Pont Georges Cinq under cover of a white flag and were taken up the Rue Royale to the eastern gate of the Citadel. While this took place, the guns were silenced for an hour. The British attitude to this respite is revealed by a report from the Q.V.R. holding the line in front of the Citadel: "The company took advantage of the lull to improve its position to give better all-round protection."

This was "B" Company of the Q.V.R. who were suffering severe casualties in their inadequate trenches. They had already been without sleep for nearly four days, and yet they were fighting hard. Opposite them also in trenches, the German infantry waited.

Schaal was still optimistic, but as a precaution, he asked Guderian for a new dive-bombing attack on the Citadel. Guderian replied that the Stukas would not be available that day. The attack would have to be made on the following morning but only if Schaal still asked for it at 10 p.m. that night. Tanks which had been resting at Guines were now brought back to link up with the 69th Rifle Regiment south-east of Calais.

Lieutenant Hoffmann demanded that French and British troops should surrender the Citadel and march out on the Coquelles road. Otherwise Calais-Nord would be reduced to a cinder by Stukas and artillery. Although he was now short of water, food, and ammunition, Nicholson had no hesitation in refusing. Lieutenant Hoffmann did not have to wait long for the answer. Those who were with Nicholson at the Citadel, say he was cold and correct. He immediately wrote out his reply which was recorded in the Tenth Panzer Division War Diary:

> 1. The answer is no as it is the British Army's duty to fight as well as it is the German's.
>
> 2. The French captain and the Belgian soldier having not been blindfolded cannot be sent back. The Allied commander gives his word that they will be put under guard and will not be allowed to fight against the Germans.

This laconic answer impressed the Germans as "soldierly" and brave. But they were very annoyed by the refusal to surrender. When Hoffmann returned over the canal at 4.35 p.m., he was slightly wounded, and the time limit for renewing the bombardment had already been twice advanced. During the afternoon Cap Gris Nez, held by the French, had fallen to a German rifle unit which was now available for the capture of Calais.

Guderian and Schaal were impatient to finish the battle before dark. A "major attack" was announced. The orders to the 69th Rifle Regiment, opponents of the Rifle Brigade and the Q.V.R. were:

"Attack over the canal and advance to the old town up the harbour and pier. Take the quadrangle jutting out to the north and south-east of Fort Risban. Clear the town south-east and south-west."

On the west side, the German infantry were to take the Citadel and "annihilate the enemy inside". There were only a few Royal Marines and 100 French infantry and they held out for another twenty-four hours.

CHAPTER FOURTEEN

Desperate Moments

THROUGHOUT the morning and early afternoon of the 25th May, the situation of "I" company of the Rifle Brigade at the Pont Mollien and on the Canal de Calais was causing great anxiety to Colonel Hoskyns. He therefore prepared to stop a breakthrough by establishing a rear line, using the Q.V.R. and Hamilton-Russell's company and by sending reserves to Major John Taylor at the Pont Mollien. In the meantime he had to hold the outer fortifications on the east and the Canal de Marck as long as he could. The Rifle Brigade and Q.V.R. positions on the 25th May are shown on the map at page 148.

When the Q.V.R. woke at dawn after their withdrawal from the outer perimeter, Hoskyns ordered them to the northern rampart. This was a bank of earth and sand twenty feet high, with steep grass slopes. At its west end was the water tower and at its east end, Bastion 2. It was separated from the Bassin des Chasses by a canal and a thin spit of land. This canal, part of the nineteenth-century fortifications went round the bastions and joined the Canal de Marck in the south,

The Q.V.R. position faced south across an open space. On their right, was the huge four-storied Cellulose Factory, a landmark for. both British and Germans in the final battle to hold the harbour. Stacks of timber fifteen feet high stood in its yard. From the top of the rampart, which had been designed for attack from the sea, rather than inside the network of streets off the Rue Mollien, the visibility was good.

Hoskyns' headquarters were still at a large bomb hole on the northern rampart. Behind him, on the shore of the Bassin remained hundreds of soldiers of many nationalities mostly without rifles and ammunition, who had been there since the last ship had left the Gare

Maritime. They had had practically no food for two days and were being kept in reserve in case the Rifle Brigade line was broken.

As the battle drew nearer to the Gare Maritime, Hoskyns began to strengthen its approaches. Men with rifles from the crowd on the shore were brought under his orders. A strong road-block under the command of Hamilton-Russell was built at the northern end of the Quai de la Loire to prevent the Germans advancing from the south.

As soon as the Q.V.R. reached the northern rampart snipers opened fire from the Cellulose Factory and from neighbouring streets. The factory was searched but the sniping continued all day. It seriously hampered the exhausted troops as they tried to dig trenches. The snipers, in civilian clothes, were well-trained and caused several casualties.

Later in the morning, Hoskyns ordered a company of the Q.V.R. to take over Bastion 2 which the French had evacuated on the 24th May after killing all the pigs and chickens inside. Lieut. Jessop's "D" Company were told to strengthen the Rifle Brigade line on the eastern rampart.

The positions of the Q.V.R. were decidedly uncomfortable. They comprised a right-angle of ramparts enabling snipers to fire on Jessop's company from behind as they faced Dunkirk. "C" Company (Austin-Brown) stayed on the northern wall, as a reserve to the 60th.

The arrival of a motley party of troops sent up from the shore of the Bassin, many of them entirely unarmed, only increased the number of targets for the snipers. According to Ellison-Macartney, these unfortunate men were obliged to scratch out sand from the banks with their steel helmets to get some cover from shells and mortar bombs. They were withdrawn after two hours.

During the afternoon about 200 disorganised French soldiers moved from the Porte de Gravelines northwards to Bastion 2, now occupied by the Q.V.R. Most were persuaded to leave and rest in the yard of the Cellulose Factory but about twenty who were armed remained to fight. Inside, men of the 6th Heavy A.A. Battery withdrawn from Fort Vert had been busy trying to mend the coastal guns spiked by the French garrison on the previous day. One gun was repaired, turned inland and fired at a German tank. There was a tremendous bang and the barrel rolled off into the sand. A roar of laughter from the Q.V.R. rose along the northern rampart. Their company sergeant-major reprimanded the men. According to Rifleman Robert C. Lane:

"He told us in no uncertain terms it was all right for us to laugh. What about the poor lads inside Bastion 2? There was a hush. Later he returned from the Bastion looking as black as thunder. 'They're laughing their heads off like you silly buggers', he said."

The gun was of 1914 vintage. A Royal Artillery major in breeches and polished boots appeared as the gunners were working on it. "Why isn't this gun firing?" he asked briskly. Someone murmured that the piece was not only ancient but dangerous. But the Major insisted. The gun exploded. "I see what you mean," he said.

This simple story amused the Q.V.R. even in the middle of a desperate battle. I heard it that afternoon as the wounded were brought down to the cellars of the Hôpital Militaire. It was one of many anecdotes which relieved the soulless tedium of prisoner-of-war camps.

A heavy artillery bombardment fell on all the Rifle Brigade and Q.V.R. positions and German infantry began to infiltrate from the south. At the Cellulose Factory, shells burst in the yard and yellow acrid smoke drifted towards the ramparts. There was a cry of "Gas!" and respirators were hurriedly put on until a few minutes afterwards it became clear that the smoke was only cordite. Several gas alarms occurred in other parts of Calais during the 25th May, all of them false.

From this time onwards, the danger of a breakthrough by the 69th German Rifle Regiment to the harbour became acute. Major John Taylor, though helped by two Q.V.R. platoons, was gradually forced back from the line of the Canal de Calais into the back streets and platoons of "I" Company on the Canal de Marck were cut off. The company position had further been weakened by the withdrawal of Bren carriers, covering the bridges, to take part in a projected flank attack on the Germans in the afternoon.

In some streets the Germans and the Rifle Brigade fought hand to hand. Grenades were thrown and many officers and men were killed on both sides. The struggle shook the Germans in its ferocity and they did not break through to the harbour for another twenty-four hours.

In this mêlée, Taylor was wounded and finding himself with only thirty men out of the original 150 who had gone into action with Major Peter Brush, he decided to retire north up the Quai de la Loire.

Platoon Sergeant-Major Stevens with sixteen men found themselves isolated and without any ammunition. They lay low in houses off the Rue Mollien for two weeks after the battle when they were forced to surrender through lack of food. Two platoons of "C" Company (Major Coghill) sent to reinforce Brush were left in houses on the Canal de Calais which they held till it was all over.

Colonel Hoskyns had now moved his headquarters back to trenches near Bastion 1. At 3.30 p.m. Taylor, despite his wounds, reached him and asked for the help of tanks to counter-attack and rescue Stevens' platoon. He had barely had time to mention this plan when a salvo of shells landed on the trench where he was talking to Hoskyns. Hoskyns was struck in the side by a shell splinter and mortally injured. Taylor was wounded a second time and unable to continue the fight.

This tragedy could not have occurred at a worse moment for the Rifle Brigade. It was now learned that the platoons on the Canal de Marck had been overrun and that the Germans would soon capture the canal bridge at the Porte de Marck.

At this critical moment, tanks and other transport had assembled on the road leading north from the Gare Maritime. Nicholson had decided during the morning that a mobile column should try to break out along the shore of the Bassin and, escorted by tanks, make a flank attack on the Germans in the south-east. His object was to help the hard-pressed 60th in the town.

Colonel Holland arrived with the orders at 1 p.m. Hoskyns was to take all available tanks and carriers and two motor platoons. Hoskyns immediately expressed his disagreement. The plan would weaken his whole front when the Germans were liable to break through from the Pont Mollien at any time. He is reported to have said: "I have my orders but I will not be responsible for the consequences."

All the evidence shows that the assembly of tanks and carriers under shellfire for this attack gravely disorganised the defence. The plan involved withdrawing from many places in the line where the Germans might penetrate at any moment. It is clear that the Rifle Brigade despite their splendid defence next day, never really recovered from the confusion.

Colonel Keller received no direct orders from Nicholson to take part with his tanks. But he favoured the plan. He wrote afterwards that he felt the few remaining tanks could be better employed in trying to break out than standing on the road behind the Gare Maritime, an obvious target for German artillery. He agreed to move off with the infantry at 2.30 p.m.

In view of his orders, Hoskyns decided to lead the column himself but it never started.

When the Rifle Brigade adjutant (Captain T. H. Acton) reconnoitred the narrow track along the shore of the Bassin, he found it blocked by an overturned truck. An attempt was made to find a way out along the north shore but this was impassable for wheeled vehicles. The plan had to be abandoned. It had no chance of success and might have meant the capture of the harbour on the evening of the 25th instead of the afternoon of the 26th.

The plight of the Rifle Brigade was extremely grave. Before he was wounded, Hoskyns was distracted by these orders from fighting his command and his battalion headquarters "never really assembled and functioned as such again".[1]

Ten minutes before Hoskyns was wounded, Major Brush, who had spent part of the day in the regimental aid post in the tunnel under Bastion 1, reappeared. His throat wound was not serious and he was impatient to return to the battle and the command of "I" Company. He made his way to Hoskyns' trenches and was lucky to be missed in the shellfire. Despite his wound, Hoskyns was able to agree that Brush should make a counter-attack along the Quai de la Loire to regain touch with his lost riflemen.

Brush was an indomitable character. He walked through the shellfire to the Cellulose Factory where he found Major Allan, the second-in-command who now took over the Rifle Brigade. It was thanks to his skill that they remained in action for another twenty-four hours.

[1] Major A. W. Allan: *Rifle Brigade Chronicle, 1945.*

Brush had only 2/Lieut. Edward Bird and fifteen men to find the remainder of his company. He started to move past Hamilton-Russell's road-block at the north end of the Quai de la Loire. He did not get far. The party were brought to a halt by intense light automatic fire. They took what cover was possible on the quay and were amazed to see a French lorry being driven towards them, under fire from the Germans. The lorry was driven by a captured fifth columnist dressed in Belgian uniform. Beside him sat Corporal Lane, pointing a pistol at his head. Lane had arrested the man, loaded the lorry with wounded and forced him to drive to within 300 yards of the road-block. At this point the driver was hit and the lorry stopped not far from Brush's party. The wounded who could move, began to crawl towards them. Edward Bird ran across the road, climbed into the driver's seat under tremendous machine-gun fire and tried to restart the lorry. There were still several gravely wounded men in the back. But he was shot in the head and staggered back, to die in half an hour. Brush wrote afterwards of his "devotion and self-sacrifice". Brush and his men ran forward and dragged the wounded to safety from the blazing lorry, taking with them Corporal Lane.

The first problem facing Major Allan was to prevent a German breakthrough from the south which would cut off the 60th and, by occupying the harbour, surround them. This is what the 69th German Rifle Regiment were now trying to achieve. At 4.30 p.m. on the 25th May, he tried, without success, to contact Nicholson at the Citadel. The fortress appeared as a great sheet of flame. The No. 9 wireless set at Nicholson's headquarters on the ramparts of the Citadel had been wrecked. From this time Allan was unable to communicate with those in the battle except by radio-telephone, though the brigade signals officer Lieutenant Millett with another set at the Gare Maritime kept him in touch with Dover. He managed to speak to Colonel Miller. Miller was under heavy fire and very hard pressed. He was worried that the Germans might capture Bastion 11 and Fort Risban and encircle the Citadel. The Rifle Brigade therefore strengthened their Bren and rifle posts on the west side of the harbour.

Allan ordered Hamilton-Russell to hold the road-block on the Quai de la Loire at all costs. Searchlight and Anti-aircraft gunners under 2/Lieut. Hawkesworth were across the railway line on Hamilton-Russell's right. Another party from the Rifle Brigade and Q.V.R. occupied the roof and upper floors of the Cellulose Factory.

An alarm was raised that German tanks were already in Calais-Nord. Allan sent 2/Lieut. Rolt across the Pont Vétillard into the town to block the streets with carriers. In 1940, the Pont Vétillard consisted of two swing bridges over the lock leading to the Bassin Carnot. Rolt was warned that the southern bridge might have to be blown behind him. The northern bridge was already blown but since the Rifle Brigade possessed only weak demolition charges it was still possible to cross on foot. In twenty minutes, Rolt returned. The report that German tanks had overrun the 60th was not correct and the two regiments were still able to keep in touch.

At 6.30 p.m. a new and violent artillery bombardment started. General Schaal observed the effect from his command post south-west of Calais. Unfortunately for his own troops, the shells directed at "A" Company of the Rifle Brigade and the Q.V.R. on the eastern bastions fell on the 2nd Battalion of the 69th German Rifle Regiment in the little wood east of Bastion 2. There were heavy casualties and a sharp reprimand for the German artillery commander.

On the canal front in Calais-Nord twenty-four guns opened up on the 60th, and precise and deadly mortar fire fell on their barricades at the bridges and the streets leading to Calais-Nord. The French engineers at the Citadel had failed to blow up the bridges which, especially the Pont Georges Cinq, were strong and broad. Their schemes for placing large quantities of explosive beneath them seemed to Miller to be "harebrained" and they were abandoned.

About 7 p.m. the noise of bombs and shells suddenly ceased and tanks appeared at each of the three bridges. At the Pont Faidherbe on the left of the 60th, three tanks began to cross followed by a saloon car. One tank forced the road-block but was put out of action. The second was also hit and stopped. The third withdrew to cheers from the riflemen. The saloon car was destroyed at the German end of the bridge.

Major Owen and many others were killed during this attack which was beaten off. At the Pont Georges Cinq—the centre bridge—the leading German tank blew up on a mine. German infantry, installed in houses on the opposite quay, opened a murderous fire on Lord Cromwell's company, but the bridge remained in control of the 60th.

At the Pont Freycinet, on the right of the 60th, one tank and some German infantry crossed the bridge and, helped by heavy mortar fire, forced the 60th from their positions nearest the Citadel, but a spirited counter-attack forced the German tank to withdraw, though some of their infantry remained in houses near the Citadel as it grew dark.

CHAPTER FIFTEEN

To the Last Man

THE evening of the 25th May found General Weygand pursuing the plan which he had announced on the previous day for "a vast bridgehead" round the ports of Calais, Boulogne and Dunkirk. The object of the bridgehead would be to tie down "important enemy forces" and gain time to organise resistance on the Somme. Faced by the British withdrawal from Arras, Weygand was concentrating on the defence of these ports to maintain supplies for the armies of the North. During the day, the French Government maintained their pressure on Churchill to reinforce their defence.

But the British had already decided that a French offensive on the Somme would never succeed. On the 25th May, in Paris, Major-General Sir Edward Spears, Churchill's personal liaison officer, warned Paul Reynaud that a British withdrawal by sea might have to be attempted if a breakthrough to the Somme were impossible.[1] A few hours later, at 10.30 a.m. on the 26th, Eden would authorise Gort to fight his way back to the west, "where all beaches and ports east of Gravelines will be used for embarkation".

The defence of Calais to the last had become, after much hesitation, the policy of the War Cabinet.

"The CIGS [Ironside] and I," wrote Eden, "went across to see the Prime Minister and reluctantly agreed that the garrison must hold out until the last, so vital had it then become to delay the German armoured advance along the coast to Dunkirk."

He added: "We should have seen this more clearly and sooner when Boulogne was evacuated."[2]

Churchill's own account of the decision is characteristic:

[1] Spears: *Assignment to Catastrophe*, Vol. I, p. 180.

[2] *The Reckoning*.

"We three came out from dinner and at 9 p.m. did the deed. It involved Eden's own regiment in which he had long served in the previous struggle. One has to eat and drink in war, but I could not help feeling physically sick as we afterward sat silent at the table."[3]

For years afterwards, he was unable to speak of Calais without emotion.[4]

By nightfall, the defenders were very weary. Colonel Miller said the 60th were "cheerful but very done". Allan described the position of the Rifle Brigade as "far from happy". Both regiments had made a remarkable stand and every clerk and cook was now in the line.

The 60th had little alternative to holding the canal bridges as long as this was humanly possible. There was nowhere to withdraw except possibly the Citadel. But the Rifle Brigade could shorten their line and hope to hold the harbour approaches for another day. Hamilton-Russell prepared a plan for bringing back Rifle Brigade companies and the Q.V.R. to a line behind the Cellulose Factory and to prevent the Germans from capturing the Bastion de l'Estran.

Orders to start the withdrawal reached Ellison-Macartney at 8.30 p.m. Only half an hour of daylight remained and there was little time to get in touch with the Q.V.R. company in Bastion 2 in the north-east. They had already been evacuating their wounded by boat across the canal which flowed round this bastion. It was now planned to withdraw the rest of the riflemen in this way. But there was only one boat and it became a dangerously slow operation even in darkness.

At 9 p.m. German aircraft made a dive-bombing attack on this bastion and machine-gunned it. They caused no casualties among the Q.V.R., but shot up their own troops in the wood on the side of the canal. But the attack led to confusion among the Q.V.R. as they withdrew and in the dark they lost their way. When they crossed the canal, they went east instead of west and dug in for the night east of the Bassin. One party moved to a French blockhouse on the north-east corner where "C" Company of the Rifle Brigade (Major Knollys) were also in position. Another started to dig trenches on a track leading

[3] *The Second World War*, Vol. II, p. 73.

[4] Private information.

to the beach. They found themselves in a dangerously forward position next morning.

Austin-Brown's Company of the Q.V.R. who had been on the northern rampart, moved west along the canal bank to the Gare Maritime. They were ordered to hold a line between the road-block at the north end of the Quai de la Loire and the water tower. In darkness it was impossible to do more than make hasty plans to cover the Quai de la Loire with rifles and machine-guns.

"A" Company of the Rifle Brigade under Captain Peel were also withdrawn during the evening after holding the fortifications from the Porte de Marck as far as Bastion 2 in the north-east corner for the whole day. When the defence was broken on the Canal de Marck during the afternoon, they came under fire from front and behind. A French machine-gun post tried to surrender. They were prevented by 2/Lieut. Welch, later killed, who set fire to their white flag.

When it was clear that these positions could no longer be held, Peel moved with his company along the northern rampart to the Gare Maritime. The withdrawal went smoothly. As on previous nights, the German attack died away but the Q.V.R. and Major Knollys' company east of the Bassin could not be reached.

From now on, the Rifle Brigade were without tank support. Just before Colonel Hoskyns was wounded he asked Colonel Keller for a patrol to help Brush's counter-attack along the Quai de la Loire. Keller sent a cruiser and two light tanks. The cruiser had great difficulty in turning round as the road to the Bastion de l'Estran was crowded with transport. The patrol moved off towards Hoskyns' trenches at the junction of the road to Bastion 1. They had hardly reached there when the shells landed which wounded Hoskyns and Major John Taylor. An officer shouted to Keller that Hoskyns had been killed and that one of his tanks was hit. Keller wrote afterwards:

"I saw that the tanks would all be knocked out if they remained where they were and decided that the only thing to do was to evacuate—try and save what was left of my unit and gain touch with the French at Gravelines. I therefore told 2/Lieut. Mundy to get his tanks on to the beach and told my second-in-command to get all the men along the beach and try and contact the French."

Keller and his second-in-command had already decided that their "sphere of usefulness" was over. They had spent the night in the sand dunes but had been able to send a number of tank patrols to help the 60th. By the morning of the 25th under very heavy shelling, it had become difficult to get any clear orders and they had lost tanks knocked out in the town by German anti-tank guns fired at street level from cellars. These casualties together with the misunderstanding when five tanks were destroyed on the previous morning, had reduced the Third Royal Tank Regiment to a handful of mobile tanks. The crews, parked on the roadway leading to the Bastion de l'Estran were totally exhausted and subjected to continuous and accurate shellfire.

The situation looked threatening to Keller. He believed that Hoskyns was dead, and, knowing nothing of the fate of the other Rifle Brigade officers, assumed command. He ordered the wounded at the regimental aid post in the tunnel under Bastion 1 to be evacuated along the beach. The wounded, about a hundred in number, from the Rifle Brigade and Q.V.R., were taken in ambulances and trucks. The drivers were ordered to hurry but two vehicles were hit and the wounded in them killed. A tank escorted them on to the beach along the north side of the Bassin accompanied by a crowd of French soldiers and refugees. Under mortar fire, stretcher parties were organised and the wounded taken a further half-mile into the sand dunes towards Dunkirk. Shortly afterwards they were all captured.

Keller ordered his second-in-command to move along the beach with the remaining tanks. He then jumped on to a light tank which carried him half a mile along the dunes until he came to the Rifle Brigade trenches, north-east of the Bassin. He told their occupants that he believed Hoskyns was dead and suggested a plan for both tanks and infantry to fall back eastwards at dusk. They agreed to meet again, but lost touch later.

Unarmed French and Belgians were plodding through the sand towards Dunkirk and Keller, through field-glasses, saw that they were being rounded up by German motor-cyclists. At this point, the light tank on which he was riding went out of action. It refused to start again and as it was under fire, he was compelled to move on foot through the dunes. Some of the tank crews and their officers, also on foot, were taken prisoner.

Except for one of his squadron commanders, Major Simpson, Keller was alone. Both of them continued walking along the shore. About four miles from Calais, three tanks were found abandoned in the sea, their engines, machine-guns and wireless sets destroyed. They were also out of petrol. At nightfall, two miles from Grand Fort Philippe they met four of their crews who had been ordered to split up and make their way to Gravelines on foot.

At 10.30 p.m., the party reached a pier on the west side of the harbour entrance. A German sentry had been posted on it, and they could hear his footsteps. When he reached the end of his beat, nearest to the shore, they scrambled underneath the pier and came to the River Aa where it flowed swiftly out to sea. Keller tried to wade over but soon went up to his neck in the strong current. A chain was formed but one man let go, and they were swept back to the western bank. The remaining men refused to make the attempt again but Keller and Simpson managed to struggle across. Exhausted and very cold, they spent the night in a beach hut.

On the morning of the 26th, they walked into Petit Fort Philippe where French troops disarmed and arrested them, since they had no identity cards, and sent them under escort to Gravelines. The French commander sent them into Dunkirk from where, after reporting to the B.E.F., they were taken by trawler to Dover. As they passed within a few miles of Calais late that afternoon they could see the British cruiser *Galatea* firing shells into the town.

Despite their losses near Guines on the 23rd May, the Third Royal Tank Regiment played a distinguished part in the defence of Calais. They had never been trained to work with infantry, they had never co-operated with Nicholson's brigade before and their tanks were very vulnerable in street fighting. But their patrols encouraged the infantry throughout the battle. On the morning of the 25th, a troop of three cruisers, under Captain Howe, destroyed six German tanks. During the heavy artillery fire in the afternoon, a British troop of four light tanks went to the aid of the Rifle Brigade. They attempted to cross the Pont Mollien, believing that "D" Company and Major John Taylor were still on the Canal de Calais though they had by then withdrawn.

A cruiser tank which helped them to force the block was hit in the turret by two shells from a German anti-tank gun opposite the Hôtel de Ville and set on fire, killing three of the crew. The driver though badly burned, brought the tank back to the sand dunes. 2/Lieut. McCallum climbed up and put the fire out. He wrote to me in 1971:

"On the bottom were two severed heads. My squadron commander told me to get the bodies out and bury them. I told him this was impossible. He climbed up to look for himself and I felt some satisfaction that when he got down he obviously felt sicker than I did and he had been in the First World War."

McCallum also experienced the "gas alarm" which seemed to him to be caused by a strong smell of chlorine gas from the batteries of a group of burning German and British tanks.

Liddell Hart has written that the most valuable contribution of the Third Royal Tank Regiment was to check the First Panzer Division at Gravelines on the night of the 23rd–24th when Major Reeves led the patrol already described, right through the German lines. Hitler's order to the German Panzer forces to halt was sent out in clear at midday on the 24th May. Had Reeves and the French troops at Gravelines not stopped the Germans at 8 a.m. on that day, the First Panzer Division might have been in Dunkirk that morning.

"Analysis shows," wrote Liddell Hart, "that its [the stand made by Allied troops at Calais] only influential contribution to the main issue was confined to May 23–4 and that was due to the brief mobile action of the Third Royal Tank Regiment."

He considered that "three fine mobile infantry battalions, trained for the new mode of warfare were cast away in a hopeless task of static defence."[5]

Liddell Hart was writing in the context of his lifelong campaign (closely studied by Guderian) to get the British War Office to create armoured forces. He was criticising them for splitting the only British

[5] *The Tanks*, Vol. II.

armoured division into two. One part was totally destroyed at Calais and the remainder landed in France too late, though they were evacuated at Cherbourg on the 18th June, closely pursued by Rommel.

He did not doubt the gallantry of the British infantry and he rightly praises Keller for taking the initiative in trying to get his remaining tanks out of Calais on the 25th. But the view which he expresses that the action on the 23rd and 24th May by the Third Royal Tank Regiment, was the *only* influential contribution is surely exaggerated. No one can doubt the fine performance of the tanks under intolerable conditions nor what the sacrifice of the infantry battalions meant to the British Army in 1940. But to describe this sacrifice as "useless" and "hopeless" is to beg many questions.

It is for example to ignore the situation of General Schaal, Commander of the Tenth Panzer Division, as the sun set over Calais on the 25th. Schaal had had a disappointing day and severe losses. As the Rifle Brigade and Q.V.R. on the east of the town withdrew to a shortened line near the Gare Maritime at dusk, there was disappointment in the German ranks. The battalion of the 69th German Rifle Regiment opposite Bastion 2, which had scattered by their own artillery, had not reassembled for a new attack. Three German tanks had been put out of action by the Rifle Brigade. The German regiment was also complaining that they were fighting in an area of factories and gardens where there was poor visibility. They claimed to be about 800 metres south of the Bassin des Chasses, which would mean they were still on the line of the Rue Mollien after a hard day's fight.

The Tenth Panzer Division staff announced: "The attack on the Old Town has been held back. The enemy fights in a most tough and ferocious manner."

On the west, it was much the same picture. German infantry reported that although artillery and mortars had been seen to cause heavy losses to the defence, the attack on the Citadel had not advanced. They paid this tribute to the 60th and their allies:

"The Enemy fights with a hitherto unheard-of obstinacy. They are English, extremely brave and tenacious. They have at least one reinforced infantry regiment,[6] armour supporting them and naval guns firing from ships in the Channel."[7]

Although the 86th German Rifle Regiment on the west were only a few hundred yards from the Citadel, their commander told Schaal that a new attack would be "worthless" as the defenders had not been ousted and there was too little time before darkness. This was at 9 p.m. and artillery fire on the Citadel and Bastion 11 had already been held up for half an hour through shortage of ammunition. Further reports from the 69th German Rifle Regiment on the east said that the town there was "more heavily defended than anticipated".

Faced with these reports Schaal decided at 9.45 p.m. to call it a day. He had good reason. As he reported:

"Today's attack has shown that the enemy will fight to the last man and holds strong and up to now unshaken positions. The attack itself is at present at a standstill."

He thought that the attack could only be continued after a renewed artillery preparation of which the assault groups could take advantage. There was no possibility of co-ordinating such an attack at the late hour and he ordered that the positions taken should be held. It was to be renewed next morning with a "well planned artillery barrage" and Stukas.

At 11 p.m. the commanders arrived at Schaal's headquarters to receive their orders. The report of this conference in the Division's War Diary shows that the Germans were not only disappointed by their slow progress on the 25th but apprehensive. They still believed that the British meant to land further troops at Calais and the guns of the destroyers had taken a heavy toll in German casualties.

This does not suggest that Liddell Hart's appreciation is the correct one. Here was a Panzer division pinned down a short distance from Gravelines, which, but for this stout defence might have captured Calais two days before, and joined in threatening the whole Dunkirk operation on the Aa Canal.

His infantry commanders told Schaal that the resistance at the bridges over the canal which led to Calais-Nord was "very violent".

[6] i.e. the equivalent of a British infantry brigade.

[7] Tenth Panzer Division: War Diary.

There was even a difference of opinion as to whether the attack should not be postponed for two days. Some commanders said that their troops were "finished" and that it would be better to plan an attack for the 27th. But Schaal was adamant. He refused categorically to postpone the attack.

"It is of the utmost importance," he said, "not to give them time for rest or to reinforce their troops from the sea. The last defended positions must be taken tomorrow."

He telephoned to Guderian and asked for more heavy artillery to combat the destroyers and reduce the Citadel. He was hoping, too, for strong help from the Luftwaffe. The discussion lasted a long time and it was after midnight before orders were issued.

The picture on the other side was different. As they took up their new positions around the Gare Maritime, the Rifle Brigade could see flashes from guns of the destroyers in the Channel and they were heartened by the sound of naval shells going in the direction of the Germans. But Major Allan knew that German infantry were moving north and preparing for an attack along both shores of the Bassin. So loud had been the explosions that it had been difficult to find out the true position. At one time, Hamilton-Russell and Allan each believed he was the senior officer left. These messages received at Dover during the fighting reveal the situation:

1900 hours 25th May.

"Rifle Brigade driven to quay—All available bombing and shelling required to support us. Given 1 hour to surrender but fighting on."

Shortly afterwards Dover ordered No. 12 wireless section at the Gare Maritime to destroy all codes. In his last message of the evening Allan reported:

"Citadel a shambles stop Brigadier's fate unknown stop Rifle Brigade casualties may be 60 per cent stop Being heavily shelled and flanked but attempting counter-attack stop am attempting contact with 60th fighting in the town stop Are you sending ships stop Quay is intact in spite of very severe bombardment."

The messages were sent from the Gare Maritime. Lieutenant Evitts' set at the Citadel had been put out of action by shellfire. The first message was not acknowledged by Dover as it was thought to be suspicious. Half an hour afterwards, another was received from the Gare Maritime:

"1930. Take no notice of message there is a spy stop Major Allan is in command of Rear H.Q. on the quay."

The calls were now accepted at Dover although it was followed by the words "All codes destroyed."

Henceforward until the battle was almost over there was communication between Calais and Dover but it had to be in plain language.

CHAPTER SIXTEEN

"A Good Day"

WE have no records of the 60th casualties on the 25th, but they were severe. Many wounded remained at their posts throughout the night and refused to go to hospital even after they were captured. So strong were regimental feelings that some had to be taken out of the prisoner-of-war column by the Germans for treatment, even when they had been on the march for days.

They had held all their positions under tremendous fire. But they were exhausted and handicapped by the blaze which raged everywhere around them, the old houses off the Rue Royale and along the quays were in flames and many of the forward posts of the 60th were forced out by the heat, dust and smoke.

Towards 9 p.m., the wind grew stronger, fanning the flames and blowing dense clouds over the town. It was difficult to move in the narrow streets blocked with rubble. Worst of all was the shortage of water, for the mains were broken. Many found that drinking champagne and wine only increased their thirst. Food and ammunition were becoming scarce and the wounded were moved with difficulty to the Hôpital Militaire, since the Rue Leveux was now alight from end to end. When they arrived they were brought down to the cellars and I heard their groans and cries above the crackle of the burning houses.

At darkness, the attack died away and Colonel Miller visited all companies. Without artillery and only scanty tank support they had put up an amazing fight. It was obvious to Miller that they could not last another day without "active support from sea and air". But would this be forthcoming? It had been hourly awaited since the 24th. The destroyers had done their best to silence German batteries outside Calais but they could do little to help in the defence of Calais-Nord.

Miller's signal officer made his way to the north-west corner where "C" Company of the 60th were still in position. After the artillery bombardment which followed Nicholson's refusal to surrender, no German attack had been pushed home. But German tanks and infantry had been moving up in front of the Citadel on the company's left. Some of these tanks had advanced, one had been put out of action with anti-tank rifle fire, others engaged with mortars. At darkness, this attack was not pursued, and the small group of French sailors and soldiers under Capitaine de la Blanchardière was still defending Bastion 11 with the party of the 60th under Captain Radcliffe.

At Bastion 12, the shelling had been so severe, that de Lambertye ordered the naval crews to abandon the coastal guns. He told their commander Enseigne de Vaisseau Georges Wiart to seek means of getting away to Cherbourg. Finding a small boat, Wiart and some of his men reached Dover. He spent the night in London at St. Stephens Club in Westminster and soon recrossed the Channel where he was reunited with other gun crews.

When the Germans seemed likely to advance over the canal on the right of the 60th, at the south-east corner of the Citadel, Miller rushed two reserve platoons into the gap to cover the Pont Freycinet where a tank was trying to cross. Captain Charles Stanton commanded them. Half an hour later, he returned, mortally wounded, to report. He had been struck twice in the body and fell dying.

Men from the 60th headquarters in the Rue des Marèchaux and the remains of Major Trotter's "A" Company raced to defend a line of posts in the streets leading to the Citadel. They were led by Trotter himself, who, after his sudden departure from my ward in the Hôpital Militaire in the morning, had been in action all day long. They managed to hold on till it was dark and prevent the Germans from making more progress.

At 11.30 p.m., Brigadier Nicholson came to the Gare Maritime and saw Major Allan. For hours his fate at the Citadel had been unknown, and he was believed to have been killed in the bombardment. Several times that day senior officers had been reported dead. Earlier, Allan had spoken to Captain Williams the adjutant of the 60th who did not know if Miller was alive. These were experienced officers and their abrupt messages now on record show how desperate the position seemed to them.

Nicholson congratulated the Rifle Brigade on their action during the day. He expressed himself as "highly pleased and satisfied" that they had held the Germans. Allan explained his dispositions for the defence on the following morning and obtained permission to wireless for a hospital carrier to move the wounded from the tunnel under Bastion 1. Despite its evacuation on Colonel Keller's orders during the afternoon, the tunnel was now full again. There were fifty or sixty cases, some very serious and others in different parts of the town.

Nicholson repeated the order that Calais was to be held to the last, that there would be no evacuation. The shells had stopped and in the quiet of the night, the full meaning of his words fell on his hearers. Till now there had seemed some chance that the Navy would be allowed to take them off. Tomorrow the alternatives were death, wounds or capture. And yet, tired as they were, no one in any unit considered surrender. They were still good for many hours' fighting.

Nicholson discussed the possibility that they should withdraw into the town and make a last stand with the 60th in the Citadel. Allan thought it would be "most difficult". His tiny force was too dispersed. He had sent officers to report the whereabouts of several Rifle Brigade groups who had not come in. He had no news of Major Knollys' company east of the Bassin nor of Keller and the tanks. The Q.V.R. company from Bastion 2 was still missing. Nicholson agreed that the plan for a final defence of the Citadel was not likely to succeed. He wished the Rifle Brigade luck and went back through the fire and smoke of the town.

During the 25th, the Rifle Brigade had used all their ammunition, including reserves, and had issued the 20,000 rounds landed by the Navy a few hours before. Most of these had already been fired. They were short of Bren guns which became easily clogged, like rifles, in the sand. The weapons had to be constantly cleaned. Only a few 3-inch mortar bombs were left and the last was fired many hours

before they were compelled to give in. Allan estimated that next morning he would have these numbers to continue the fight:
"A" Company (Peel): Three officers and eighty men with two Brens.
"B" Company (Hamilton-Russell): Two officers and forty men with one Bren.
"I" Company (Brush): Two officers and thirty men with two Brens.
"C" Company (Knollys): One officer and twenty men with one Bren (whereabouts unknown).
H.Q. Company (Coghill): Four officers and eighty men with one Bren.
Captain Gordon-Duff's party: Two officers and forty men with one mortar and two or three Brens. (This party consisting of two platoons of spare drivers who had been charged with protection of the quays and harbour bridges from the 23rd.)

In all fourteen officers and 290 men, showing that the figure of sixty per cent casualties was if anything an underestimate.

The Q.V.R., Anti-aircraft and Searchlights now under Allan's command had about four officers and 200 men, only half of them armed. The shortage of weapons and ammunition was more serious than the shortage of men. With these depleted and tired forces, without field artillery or mortars, the Rifle Brigade calmly prepared to fight another day.

A patrol was sent out at 1 a.m. along the beach. They returned after five hours to report. The H.Q. Company of the Rifle Brigade was dug in at the Bastion de l'Estran and near them twenty-five riflemen were in trenches under the command of two young officers, 2/Lieuts. Surtees and Prittie. At the north-east end of the Bassin, the French blockhouse was occupied by the missing company of the Q.V.R. Of Knollys' company there was no sign. They were in fact further to the east.

Some time afterwards, the tangled events of the night were sorted out. The first party of Q.V.R. to leave Bastion 2 on the evening of 25th went north-east in the darkness instead of north-west. They met Knollys' company in their trenches and took up positions for the night. When dawn broke they could see warships in the Channel and hoped that boats would be sent to collect them. They were in very advanced positions, with Germans 200 yards away signalling them to surrender. But Knollys counter-attacked and dislodged the Germans. This enabled the Q.V.R. to move forward in the forlorn hope of escaping to Gravelines. Within a mile, they were surrounded by light tanks and forced to surrender. Shortly afterwards Knollys was overwhelmed by a tank attack without having regained contact with the Rifle Brigade.

The second party of Q.V.R. under 2/Lieut. Jabez-Smith who withdrew from Bastion 2 with several wounded, also lost their way and had an exhausting march in the sand. They reached the French blockhouse where they were discovered hours later, by the patrol which Allan had sent out. They agreed to withdraw to join the Rifle Brigade in the morning.

Jabez-Smith has left us a note of the scene from the top of the blockhouse:

> It was a very clear, warm night. At sea were the dark forms of the warships and the sky in their direction was crossed and recrossed with the beams of hundreds of searchlights from the English coast and from the ships. Calais was on fire. Red, orange and yellow flames burned skywards from various points in the town. From our platform it seemed that the whole city was burning. Between us and the city was a lake called the Bassin des Chasses and in this the flames were reflected. The scene made me think I was witnessing the sacking of some medieval walled city.

During the night they signalled with a torch to warships off Calais. After some hours, they seem to have attracted attention and were told "to await a reply". The result was a heavy air attack on the blockhouse by the Luftwaffe, but fortunately it escaped a direct hit. At dawn, they tried to retire but were forced back towards Gravelines, surrounded and captured.

Much the same fate befell a third party of Q.V.R. They struggled for hours in thick mud and weeds on the edge of the Bassin after leaving Bastion 2. During the night they reached the coast and saw a fully-lit hospital ship putting to sea. They lay under cover during the day and at nightfall, while trying to escape to Gravelines, ran into a hidden German position and were forced to surrender.

Ellison-Macartney was not sure of the fate of these men till it was possible to piece the story together in a prisoner-of-war camp. He had the remnants of two companies, and gave them orders to take up positions in support of the Rifle Brigade. A hundred and fifty Q.V.R. manned blocks, made by vehicles, across the railway lines by the water tower. During the night they received fresh orders. These were to occupy the pumping station opposite the Pont Vétillard and the rampart behind the water tower along the south-west shore of the Bassin. From the top of this, they could cover any approach from Calais-Nord.

Thirty or forty men helped to block the roads to the Bastion de l'Estran and Bastion 1. Hope that they would be evacuated, despite clear orders to the contrary, still sustained them and continued till the last round was fired next afternoon. In sight of the cliffs of Dover, they could not believe that in the last hour, the Navy would not come to their rescue. Many company commanders half-believed this. For some, disillusionment would be bitter.

At 2.30 a.m. on Sunday the 26th, Commodore W. P. Gandell, R.N. the principal Sea Transport Officer who had been at Bastion 1 during the night, met Allan. The wireless message for a hospital carrier was sent. It arrived two or three hours afterwards taking with it over a hundred wounded. It may have been the brightly lit ship which the Q.V.R. saw from the dunes. With it went Hoskyns, gravely wounded, to die in England. Gandell, like Admiral Ramsay, was anxious to take off as many men as possible. But when the final orders came from Churchill, Nicholson made it plain that there could be no evacuation save for the wounded.

By midnight, but for the roar of the flames around the Place d'Armes, the old town of Calais was quiet. At the Citadel, Lieutenant Evitts saw the shapes of three destroyers lying just offshore in the stillness of the night. There was a wild cheer. Could this be the "final evacuation" after all? For more than an hour the destroyers bombarded the Germans. But when Evitts awoke at the Citadel at dawn, they had vanished.

At midnight, Miller decided to see Nicholson at the Citadel. He struggled through the streets to the entrance and with difficulty got past nervous French sentries. The fortress was on fire at many places and he found the Brigade Staff, shrouded in smoke, sheltering in slit trenches on top of an embankment. Nicholson was not there. He was still visiting the troops which he had been tireless in doing all day despite his apparent isolation by making his headquarters at the Citadel. He did not see Miller at the Rue des Marèchaux until 1.30 a.m. when he brought with him a copy of Eden's message.

Though evacuation was out of the question, many false hopes were raised by the presence of the destroyers. Miller reported that the battalion had had "a good day" but it could not go on indefinitely. The fires raging in the town were a serious handicap and might be the deciding factor. Nicholson nodded. Wearily he made off through the burning streets. His last orders to Miller were that should his present positions become untenable, he was to join with the Rifle Brigade and make a "last effort" at the Citadel. This was the plan which Allan had thought too difficult and it was never attempted.

In the dignified tragedy of the last hours at Calais, individual soldiers showed a splendid contempt for danger. At 1 a.m. on 26th May, Lance-Corporal Humby and Rifleman Ewings of the 60th were sent across the Pont Faidherbe to search the saloon car which had followed behind the German tanks on the previous evening. It now stood wrecked at the end of the bridge. They found it only 100 yards away from a German post on the Quai du Danube whose voices they clearly heard. They reached the car, finding inside the body of a German pioneer officer, and returned across the bridge with his papers which contained valuable information. It took them two whole hours to cross and recross the bridge in the darkness under continuous small arms fire. Humby had already distinguished himself earlier in the day. He was in command of a detachment of the 60th in one of the houses on the canal front which was entirely destroyed by enemy fire and he continued to fight from the ruins.

At 3.30 a.m. all companies of the 60th stood to on the last morning of the battle. As it grew light, their white faces beneath steel helmets could be seen in shattered windows and doorways and behind the final road-blocks. Every man knew that this Sunday morning, when the bells of Notre Dame were silent, would test the stoutest hearts. Sheer weariness, hunger and thirst made some wonder if the fight could possibly continue. There was little time to falter. At 5 a.m. the whole of Guderian's corps artillery, about double the number of guns of the previous day, bombarded the 60th on the waterfront and "C" Company in front of the Citadel and Bastion 11. Many fresh guns brought up from Boulogne were firing into Calais from the west.

Churchill, Eden, and Ironside had taken their terrible decision to sacrifice the garrison. But Admiral Ramsay did not give up hope of saving some of them. His father had been a soldier and he was distressed by the thought of their fate. During the morning he received this message from Commodore Gandell who had left Calais Quay about 8 a.m.

SECRET

Immediate Situation at Calais up to 0800 this Sunday morning

1) Enemy hold greater part of Northern town. They have one heavy and one light battery and plenty of ammunition. Quay and harbour under machine-gun fire.
2) Our troops in Citadel and round Outer Port. Troops dead beat and no tanks left.
3) Water essential also food if decided to reinforce.
4) Naval gunfire and air attack effective for temporary neutralisation only of artillery fire.
5) Very difficult to get anything in but personnel. Personnel not impossible provided air attack and gunfire can be neutralised. Any ships drawing more than 14 feet would be aground at low water.
6) French troops at Fort Risban in large numbers but quite demoralised.
7) Reinforcements would have to be on a considerable scale as present garrison dead beat. They will have to compete with artillery, machine-guns and tanks. Enemy are definitely weary.

8) Reinforcement probably a forlorn hope and liable to heavy casualties. Ships liable to be sunk alongside thus blocking quay.
9) As regards evacuation we might get off a proportion amounting at a rough estimate to three hundred by ferrying troops off in boats to waiting trawlers and Destroyers. This number might well be exceeded.
10) A decision essential today as to either reinforcement or evacuation.

According to Lord Moran, Churchill said: "I gave that order: it was my decision, although it sickened me to have to do it. But it was Calais that made the evacuation at Dunkirk possible." But he did not do it alone. Both Eden and Ironside shared the responsibility and the anguish.

Gandell's report underestimated the hopeless situation of the defenders. The 229th Anti-tank Battery had lost all eight guns. Captain Woodley and the surviving gunners were fighting with the Rifle Brigade. There were no British tanks left in action. Infantry battalions were down to about 250 men each. It was evidently too late to land reinforcements. There was to be more support from naval guns and R.A.F. bombing of the Germans on the afternoon of the 26th and even on the morning of the 27th. But by then, the weight of numbers and firepower had overwhelmed the few left to defend Calais.

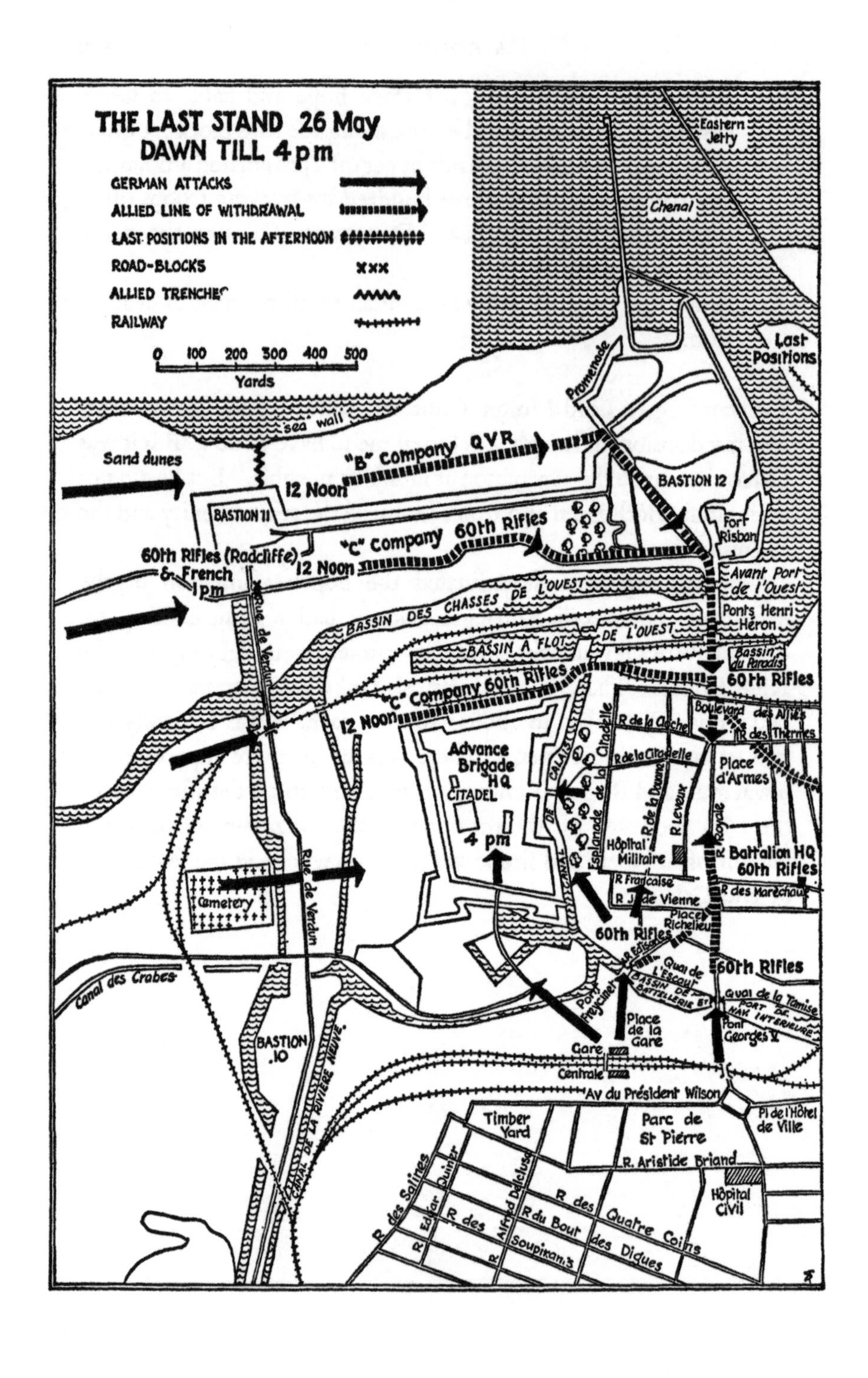
THE LAST STAND 26 May
DAWN TILL 4 pm
GERMAN ATTACKS
ALLIED LINE OF WITHDRAWAL
LAST POSITIONS IN THE AFTERNOON
ROAD-BLOCKS
ALLIED TRENCHES
RAILWAY
0 100 200 300 400 500
Yards
Eastern Jetty
Chenal
Last Positions
Promenade
sea wall
Sand dunes
"B" Company QVR
12 Noon
BASTION 12
BASTION 11
Fort Risban
"C" Company 60th Rifles
60th Rifles (Radcliffe) & French 1pm
12 Noon
Avant Port de l'Ouest
BASSIN DES CHASSES DE L'OUEST
Ponts Henri Héron
BASSIN A FLOT DE L'OUEST
Bassin du Paradis
"C" Company 60th Rifles
60th Rifles
12 Noon
Boulevard des Alliés
R des Thermes
R de la Cloche
Advance Brigade HQ
CITADEL
R de la Citadelle
Place d'Armes
Rue de Verdun
CALAIS
Esplanade de la Citadelle
R de la Douane
R Leveux
R Royale
4 pm
Hôpital Militaire
Battalion HQ 60th Rifles
R Française
R J. de Vienne
R des Maréchaux
Cemetery
Rue de Verdun
Place Richelieu
60th Rifles
60th Rifles
Quai de l'Escaut
BASSIN DE BATELLERIE
Canal des Crabes
Pont Freycinet
Quai de la Tamise
PORT DE NAV. INTERIEURE
Place de la Gare
Pont Georges V
BASTION 10
CANAL DE LA RIVIERE NEUVE
Gare Centrale
Av du Président Wilson
Timber Yard
Parc de St Pierre
Pl de l'Hôtel de Ville
R. Aristide Briand
Hôpital Civil
R des Salines
R Edgar Quinet
R Alfred Delcluse
R des Quatre Coins
R du Bout des Digues
R des Soupirants

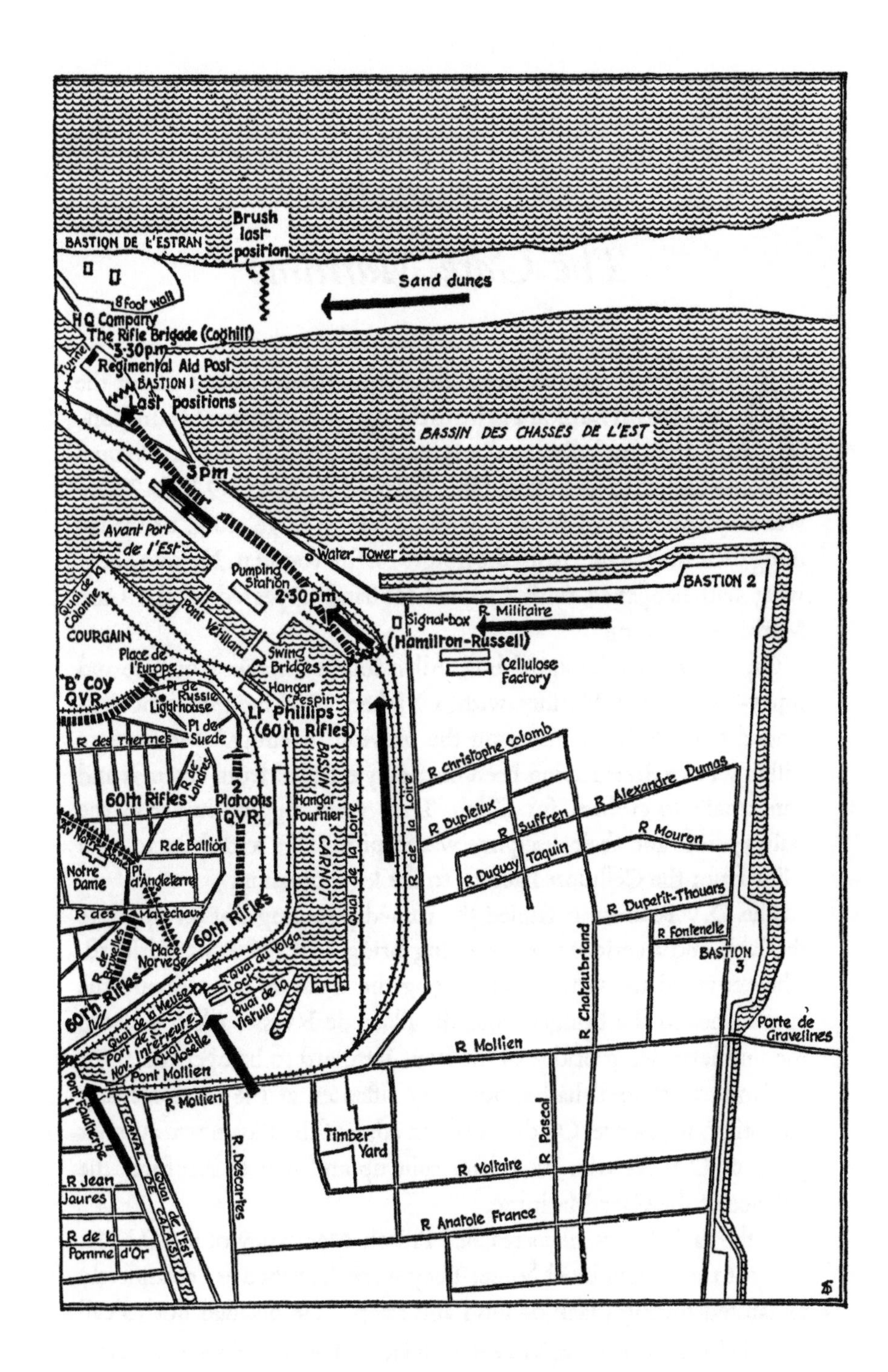
Brush last position
BASTION DE L'ESTRAN
Sand dunes
8 foot wall
HQ Company The Rifle Brigade (Coghill) 3.30 p.m.
Tunnel
Regimental Aid Post
BASTION I
Last positions
BASSIN DES CHASSES DE L'EST
3 pm
Avant Port de l'Est
Water Tower
Pumping Station
2.30 pm
BASTION 2
R Militaire
Signal-box
(Hamilton-Russell)
Cellulose Factory
Quai de la Colonne
COURGAIN
Pont Vétillard
Swing Bridges
Place de l'Europe
Hangar Crespin
"B" Coy QVR
Pl de Russie
Lighthouse
Lt Phillips (60th Rifles)
Pl de Suede
R des Thermes
R de Londres
BASSIN CARNOT
Hangar Fournier
Quai de la Loire
R de la Loire
R Christophe Colomb
R Alexandre Dumas
60th Rifles
2 Platoons QVR
R Dupleix
R Suffren
R Mouren
Av Notre Dame
R de Bastion
R Duguay Taquin
Notre Dame
Pl d'Angleterre
R Dupetit-Thouars
R des Maréchaux
60th Rifles
R Fontenelle
R de Bruxelles
Place Norvege
Quai du Volga
Lock
Quai de la Vistula
BASTION 3
R Chateaubriand
60th Rifles
Quai de la Meuse
Port de Nav. Intérieure
Quai du Moselle
Porte de Gravelines
R Mollien
Pont Mollien
Pont Faidherbe
R Mollien
CANAL DE CALAIS
Quai de l'Est
R. Descartes
Timber Yard
R Pascal
R Voltaire
R Jean Jaures
R Anatole France
R de la Pomme d'Or

CHAPTER SEVENTEEN

The Gare Maritime

AT the first light on the 26th, Major Allan walked along the road from Bastion 1 as far as the signal-box to meet Hamilton-Russell and discuss the Rifle Brigade dispositions. Colonel Ellison-Macartney went with him to give orders to the Q.V.R. There was no further word from Nicholson, and a huge cloud of smoke hung over the Citadel from the houses on fire round it. No one knew what had happened until Colonel Holland appeared at the Gare Maritime at 1 p.m.

On the way to the signal-box, Allan found Captain Courtice and thirty-five Royal Marines with a Vickers machine-gun who had landed from H.M.S. *Verity* on the previous evening.[1] Many were still in service dress having been hurriedly recalled from cinemas and dance halls to embark for Calais. They were digging in across the railway lines and their discipline was inspiring. He told them to hold a line from the Cellulose Factory to the level crossing.

The Q.V.R. now occupied the ruined pumping station opposite the lock and overlooking the swing bridges of the Pont Vétillard. They covered the railway lines along the Quai de la Loire and the approaches to the bridges from the Place de Russie. Allan ordered the southern swing bridge of the Pont Vétillard to be opened.

Hamilton-Russell had about forty riflemen at the level-crossing and others in reserve. On the northern edge of the Bassin was another party of Q.V.R. who were later split up and sent to reinforce the defence of the Gare Maritime.

In the early hours, news reached Ellison-Macartney of the Q.V.R. party at the French blockhouse. They were described as "completely exhausted through lack of food and sleep". He decided not to call

[1] Including those at the Citadel, *Verity* landed four officers and sixty Royal Marines.

them in. They were as well placed in the sand dunes and safer than at the overcrowded Gare Maritime. But they were much nearer the enemy and he did not see them again during the battle.

"During the past forty-eight hours," wrote Ellison-Macartney, "the Gare Maritime had become the focal point for all stragglers and leader-less personnel."

Some had drunk deeply from the hundreds of bottles of wine and champagne in the cellar of the hotel. They were now ordered to get out and fight. Two hundred men from different units who had been on the shores of the Bassin were also armed with rifles and moved in as reinforcements to different parts of the line.

Hamilton-Russell, with headquarters at the water tower, was in charge of the defence of the Gare Maritime. Besides men of his own company, at the level-crossing and signal-box, he had three officers and about 120 men under Major Brush and Captain Peel. These were on the quay and "able to fire across the Bassin". They were joined by the staff of Nicholson's rear brigade headquarters at the Gare Maritime who now took their places in the line. The Rifle Brigade party commanded by Captain Gordon-Duff still faced westwards towards the town guarding the Pont Vétillard.

By 4.30 a.m., Allan had given his orders at the signal-box to all officers and men. They were very tired but confident that they could hold on for a few hours.

"All troops stay in these positions to the last. There will be no further withdrawals."

It was difficult to make further withdrawals except to the seashore. Allan repeated Eden's last order as the first shells of the day came in and crashed on the quays.

Leaving Hamilton-Russell and Ellison-Macartney at the signal-box, he went by truck to the Gare Maritime. On his way, he passed men of the Searchlights plodding up towards the sand dunes. Major Deighton their commander had been severely wounded the previous evening on the embankment near the Cellulose Factory. Their remaining officers had been ordered to move at dawn, and occupy a line of trenches in the sand between the north shore of the Bassin and the sea. Senior officers of the 6th Heavy A.A. Battery took command of them. When they reached there the area was already under shellfire.

At the Gare Maritime, Allan found a naval doctor, Lieutenant Waind, who had come ashore from one of the destroyers during the night and was now in charge of the wounded. Waind confirmed that a hundred wounded had been taken off before dawn in the hospital carrier. When the destroyers withdrew on Admiralty orders during the night, he was left behind and taken prisoner. As the situation grew more desperate, he was forced out of his dressing station at the Gare Maritime and moved to the tunnel under Bastion 1.

Allan did not yet regard the Rifle Brigade situation as hopeless. He was now forced to hurry round on foot. Before the worst of the shelling started at 7 a.m., he tried to strengthen the defence of the few hundred yards of sand dunes, smashed railway trucks and shell-torn quays which formed his command. After leaving Waind, he saw the Searchlights who now occupied trenches dug two days before by the Rifle Brigade, and faced east. Allan impressed on them that they were the mainstay of the left flank and were to hold on at whatever cost. Men who had no rifles were to take shelter under the sea wall, presumably to await the inevitable end.

As Allan left the dunes, the shelling increased in violence and accuracy. At the Gare Maritime he was joined by his young signal officer Jerry Duncanson, an intrepid character who was killed that afternoon when the last rounds were fired in the sandhills. With him too was Regimental-Sergeant-Major E. Goodey who had been, throughout these fearsome days, a wonderful example of steadiness under fire. He took over all that remained of the small arms ammunition and began to distribute it at 6 a.m.

Sunday the 26th was a morning when courage and discipline really mattered. If the town was to be held another day, the Rifle Brigade and its auxiliaries, red eyed and sleepless, would have to make a supreme effort. The Germans must be made to fight to the very finish.

The first signs of weakening came unhappily from the French. At 8 a.m. a white flag was seen flying from the French troops in trenches on the west side of the harbour near Fort Risban. De Lambertye and another naval officer were on a visit to Allan at the Gare Maritime, and about to start "breakfast". They agreed to order the lowering of the white flag, but before they could leave, the shelling in the station area became so bad that "breakfast" was interrupted. In spite of his age and poor health, de Lambertye left by the footbridge and induced the French to obey him. But they were being dive-bombed and shelled and the white flag was soon flying again.

De Lambertye was next at the Citadel and later in the morning, while crossing the Pont Henri Héron to Fort Risban, he collapsed and died of a heart attack. He had valiantly defended the sea front and without him it would certainly have been deserted by most of the French on the 24th May.

From 9.15 a.m. the Germans moved forward slowly on the canal front aided by very precise mortar fire. Two German infantry companies attacked the lock at the Arrière Bassin and were held up by the 60th and two platoons of the Q.V.R. on the Quai de la Meuse and the Quai du Volga. A third turned north-east to attack Hamilton-Russell's road-block. In the south, the Germans were not yet across the canal bridges. They were received by heavy machine-gun fire from the 60th and reported "very hard fighting" to General Schaal.

At the Gare Maritime, Allan again visited the signal-box, where an officer with a corporal from the quartermaster's stores were manning a Vickers gun. They were being fired on from a building beside the Cellulose Factory and two platoons of the Q.V.R.s moved forward to search the place. They could find no Germans. Probably a fifth columnist with an automatic weapon had been concealed there and escaped.

From the embankment by the water tower, it was possible to see across the Bassin to the eastern shore. Brush and his party could now see German infantry, working round to the north-east. They had captured the French blockhouse and were firing mortars from it and from Bastion 2. They were trying to force the Rifle Brigade back to the seashore from two directions.

At 10.45 a.m., Allan sent a wireless message to Dover asking that the blockhouse be shelled. The message was repeated by Lieutenant Millett the Brigade Signals Officer at 1.56 p.m., but not in time to save the Rifle Brigade. Both messages were in clear, for Allan had been told to destroy all codes on the previous evening. In spite of this, the Admiralty signalled at 12.48 p.m. on the 26th:

"Codes left in *Conidaw*.[2] Suggest you fetch them if any naval signalman available to work them."

Millett replied at 1.0 p.m.:

"*Conidaw* sailed did not give us codes. Require naval rating to work codes."

In the midst of a hail of mortar bombs this must have been an exasperating exchange. Millett had already had trouble with "bogus" messages by "unauthorised officers" who had given orders to his signallers without his knowledge. It is not known who these people were. In one case on the previous evening it might have been a spy, but more likely the noise of battle led to confusion. At 10.37 a.m. on the 26th a signal was dispatched to Dover:

"Please cancel bogus message. Have been heavily bombed and am fired at all round but can see no targets. Allan Calais quay."

The message referred to the difficulty of seeing the enemy in the huge clouds of smoke which continued to roll from a burning oil depot on the Rue de la Loire and to the skill with which the Germans concealed their mortar positions. By now, the number of men wounded had become a serious problem for Lieutenant Waind. He had little or no surgical equipment or trained help. Allan signalled Dover for another naval surgeon to be sent by destroyer. Though a motor torpedo boat took off some wounded at 2.30 p.m., no further medical assistance arrived.

About 11 a.m., Allan realised that the Germans might soon assault the Gare Maritime. He told Millett to destroy all the brigade signals equipment and files, leaving one wireless truck in action so that he could remain in touch with Dover. The Stuka raid on the Citadel ordered by Guderian, which set most of Calais-Nord on fire, had stopped, and German infantry were again advancing. The Rifle Brigade and Q.V.R. on the embankment of the Bassin came under heavy small arms fire from the shore. A tremendous battle could be heard raging in the town where the 60th were still holding on the canal front. From time to time messengers came from Colonel

[2] A Royal Naval echo-sounding yacht which berthed early on the 26th May.

Miller to discover the situation on the quay. It was no longer possible for him to communicate by radio for the batteries had given out on the previous night.

Reports that the 60th might withdraw north-east to the Place de l'Europe, encouraged Allan to hold on to the Gare Maritime as long as he could. There might still be a chance of joining in a final defence of the harbour.

Messengers at some peril crossed the northern swing bridge by the footway which was still intact. Though the bridge itself had been damaged, a number of anti-tank mines had been placed on it.

Just before 11 a.m. dressed only in a shirt and battledress trousers, and wearing a steel helmet, I appeared at the bridge from the direction of the Place d'Armes. My apparition caused a sensation among the Q.V.R. lining the platform of the Gare Maritime.

I had passed the night of the 25th in the cellar of the Hôpital Militaire and as the light began to show through a trapdoor, heard the first shells whine over the town. Punctually at 9.30 a.m., the Stukas screamed down. As the wounded cowered in their blankets, bombs fell among the mulberry trees of the hospital garden. Stones and plaster from the cellar roof dropped among the rows of bandaged men. In the candlelight, I could see a man with his jaw blown off, trying to speak: another blinded. The smell of wounds and fear was overpowering.

After each wave of dive-bombers there was a strange silence, only the flames crackled. Nurses sought the dying in the dust of the cellar, with the few drugs and medicines rescued from the wrecked dispensary. The English wounded laughed and made bets on the time when the next wave of Stukas would come.

Just before 10 a.m. a bomb dropped in the Rue Leveux within a yard of the main doors and blew them in (see photograph facing page 144). The cellar shook and the candles went out. I was terrified that with the next direct hit the wounded would be buried alive. When the bombing ceased, I decided that, since I was now able to walk, I would go to the Gare Maritime and get transport. I might still be possible to evacuate the wounded by sea. Anything was better for them than entombment in the ruins of the Hôpital Militaire.

Médécin-Commandant Devulder of Boulogne stood looking at the garden which the day before had been a quiet place with its mulberry trees and soft shadows. Five riflemen were buried there who had died in the cellar. The trees were uprooted: bricks, stones and glass covered the flowerbeds. Devulder, a hero of the previous war, with rows of decorations, was looking at the sky, fearing another attack. Nurses and hospital orderlies crowded round him. I climbed out of the cellar with a corporal who volunteered to join me. I spoke to Devulder: "I am going to the Gare Maritime to get help. It may be still possible to get the less serious cases out of here."

"You are crazy, mon lieutenant. You do not know what is happening in the town."

"The men will only be taken prisoner if they stay here. I believe hospital ships can still get into the harbour."

He turned to me: "You are absolutely determined to sacrifice your life?"

I was not interested in anything of the kind, nor had I any idea of the true situation in Calais. I was irrationally confident that I could get through. The corporal and I made a painful start. Watched by the hospital staff, we crawled beneath the great double doors of the Hôpital Militaire, blown in by the blast. In the Rue Leveux we leant against a wall, exhausted. The building next-door on the corner of the Rue Française had received a direct hit. Opposite, a whole row of houses burned. Charred paper blew like leaves along the narrow street. We walked slowly northwards. I was doubled up by the wound in my side and the thick smoke made it hard to breathe. My companion was limping badly, as, without meeting anyone, we reached the Boulevard des Alliés and turned eastwards. To the south we could hear rifle and machine-gun fire.

Calais-Nord seemed empty and silent after the dive-bombing. Then, without warning, shells whistled and burst near us as we passed the Courgain. The corporal vanished in the blinding flash and dust. I fell to the ground unhurt and crawled to the side of the street where a hand stretched out from a cellar window, holding a bottle of cognac. I drank from it, and staggered on towards the lighthouse.

I had not met a soul save for the occupant of the cellar, an old

Frenchman. I wandered, dazed, across the Place de Russie as far as the footway at the northern swing bridge at the Pont Vétillard. I could see the figures of British troops in front of the station. I waved to them and began to make my way slowly across towards a row of rifles pointing straight at me.

"Hurry up," shouted an officer.

This was Major Timpson, second-in-command of the Q.V.R. I came face to face with the riflemen lying on the platform and across the tracks, ready to open fire. The Gare Maritime was a scene of disorder, the platform thick with broken glass and the bodies of British soldiers. Below, cognac was dispensed to me as I told the Q.V.R. my story. I was viewed with suspicion and my identity card was inspected several times.

My statement that I had met no one in the town, that transport should be sent to collect the wounded from the hospital cellar, was thought to be peculiar. Obviously I was either a fifth columnist or delirious. In my shirt were two jagged holes and large bloodstains on my left side. None of these outward signs inspired confidence in my judgment of the situation. I was ushered to the cellar of the Gare Maritime, where other wounded lay. In a few minutes the whole area was furiously mortared and I was rushed to the tunnel under Bastion 1 which now became the regimental aid post under Lieutenant Waind.

CHAPTER EIGHTEEN

The Final Stand

GENERAL SCHAAL's plan for the capture of Calais included heavy shelling of the Citadel and Calais-Nord from 8.30 a.m. to 9 a.m. Infantry were then to attack the Citadel over the Canal de la Rivière Neuve and capture the key Bastion 11. There was to be further heavy shelling from 9.30 a.m. to 10.15 a.m., followed by an infantry attack over the three bridges and entry of the Citadel by the eastern gate. The attacks were carried out methodically but they took much longer to achieve results than Schaal expected.

The artillery barrage fell most heavily on the companies of the 60th in the centre, commanded by Lord Cromwell and Major Trotter. They were holding on, precariously, at the Pont Georges Cinq and the Pont Freycinet. It was here that the Germans concentrated their efforts to force the bridges and capture the Citadel. They claimed at 10.50 a.m. that their gunners had scored direct hits on the 60th road-blocks and were crossing the bridges. Half an hour later, Schaal thought the position so favourable that many tanks were pulled out of the battle.

The situation of the 60th was desperate. A death-struggle developed at the bridges. Barricades of burned-out lorries and trucks off the Rue Edison and the Place Richelieu were manned by the surviving officers and riflemen. Houses in this area had long since been devastated by the flames and blown by shellfire into heaps of rubble behind which the defenders fired on the Germans. The mortar bombs came in an endless stream exploding dead on the road-blocks.

The 60th, lying without cover in the streets, had little protection from the Stukas. No one who experienced the attack on the morning of the 26th is ever likely to forget it. A hundred aircraft attacked the Citadel and the old town in waves. They dived in threes, with a prolonged scream, dropping one high explosive and three or four incendiary bombs. They machine-gunned the streets and dropped a few heavy bombs between the 60th headquarters in the Rue des Marèchaux and the docks. Each of this series of attacks lasted twenty-five minutes. The first effects on the defence were paralysing but, as others had experienced with Stukas, the damage was moral rather than physical. Within a few minutes the riflemen eagerly fired Bren guns and engaged the Stukas, one of which was brought down on the seashore.

But the air attack hit the 60th in Bastion 11 and round the Citadel especially hard. The French, under de la Blanchardière at Bastion 11, lost three officers and many men killed in a single raid. The Stukas came and went, leaving Calais-Nord a furnace, and then German infantry attacked again. They were once more thrown back at the Pont Freycinet where they had crossed into the streets of Calais-Nord and were advancing along the esplanade in front of the Citadel.

Schaal complained that the British were shooting *his* troops in the back from the houses. But it was German sniping at the 60th road-blocks from across the canal which finally made them untenable.

Like the Rifle Brigade at the harbour, the regiment fulfilled those great traditions to which Eden had referred in his signal.

At the Place Richelieu, Lord Cromwell, firing a Bren gun, was three times wounded that morning. He had already shown all those qualities that add up to real leadership in war. He was hit by bullets in both arms and in the head, the sight of one eye being badly affected. And yet he remained in command when all men at his barricade, save himself and two riflemen were dead. At 11.30 a.m. he was compelled to fall back to the line of the Rue des Marèchaux.

At the corner of the Rue Edison (see photographs facing page 145) Claude Bower was defending a barricade of vehicles and sandbags until he fell mortally wounded, after showing the greatest courage for hours on end. The street was lashed by machine-gun fire which made it suicide for stretcher-bearers to cross and bring him in. Rifleman Matthews drove in a truck across the open street. He backed it into position to rescue Bower, but he was already dead. Matthews removed several others badly wounded, and got away unscathed.

Those who witnessed this wonderful achievement never forgot it and it appears in many private accounts of the battle. Matthews was awarded the Distinguished Conduct Medal.

To the east in front of the Pont Faidherbe, the 60th were forced out of flaming buildings on the Quai de la Tamise at 7 a.m. but later reoccupied the ruins. They held grimly on with the few riflemen who remained since the death of Major Owen on the previous evening.

At 10 a.m. a tank attack was launched on the Pont Faidherbe. It was closely supported by mortars and German infantry who accompanied one of the tanks on to the bridge. They were driven back by Captain Duncanson and Lance-Corporal Pickett. Firing an anti-tank rifle and a Bren gun they killed six German infantrymen and the tank withdrew. Both men were already wounded.

On the left, "B" Company of the 60th under Poole were subjected to continuous shelling and sniping at the Place de Norvège and on the quays. About 10 a.m., German infantry began to work forward and cross the canal. The survivors of a scout platoon commanded by 2/Lieut. Warre, who was killed shortly afterwards, were shelled out of their posts for a time. They were reoccupied and held until 3 p.m. when a general withdrawal of the 60th from forward posts had already taken place.

When Cromwell reported that the barricades in the centre could no longer be held, German troops were already in the Rue Jean de Vienne and the Rue Française and firing down these streets against his company's flank. After Bower was killed, their tanks crossed the Pont Freycinet and crushed a section under Lieutenant Perkins of the R.A.O.C. Perkins was in a building overlooking the bridge. With drivers and ordnance men he had held out since the morning of the 25th. He was killed and his body buried under piles of masonry. Staff Sergeant Wass was severely wounded but refused to leave his post.

With men like these, Miller could still contemplate holding on. Though every house around him was on fire, and no support from tanks, aircraft, or naval guns was forthcoming, he planned and carried out an orderly withdrawal. This was to be done in stages, the first rearguard position being the line of the Rue des Marèchaux. Miller went with his adjutant to the lighthouse, looking for a final position to keep in touch with the Rifle Brigade. He searched the area but found it too exposed. He tried the Citadel, and went to see if it were still possible to enter from the east, but the roads leading to the entrance were swept by machine-gun fire. The moat and bridge over the canal at its eastern face were impassable and its fall could only be a matter of time.

Miller retraced his steps and decided to make his final stand on a line of posts in the north-east corner of Calais-Nord from the Boulevard des Alliés to the Place d'Angleterre. Here he hoped to hang on till dark and make contact with the Rifle Brigade. This cool and deliberate preparation for what everyone knew must be the end of the battle, included the withdrawal of most of "C" Company of the 60th on the western side, from their positions in front of the Citadel and Bastion 11. The last reserve of one section had been sent to help them and they held on till noon despite severe losses.

Captain Radcliffe, who commanded Bastion 11, volunteered to remain in this exposed position with eighty riflemen and a handful of French officers and sailors to cover the retirement of "C" Company.

The defence of Bastion 11 was truly heroic. Since the 25th May Capitaine de la Blanchardière and Capitaine de Metz had placed themselves under Radcliffe's command. At 3 a.m. on the 26th, they heard the hoot of an owl from the German lines. Shells and mortar bombs followed, blowing great clouds of sand into the air. At 7 a.m. de Metz was killed and de la Blanchardière badly wounded. Aspirant Pierre Nielly, a Dominican (now the Révérend Père Nielly) took command of the French. He too was hit in the chest. "The Volunteers of Calais" fought with the greatest gallantry.

When the Germans surrounded Bastion 11 at 1 p.m., very few unwounded men remained. British and French refused to surrender but their ammunition finished, they could not prevent the Germans from storming the bastion with hand grenades. Of the French sailors and soldiers, only seventeen remained alive and André Berthe recalls that, just before the end, Capitaine de la Blanchardière, lying on a stretcher, addressed them: "We have fought for the honour of France."

De la Blanchardière lived up to his beliefs. Later in the war, he joined the French Resistance and died in Mauthausen concentration camp after torture.

Only thirty of the eighty riflemen of the 60th were unwounded. Radcliffe, who many remember coolly blowing the sand out of his revolver, was faced by a furious German officer. The German casualties had been heavy and the officer made a cut-throat gesture at Radcliffe, who slapped his thighs and roared with laughter. The German walked off, nonplussed.

Miller commended Corporal McBride and Rifleman Dinnie for their brave and unselfish conduct while serving in "C" Company before they withdrew. McBride commanded a section at Bastion 11 for two days in continuous danger. He carried a severely wounded man for 200 yards under fire, and having placed him under cover, returned to his section.

One of two trucks loaded with small arms, ammunition and mortar bombs, which were parked touching each other, was hit by an enemy shell and burst into flames. Under heavy fire, Rifleman Dinnie got into the other truck and drove it safely away. These are examples among many others, of the personal gallantry shown by the riflemen.

"C" Company withdrew along the Sangatte road and occupied a new line from Fort Risban to the north-east corner of the Place d'Armes. Covered by Radcliffe's sacrificial defence of Bastion 11, they established themselves at a few last, hopeless posts. The remaining men of the Q.V.R. company who had fought with them and a few Searchlight troops, also withdrew by the Ponts Henri-Héron—the swing bridges leading from Fort Risban. These bridges were blocked with vehicles and an officer was sent to the Gare Maritime to make contact with Ellison-Macartney. Another Q.V.R. party which had since 8 a.m. endured a heavy bombardment on the beach north of Bastion 11, retired along the shore, to rejoin the rest of the company in Calais-Nord.

By 1 p.m. what remained of the 60th were in their last positions. Trotter's company was on the west and south side of the Place d'Armes and Cromwell was along the Rue Notre Dame. The Head-quarter Company (Duncanson) was east of Notre Dame near the

Place d'Angleterre. It had been intended that "B" Company (Poole) should complete this line to the Place de Norvège. But they were still under terrific shellfire on the canal quays. In the confusion the orders to retire had not reached them. Perhaps a runner had been killed. Miller and 2/Lieut. R. Scott (the same officer who was wounded at Coquelles on the 24th) left the Place d'Armes to find out what had happened. They entered the Rue des Marèchaux from the Rue Notre Dame and then separated, Scott making for "B" Company headquarters in the direction of the canal. As he reached them, a sniper shot him dead in the street. He was twenty years old. Of its six officers, "B" Company now had three killed.

A platoon of "B" Company was at a very difficult and exposed block of houses on the Quai de la Meuse. The whole area of the canal front was swept by close-range mortar and machine-gun fire. The platoon commander 2/Lieut. Davies-Scourfield was struck by three bullets in the head, arm and body but still remained at his post.

The fierce resistance by the 60th was really worrying the Germans. Earlier in the morning, Schaal had thought the position so favourable that tanks were withdrawn to cover the coast in case another British landing took place. By 11.30 a.m. a heavy battery had to be brought up to Coulogne "to increase the pressure on Fort Risban". Guderian's chief of staff rang up to ask whether the division expected to take Calais that day. If not, the attack was to be stopped and "the town destroyed by the Luftwaffe". Schaal replied optimistically that he was quite sure that Calais would fall during the day. Fifteen minutes later, the Germans were driven back again at the Pont Freycinet. Tanks had to be restored to the battle to support the infantry in the house-to-house fighting which was certain to develop once they regained their foothold in Calais-Nord. At noon, there were requests for the Citadel to be shelled again. Such was the spirit of Le Tellier's troops and the Royal Marines, even after the horrific bombing of two hours before, that this entry appears in the Tenth Panzer Division War Diary:

"Enemy gives impression of being fresh, seems to have received reinforcements."

In reality, the defenders of the Citadel, though protected by the strength of Vauban's cellars, were in a hopeless position. The size of the fortress itself was a serious disadvantage when there were barely 200 men to man the ramparts.

At 12.40 p.m. Guderian himself arrived on the scene of the fighting. He was told that, although the attack was going slowly, the division had "the impression that they can still take Calais today".

There must have been some anxiety on this score, for Guderian discussed whether there should be a renewed attack by Stukas on the following day "in case the taking of Calais by the Tenth Panzer Division does not succeed today". He asked Schaal to report to him by 3 p.m. whether the town could be taken or whether the Luftwaffe should be called in on the next day. He remained in the neighbourhood, apparently in some concern about the outcome of the battle. He had already wasted valuable days and lost many officers and men killed in taking Calais.

Schaal was "absolutely convinced" that Calais would soon fall. And he was right. From 1 p.m. onwards the position of the defence quickly worsened.

At the Gare Maritime, Allan saw that the Germans were advancing and would soon cut off all retreat. As the Anti-aircraft and Searchlight men were forced back to the Bastion de l'Estran, he sent Brush with thirty Rifle Brigade reinforcements to the north shore of the Bassin. There Brush took up his last position, joining the twenty-five riflemen already in trenches 200 yards east of the Bastion de l'Estran.

The Q.V.R. in the Cellulose Factory were overrun and the Royal Marines were forced out of their positions on the railway track. Captain Courtice and Lieutenant Bruce of the Royal Marines brought back the Vickers machine-gun, which they mounted on Bastion 1 and continued firing at the enemy till the last moment. The remaining troops of the Rifle Brigade were forced to withdraw from the embankment past the water tower to the top of the Bastion.

Allan set out on foot for the signal-box to find Hamilton-Russell. It was difficult to cover even short distances. The way was blocked by shattered rolling-stock and burned-out vehicles. Near the water tower, he stopped to order 2/Lieut. Rolt to take the only 3-inch mortar to the sand dunes, where it was used to silence a German post until it was itself knocked out.

Allan and Hamilton-Russell missed each other in the chaos of this savage battle. Hamilton-Russell had already moved back from the signal-box to the fork in the road to Bastion 1. He may have believed a rumour that Allan had been killed, and been concerned to watch the beach where the Germans were advancing. In the smoke and din, it was impossible to be sure what was happening. At about 1.30 p.m., he was mortally wounded and although he was put aboard a small ship at the eastern jetty, he died in hospital at Dover.

Everything that soldiers could do without artillery or other aid had now been done to carry out Eden's orders. At 2.30 p.m., the German infantry commanders told Schaal that the fall of the Citadel was a matter of one or two hours and the rest of the town would be swiftly captured. They urged that an attack by Stukas next day was unnecessary. Their prediction was correct.

CHAPTER NINETEEN

"Every Man for Himself"

BRIGADIER Nicholson knew that his refusal to surrender meant that further lives would be lost. But Eden's last order was clear. The loss of Calais could mean the defeat of the British in France.

In the nineteen-thirties, it had been the opinion of the Staff College that, without the Channel ports to supply them, the B.E.F. would not be able to fight. Like many senior officers in France, Nicholson had no doubt that this would mean capitulation and the end of the war. He was aware of his fearful responsibility to hold Calais at whatever cost.

After the fall of the Citadel, the Germans claimed that a French officer told them that he had urged Nicholson to surrender twenty-four hours before and that he refused this advice. Since Nicholson died in captivity, no one can be sure. But he was a man of stern principle and he did not believe in surrender. He left a pencilled comment which I have seen, on the accounts prepared in his prison camp, that he had remained at the Citadel to "steady the French". There is evidence that his presence there restored morale. He remained unperturbed, even when the fall of the town was only a matter of time, though his disappointment and frustration were deep. Till the last he was to be seen visiting the road-blocks in Calais-Nord.

When Stukas came screaming out of the sky on the morning of Sunday, the 26th May, Colonel Holland ordered all troops to leave the ramparts of the Citadel and shelter in the deep brick-lined chambers beneath the bastions. Here they endured the bombardment with a mound of earth and sand ten feet thick above them. In the dim light, Lieutenant Evitts saw two casks of red wine from which the

French filled their water bottles. There being no water in the Citadel, the British did the same.

Few ordinary soldiers in the streets and sand dunes had time to ponder the strategic importance of the battle. They were in a hand-to-hand fight—bayonets were used more than once—to prevent the capture of the town. They did not need messages from the War Office. They were fighting for their lives and never more boldly than after 1 p.m. on the 26th. From that time, there was an extraordinary conflict around the Gare Maritime until the Germans delivered the *coup de grâce* at about 3.30 p.m.

Many of the younger men of the Rifle Brigade and their officers, though tired, were still fighting as if this were the last stages of a football match. Shouts of encouragement, even laughter, came from the trenches in the sand dunes. At 1.30 p.m., the Germans were only 400 yards from the Bastion de l'Estran and were seeking by a joint attack to converge at this point by advancing on the Gare Maritime.

The last two platoons of the Rifle Brigade had withdrawn to a position in line with the clock tower on the roof of the station. They held on here for over half an hour and were gradually forced back as the Royal Marine officers continued to fire the Vickers machine-gun over their heads from Bastion 1. Allan climbed the steep sandy path to the top of the bastion and saw that the whole area south of the Gare Maritime was hidden by smoke. He fired a belt of ammunition from the Vickers gun. It could not be long before the Germans assaulted the station itself. From 2.30 p.m. he saw a deadly mortar barrage brought down, creeping along the quays and platforms. Gordon-Duff's party at the Pont Vétillard suffered heavy caualties and were withdrawn.

Two of Lieutenant Millett's wireless vehicles had already been hit and set on fire and the flames spread to other vehicles. Millett drove a third vehicle away but he was later ordered to destroy it. From the evening of the 24th May he and his signallers had stuck to their earphones with shells and bombs exploding near them, and they were in contact with Dover as late as 1.56 p.m.

The last message from Calais recorded at Dover was:

"Here is Lieutenant Millett Signal Officer, I have an emergency call for you. Tell Dover to shell between Fort 888793 to Brewery 880788. Very urgent am being shelled."

This was a request for the Navy to shell German mortar positions between the French blockhouses east of the Bassin and the Cellulose Factory described in the message as a brewery.

It was plainly impossible to hold the Gare Maritime any longer. As Allan gave orders to evacuate it, a stream of dazed, unarmed soldiers from different units who had been sheltering in the cellars emerged and were hurried into the sand dunes. Only a small group of riflemen with a few unwounded officers, were now left to fire on the Germans from the top of Bastion 1 as they moved forward through the smoke. Nicholson's staff-captain, Coxwell-Rogers, died here. The mound of earth above the bastion and the tunnel beneath have not changed since 1940. From it you can see the railway and the Cellulose Factory as the Rifle Brigade did more than thirty years ago (see photographs facing page 128).

A group of twenty Rifle Brigade and Q.V.R. under Rolt made a last attempt to form a line where the road to the Bastion de l'Estran forks to the tunnel. The Germans were at the junction, when Rolt rushed at them, with a few others, at ten yards range and drove them off. Most of his men were killed. Rolt had already won the Military Cross with his carrier section in the town. Untiring, he performed this final act of defiance. It was only after all British troops in his rear had been overwhelmed, that he handed over his two empty revolvers.

There could be no doubt of the outcome of the battle, but the Rifle Brigade remained in action for another hour. They were now shut in by the Germans among the tussocks of grass and sandhills in an area two or three hundred yards square, with the sea on either side of them.

In the trenches east of the Bastion de l'Estran, Brush, Peel, and fifty men were under heavy mortar fire. Most of them had rifles, but the party had only one Lewis gun and one Bren gun which were frequently choked with sand. In their rear at the Bastion de l'Estran, was Major Coghill with four officers and sixty riflemen. In the confusion, he seems to have been unaware of Brush's position. The bastion was only a walled-in enclosure of grass which gave little protection from the shells.

When Allan withdrew from the Gare Maritime, he sent two officers to collect men and join Brush in preventing the Germans from surrounding the Bastion de l'Estran. With these meagre reinforcements, Brush counter-attacked and recaptured a commanding dune. At 3 p.m. he was again forced back. The Germans had now broken through between him and the sea and appeared behind him. In a last, fantastic mêlée, he fought on, though Coghill and the Bastion de l'Estran were made to surrender at 3.30 p.m.

Brush had again been wounded, and he was wounded a third time before it was all over. Peel and 2/Lieut. Surtees, though unable to move from severe leg wounds, kept firing till the Germans appeared on the skyline and took them prisoner. With them was Rifleman Don Gurr, one of the best shots in the Army, who fought until his leg was shattered (it was later amputated). Rifleman Murphy, also taken prisoner beside Brush, discovered an ancient Lewis gun which he got in working order and kept firing to the last round. These few held the enemy at arm's length for half an hour. Jerry Duncanson who had enjoyed every moment of it, stood up to kill the last German in the Rifle Brigade area, and himself died fighting.

As soon as they had taken the Bastion de l'Estran, the Germans opened the entrance gates which faced west across the lock and mounted a machine-gun which dominated the entrance to the tunnel under Bastion 1. This was now crowded with men who awaited orders. Since they were quite defenceless, with Germans in control of the Gare Maritime, they had to surrender. Lying in one of the underground rooms I could hear the hoarse shouts of German under-officers and the noise of rifles being flung on the floor of the tunnel. Through the doorway came field-grey figures waving revolvers.

It was a sad ending. Allan had held the Gare Maritime till the last moment in case the 60th should try to retire from it. Once it had gone, the fall of Bastion 1, attacked from the south and the east, could not be prevented. But no soldiers fought harder and even as they were marched away, unshaven, hungry and tired out, they felt that they had done their duty. Allan and Gordon-Duff avoided capture for some time, hiding in the dunes. As they were marched off, the long-hoped-for naval bombardment started about 6 p.m. to ironic cheers from the Rifle Brigade.

At the same hour as the Rifle Brigade were compelled to bring their resistance to an end, the Germans were surrounding the Citadel. A white flag had been seen by their infantry during the afternoon but rapidly disappeared and the firing continued. By 3 p.m. with the fall of Bastion 11 and the crossing of the Pont Freycinet in the south, the Citadel was surrounded by tanks. German infantry began to infiltrate across the canal at the south-east corner. In half an hour they had forced the south gate and once inside climbed on to the ramparts. There was not a single automatic weapon left to stop them.

The shelling had stopped and it was suddenly quiet. A French officer ran to the cellar in the north-east bastion which had been Nicholson's headquarters since early morning. The French were surrendering. Then a sergeant came to the entrance, shouting that the Germans were in the huge interior courtyard.

Lieutenant Evitts noticed Nicholson's expression. "The bitter agony of defeat lay unmistakably written on his face."

As the Germans crossed the courtyard, led by a Feldwebel with a revolver, the British came out with their hands up. An angry German officer threatened to shoot them if there were more deaths from the naval guns offshore. Two machine-guns were put in position thirty yards away. But nothing more happened and Nicholson and Holland were taken off. The rest were told to bury the dead including the horses killed by shells.

With Nicholson a prisoner, the Germans were soon able to announce that Fort Risban was in their hands. They claimed to have captured over 20,000 Frenchmen, Belgians and Dutch. Many of these, reported Guderian, had been locked up in the basements of the houses by the English. This is an exaggeration. Only suspected fifth column or those who persisted in showing the white flag were actually locked up. The English were numbered at three to four thousand and inaccurately described in the Tenth Panzer Division War Diary as belonging to the "Queen Victoria Brigade, well known in English and Colonial history".

The 60th held their line across the north-east corner until after 4 p.m. and they fought on afterwards in small parties.

An hour before, Colonel Miller had made his way east along the canal to a warehouse, known as the Hangar Crespin, overlooking the Bassin Carnot. This was held by Lieutenant Norman Phillips and his platoon. They had been able to fire on the Germans as they overcame the Rifle Brigade road-block on the Quai de la Loire and advanced on the Gare Maritime. The 60th were well concealed but all the approaches to the building were under constant machine-gun fire. From this place, Miller could see across the Bassin Carnot. At 3 p.m., he saw Very lights fired in quick succession from the Cellulose Factory and German infantry swarm over the quays and on to the platforms.

Within half an hour, it was obvious that Bastion 1 would be in their hands. It must have been a grim moment for the commander of the 60th. The enemy was now on all sides and getting very close. But Miller did not think the position entirely hopeless. He felt that the 60th must make one more stand in Calais-Nord.

Miller left Phillips and never saw him again. When the Germans occupied the harbour area, Phillips and several riflemen remained hidden. At dark, he crept out to the western quay and with Corporal Jones of "A" Company and tried to swim the Bassin Carnot and escape. German sentries opened fire and Phillips was hit. He was pulled ashore but died of his wounds on the 28th May.

Miller returned to the 60th in buildings at the Place d'Angleterre and found things were getting steadily worse. The Germans clearly intended to finish things off before dark. The Place d'Angleterre was under direct observation from the Hôtel de Ville and each building occupied by the 60th and all road junctions were accurately shelled.

At the Place d'Armes, Trotter and his company were doing their best to fortify the west and south of the square, but raging fires prevented them from using the old houses. All they were able to accomplish were a few barricades of debris from damaged buildings and to occupy some upper rooms. The area of the Place d'Armes and of Notre Dame was filled with clouds of dense smoke. The flames had swept from the Rue Leveux to the Courgain. Calais-Nord was in ruins.

Nothing could stop the German tanks from crossing the Pont Faidherbe to join up with their infantry on the west side of the town. They crept round street corners and opened fire at close range. Slowly they worked their way towards Notre Dame.

At 4 p.m. organised resistance was obviously hopeless and there was no contact with the Citadel. Miller ordered the Battalion to scatter and hang on in buildings or cellars in small parties and then if possible to get out of the town. He suggested that escape to the south presented the best chance since the Tenth Panzer Division would be moving on towards Dunkirk. Many attempts were made but few succeeded in getting very fat. The men were forced by exhaustion and the heat from their hiding places.

After Miller gave the order, it was passed on in the bitter cry: "Every man for himself!"

Two platoons of the Q.V.R. who had been detached to hold the Quai du Volga and the Place de Norvège in support of the 60th on the 25th May, sought to retire north to the lighthouse at the Place de Russie and made a final stand. One of them was forced to surrender on the way there, coming face to face with German infantry only fifteen yards away. The other manned a hastily prepared obstacle at the Place d'Angleterre. For an hour they were subjected to heavy mortar fire until they heard Miller's orders and withdrew to the Place de Russie where they were taken prisoner.

Those Q.V.R. of "B" Company who, in the morning, had been in position at the Ponts Henri-Héron and on the Quai de la Colonne received the orders to scatter. Under Captain Bowring, they planned to keep together and escape towards Dunkirk. They began to move southwards from the Quai de la Colonne but, when they reached the Place de l'Europe, they found it swept by machine-gun fire from the lighthouse. Bowring led the company to a school for shelter, while his second-in-command explored an underground passage leading to an adjoining street only to find a German tank standing outside.

At 5 p.m. when German tanks and infantry entered the Place de l'Europe, "B" Company of the Q.V.R. surrendered. They had been in action since Oyez Farm on the morning of the 24th and during the last two days had given the 60th invaluable support. Despite lack of weapons and training and no transport, they had, a Territorial Company, displayed stout-hearted qualities of which they were right to be proud.

After keeping out of the way of the Germans until the evening, Miller, his adjutant, and a small party of riflemen made their way back to the 60th battalion headquarters in the Rue des Marèchaux. They remained there until dark, destroying all papers and documents that could be of any use to the Germans. They then attempted to leave the town but were taken prisoner on the way to the docks. The 60th had been fighting for four days against impossible odds but like the Rifle Brigade had added another splendid action to their battle honours.

At 7.56 p.m. this message was transmitted from Dover:

To O.C. Troops Calais
From Secretary of State

Am filled with admiration for your magnificent fight which is worthy of the highest tradition of the British Army.

It was never received and as darkness fell on Calais, there was a merciful silence.

CHAPTER TWENTY

A Fitting Finish

LITTLE would have been known of the fate of the survivors but for the part played by the Royal Navy on the 26th and 27th May. While the Gare Maritime was under tremendous shellfire on the afternoon of the 26th, *Conidaw* grounded and remained until the last moments to take off 165 men. The Belgian yacht *Semois* went in four times and each time brought away wounded.

There was a remarkable rescue in the early hours of the 27th. Signalman Leslie W. Wright had fallen off the jetty in trying to escape. He swam to the end of the pier to find a group of forty-six men hiding underneath it. Some were in the port room which was reached by an iron ladder, others clung to the pier beams. The jetties were in German hands and there was a machine-gun on the pier above them. When it was dark, a Royal Marine sergeant signalled out to sea with a lamp. At 2 a.m. there was a cry. "They are here!"

H.M. Yacht *Gulzar*, which had already been in Calais harbour for much of the battle, had returned. Lieutenant-Commander Brammall sent some of his crew ashore to search for survivors. But the yacht came under machine-gun fire and they had to put back to sea. Then they heard shouts from under the pier and came back. As he swung the yacht past them, Mr. W. Shepherd of the Light Aid Detachment attached to the Rifle Brigade, heard Brammall say through a loud-hailer: "I cannot stop to pick you up. I will go out and turn. As I pass you must jump for it."

Despite the machine-gun bullets, all forty-seven men including three officers jumped on to *Gulzar*'s deck and safely reached Dover. Brammall and his coxswain, Jack Woodhead, were both decorated.

The cruisers *Arethusa* and *Galatea* shelled the Germans and caused heavy casualties. Early on the morning of 27th May, after spending all night in the tunnel under Bastion 1, I was taken by ambulance into Calais. With a noise resembling an approaching train, a naval shell burst quite close. The ambulance was nearly overturned and the crew fled for shelter. When they came back they drove me to a covered market in Calais-St. Pierre where my stretcher was placed on a slab, as if I were a piece of meat.

During the four days of fighting, there was strong R.A.F. fighter opposition over Calais which drove off many bombing attacks. Thirty-six Blenheims and ten Swordfish bombed the Germans. Twenty British aircraft were lost including two Blenheims. On the 26th, aircraft of No. 613 Squadron R.A.F. (Squadron Leader A. F. Anderson) with Hawker Hectors and twenty-four Lysanders were in action. The Lysanders dropped ammunition and water in ten-gallon containers on the Citadel. The Hectors attacked German anti-aircraft positions.

On the 27th this force returned, not knowing that the town had fallen. At 10 a.m. thirty-eight Lysanders dropped water, hand grenades and 22,000 rounds of ammunition on the Citadel and three did not return. The Hectors bombed German artillery on the coast, and several were lost.

It was a brave effort to help Nicholson. The Hectors were old-fashioned. Anderson had flown his at the Hendon Air Display in 1937. The Lysanders were vulnerable by day and none of the planes had radio. Anderson wrote to me:

"Some of our aircrew were straight out of flying training school, had never flown in a Hector, fired a gun or dropped a bomb."

There were some striking escapes from the line of march. News of the garrison had come from 2/Lieut. T. Lucas of the Q.V.R. who crossed the Channel alone in a dinghy. On the 17th June, Captain E. A. W. Williams, adjutant of the 60th, Captain Dennis Talbot, Nicholson's Brigade Major, Lieutenant Millett the Signals Officer at the Gare Maritime, Lance Corporal R. Illingworth, Q.V.R. and Rifleman Harington, 60th, were picked up by the destroyer *Vesper* eight miles off Folkestone.

They had reached the coast, joined a party of six Frenchmen, and with them crossed in an old motor-boat. Gunner G. Instone, Second

Searchlight Battery, after knocking out two sentries, reached southern France and later crossed into Spain.

These were the few who escaped five years in the prison camps of Nazi Germany.[1]

As the garrison was marched away, at sunset on the 26th the great Dunkirk operation began. Three hours after the fall of the Citadel, the Admiralty ordered:

"Operation Dynamo is to commence."

The flow of personnel ships from Dunkirk had already started and at 10.30 p.m. the first troops disembarked at Dover. No one was optimistic. Admiral Ramsay was told that:

"It was imperative for Dynamo to be implemented with the greatest vigour, with a view to lifting up to 45,000 men of the British Expeditionary Force within two days, at the end of which it was probable that evacuation would be terminated by enemy action."

That evening, Guderian stood with his staff, only a few miles from Dunkirk, watching "the armada of great and little ships by means of which the British were evacuating their forces". He was bitterly disappointed. The resumption of the armoured attack, on the 27th May, came too late. The British Army slipped through a gap only ten miles wide, held open for them by their Second Division who were cut to pieces. Guderian's corps regrouped on 29th May for the breakthrough to the Aisne and never took part in the final battle for Dunkirk which finished on the 4th June with the evacuation of 330,000 men.

The stand of Nicholson's brigade against impossible odds can be compared with other actions in the history of war. All through the episode there runs a thread of poor intelligence and indecision. Nicholson was landed much too late to be able to do more than block the entrances to the town. The tanks had no chance of getting ready. There are those who think that a tank brigade could have been landed at Calais. Had it been in time, it might have delayed the Germans much longer. Much blame must lie with those who failed to provide the War Office with information of Guderian's advance. When he

[1] On the 5th January 1942 the author escaped from Colditz Castle in Saxony and reached England in May of that year.

turned north from Abbeville to the Channel ports, he was followed and bombed by the R.A.F. They put in a big effort to cover the coastal area during the battles for Boulogne and Calais. Why did the British Army staff not know of his movements? Co-ordination of Intelligence with the R.A.F. had evidently a long way to go.

Then there was the psychology of the moment. The War Office had already determined that the B.E.F., except for some thirty to forty thousand men, was lost. There was some justice in Churchill's charge of defeatism. They were opposed to the defence of Calais and they wanted Nicholson's troops for Home Defence. The whole operation was carried out in a half-hearted fashion.

Gort's decision to withdraw to the coast led Churchill to cancel the "evacuation in principle". But it was not until the 25th May that the value for the B.E.F. of delaying the Tenth Panzer Division became clear. Even then Nicholson received neither field artillery nor reinforcements. As Eden, very fairly, wrote:

"We should have seen this more clearly and sooner when Boulogne was evacuated."[2]

It is unfortunate that the French, who had urged Churchill to reinforce the ports as part of Weygand's plan for a "vast bridgehead" did not do more to defend Calais. But, today, we should remember de Lambertye and those who stayed to fight. Afterwards, Weygand was generous in his appreciation of their courage.

Despite their heavy losses when they entered Boulogne harbour to take off the Guards on the 24th May, the Royal Navy were disappointed at not being able to carry out a similar rescue at Calais. Admiral Ramsay felt strongly about this. During the battle he wrote to his wife:

"What we are experiencing is nothing to what the poor devils are going through in Calais."

Only the sourest military historian could seriously attack Nicholson's conduct of the defence. He had an impossibly large perimeter to protect and due to the orders of others, most of the tanks were lost before he landed. His headquarters at the Citadel in the most exposed position cannot be fairly criticised. He was afraid

[2] *The Eden Memoirs. The Reckoning*, p. 109.

that, if he remained at the Gare Maritime, the French would surrender. Unfortunately he had reason for this, as incidents on the last morning were to show.

The fault lay with "higher authority". By the time that Nicholson's brigade was landed, confidence in the French had been lost. The General Staff concentrated on extracting the B.E.F. Preoccupied with these vast problems, they had no plan for Calais. Indeed, it is not clear who was in charge of the operation.

Few commanders, since the days of Balaclava, have issued such suicidal orders as General Brownrigg, who, as late as the 24th May, wanted the Third Royal Tank Regiment to go to Boulogne.

Ironside at first supported the landing. On the 23rd May he wrote in his diary:

"I have only just got my three battalions of motorised infantry, and the Tank Regiment into Calais in time."[3]

Yet it was he who approved General Dewing's "evacuation in principle", when the news came that Boulogne could not be held. On the same day, the 24th May, after Dewing had got his approval at 6 a.m., Ironside wrote of General Fagalde at Dunkirk:

"He has been appointed C-in-C in the North. His first order was to our people in Calais to stand fast. A good sign. The first order of co-ordination which has been given by the French command in the north for ten days. Let us hope it is the beginning."

This seems to establish beyond doubt why "evacuation in principle" was postponed and then abandoned next day.

When Churchill suggested on the 25th May that there was "defeatism in the General Staff", Ironside replied:

> No order was issued for the evacuation of Calais. This now held by some 4 Battalions in the inner perimeter of the town.
>
> An order was issued by me for the evacuation of all non-fighting people at Calais. These contained some *2,000* men from Admiralty Staffs, Pioneer Corps, and many unarmed men. There were also *400* wounded.

[3] *The Ironside Diaries*, p. 330.

We are still in touch with Brigadier Calais and I have sent him a telegram in the sense you have on your paper.

There is no defeatist element in the General Staff.

Churchill countered by asking who had sent the telegram—"evacuation *decided* in principle". General Dewing's answer is reproduced in full in the Appendix to this book. The paper went round till the 20th June when it was marked "no further action required".

The only fair conclusion is that Churchill felt bound to support Weygand and Fagalde, especially since the B.E.F. had begun to withdraw to the coast. It was he who first countermanded the evacuation, though he poured scorn on the "Allied solidarity" message. None the less, the decision was not final until 9 p.m. on the 25th May. Until then, Nicholson was in a state of uncertainty, faced with a flow of telegrams which were more exhortations than orders.

It is necessary to criticise but it was a painful dilemma. Those in authority wanted to save the Calais garrison if they could. To Eden the decision was one of the most cruel of the war.

"I had served," he wrote, "with one of the regiments (the 60th) and knew personally many of those whose fate I now had to decide."[4]

Ironside, a generous and humane man, was much moved. He pasted in his diary the cartoon in the *Daily Mirror* reproduced in the illustration facing page 161.

On 5th June when Dunkirk was over, he expressed his feelings about the stand at Calais:

A great effort which I hope we shall never forget. It would not have been possible to have used Dunkirk as a point from which to evacuate the B.E.F. and the 1st French Army without this stand. The most famous regiments in the British Army. They fought it out to the end. When I sent them into Calais I was sure they would do their duty and they did it. A fitting finish to their history. Requiescant. The historic name of Calais should be written once more on British hearts.[5]

[4] *The Reckoning*, p. 109.

[5] *The Ironside Diaries*, p. 354.

CHAPTER TWENTY-ONE

Calais: An Epilogue

WHAT part did the stand at Calais really play in the deliverance of Dunkirk? The short account published by Eric Linklater in 1941, set the tone for wartime opinion of the battle which inspired a good deal of bad poetry published in *The Times*. References to Queen Mary's heart were worked to death. The Press seized on Calais as a gleam of light in dark days.

Linklater wrote:

"The Fury of the death struggle engaged, during four vital days, the whole strength of at least two Panzer divisions that might otherwise have cut our retreating army's road to the sea . . . the scythe-like sweep of the German Divisions stopped with a jerk at Calais. The tip of the scythe had met a stone."

This was a big claim and it later met with opposition from two important quarters: Guderian himself and Liddell Hart.

Guderian remarked:

"The Tenth Panzer Division then under my command, took Calais on the 26th May *without waiting for the Air Force* which by the way, with the bombs available at that time would have no results against the forts and the citadel of Old General Vauban."[1]

Survivors of Calais will be surprised after undergoing the horrific Stuka bombardment of the 26th May (see photograph following page 144) to hear this. It is true that the cellars at the Citadel withstood heavy bombing at this time and later the R.A.F. bombardment of 1944. But Guderian made this remark in the context of Hitler's decision to halt the Panzers on the 24th May and leave Dunkirk (and Calais) to the Luftwaffe.

[1] Quoted by Liddell Hart in *The Other Side of the Hill*.

"I think," he said, "it was the vanity of Goering which caused that fateful decision of Hitler's."

Is Guderian right to say that Calais had *no* influence on the operations against Dunkirk to which he had wished to send the Tenth Panzer Division as early as the 21st May? The 21st and 22nd May were days when scarcely a battalion could be found between Calais and Dunkirk. Guderian wrote of the 21st May:

"I wanted the Tenth Panzer Division to advance on Dunkirk by way of Hesdin and St. Omer, the First Panzer Division to move on Calais and the Second on Boulogne."[2]

This was his original plan. It had to be abandoned but the First Panzer Division could have taken Calais on the night of the 22nd May without difficulty as their War Diary shows. The Tenth could have been sent forward to Dunkirk on the 23rd, twenty-four hours *before* Hitler and Rundstedt intervened with their famous "Halt Order". It was Guderian who missed his chance at Calais, however much subsequent events prevented his triumph at Dunkirk. Hitler's order was not issued until 11.24 a.m. on the 24th May, when Guderian was already over the Aa Canal.

None the less, he wrote after the war:

"As the commander on the spot I am able definitely to state that the heroic defence of Calais, although worthy of the highest praise, yet had no influence on the development of events outside Dunkirk."

This is not accurate. On the 26th May, when the First Panzer Division was waiting on the Aa Canal, units of it were being sent to the siege of Calais.

Eden wrote:

While Ironside and I were still grieved at what we had had to do, General Percival, who was then Assistant C.I.G.S., came into my room. He brought an intercepted German message and remarked: "Here is the justification for your decision."

The message was an instruction from the German High Command to an armoured division, then moving eastwards against

[2] Guderian: *Panzer Leader*, p. 114.

Gort's communications to change directions and reinforce troops attacking Calais. The order added that Calais must be reduced at all costs.[3]

The XIXth German Army Corps War Diary refers to the transfer of a heavy artillery battery from the First Panzer Division at Gravelines. The Tenth Panzer Division orders for 25th May signed by General Schaal show *three* heavy batteries of corps artillery. Infantry may also have been brought in from Gravelines, for Major Allan noticed that the Germans on the eastern front were fresh and had recently shaved.[4] Yet Guderian continues:

"The British defence of Calais had no effect on the operations against Dunkirk. No delay in the advance arose from the defence of that fortress."

One thing is indisputable, the Tenth Panzer Division was delayed at Calais for four days and not by Hitler. Guderian is not giving us the whole story. He is covering up his failure to take it earlier.

Guderian has been corrected by Dr. Hans-Adolf Jacobsen in his essay on Dunkirk 1940 in *Decisive Battles of World War II: The German View*. Discussing why the Germans failed to cut the B.E.F. off at Dunkirk he writes:

"A factor which must not be overlooked in this connection was the courageous defence of Boulogne and Calais. This was by no means useless, since it delayed the attack of XIX Corps on Dunkirk for a number of crucial hours."

He did not consider Calais the decisive factor. Like Guderian, he blames Hitler and the German High Command. But if Calais had never been fought, wrote David Divine:

"It seems inconceivable that in the circumstances, Guderian would not have gone straight through to Dunkirk, his avowed objective."[5]

Many will agree with this assessment.

After the war Churchill repeated his claim that the defence of

[3] *The Reckoning*, p. 109.

[4] Eden also quotes the Commander of the British 48th Division at Cassel as saying that German armoured troops were suddenly withdrawn.

[5] *The Nine Days of Dunkirk*.

Calais had brought time to build up the Dunkirk perimeter and that "without this, even in spite of Hitler's vacillations and Rundstedt's orders, all would have been cut off and lost."[6]

Liddell Hart's comment has a patronising tone.

"While it is natural that Mr. Churchill," he wrote in *The Other Side of the Hill*, "should wish to justify his personal decision to sacrifice the force landed at Calais, it is hard to understand how he can still make such a claim for the effect of this action. The Panzer division which attacked Calais was only one out of the seven in the area. It was employed there because it had nothing else to do during the halt which Hitler had ordered."

There were two Panzer divisions within reach of Calais many hours before Hitler issued his fateful order. Liddell Hart was moved by "the gallant stand of the British troops at Calais" but he called it a "useless sacrifice"[7]—a most opinionated view.

There was nothing useless about the stand at Calais. It hampered Guderian during crucial hours, especially on the 23rd and 24th May, when there was little to prevent his taking Dunkirk. It formed part of the series of events, some foolish, some glorious, which saved the B.E.F.

"To create heroic legends, successful and heroic objectives are necessary, and what better one can there be, than to sacrifice oneself so that others can escape."[8]

In 1940 the battle of Calais was fought with that objective. When the reader next crosses the Channel by boat, lands at the Gare Maritime near Bastion 1 and sees the new houses round the Place d'Armes, let him spare a thought for those who fought and died in the flames of Calais.

[6] *The Second World War*, Vol. II, p. 73.

[7] *The Tanks*, Vol. II, p. 23.

[8] *Annals of the King's Royal Rifle Corps*, Vol. VI, p. 94.

Questions asked by Prime Minister. *Enclo. 1A.*

C.I.G.S. thro A.C.I.G.S. (A)

With reference to the questions by the Prime Minister written on attached note.

Question 1. "A telegram was sent saying evacuation decided in principle on the night of 23rd. Who sent this telegram?"

A signal to the following effect was sent from Dover to Brigadier Nicholson in Calais about 3 a.m. on the morning of the 24th—

> Evacuation decided in principle. When you have finished unloading your two M.T. ships commence embarkation of all personnel except fighting personnel who will remain to cover final evacuation.

This signal was authorised by me. About 6 a.m. the same morning I spoke to C.I.G.S. in his room. He agreed with the principle. I then spoke to Nicholson by telephone, making it quite clear that evacuation was approved in principle, but that final evacuation would not be for at least 24 hours; that is at the earliest the morning of Saturday, 25th.

During the 24th the British and French troops at Calais were placed under the orders of General Fagalde who ordered no evacuation. Attached is a copy of a signal which was sent to Nicholson on the evening of the 24th, since it was perfectly clear that the military purpose for which the force had been put into Calais, namely to keep the port and communications forward from it open for the B.E.F., would not be achieved.

Question 2. "When were the non-fighting people evacuated from Calais?"

They were evacuated during the morning of 24th, for the most part in the two M.T. ships referred to above.

27/5/40 R. H. Dewing
D.M.O. & P.

Office Note
No further action required.

A. E. Percival
20/6/40 A.C.I.G.S. (A).
21/6/40 R.H.D.

INDEX